KARMA & REINCARNATION

TORKOM SARAYDARIAN

T.S.G. Publishing
Foundation, Inc.

Karma and Reincarnation

© 1999 The Creative Trust

All Rights Reserved: No part of this publication may be reproduced, stored in a retrieval system, or transmitted in any form, by any means, electronic, mechanical, photocopying, recording or otherwise, without permission in writing from the copyright owner or his representatives. Contact publisher for details.

ISBN: 0-929874-23-4

Library of Congress Catalog Card Number: 99-73858

Printed in the United States of America

Cover Design: *Tim Fisher*
                   Cave Creek, Arizona

Printed by: *Data Reproductions*
                   Rochester Hills, Michigan

Published by: T.S.G. Publishing Foundation, Inc.
                   Post Office Box 7068
                   Cave Creek, Arizona 85327-7068
                   United States of America

Note: Meditations, visualizations, and other health information are given as guidelines. They should be used with discretion and after receiving professional advice.

The Water Pitcher

My Teacher gave me a pitcher and said, "Go and fill this from 'the green spring,' the fountain, and bring it back." It was a heavy pitcher. The spring was half a mile from his home. I went and filled the pitcher, but to my surprise the pitcher was leaking. With one hand I tried to stop the leak; with the other I tried to carry it home. By the time I reached his house there were only two inches of water left in it.

"Did you bring water?" asked the Teacher. "Yes," I said, "but the pitcher leaked very badly." "Yes, yes, yes," he said, and began to laugh. Suddenly, stopping his laughter, he said, "That is what happens to those who are given the Teaching but cannot contain it due to their leaks. Leakage is fear, anger, jealousy, revenge, hatred, self-interest, earthly desires, hypocrisy, and vanity. If these cracks exist in a man-pitcher, it is impossible to fill such a pitcher."

I forgot many things he said during those school days, but I never forgot the Teaching he gave me about the pitcher.

Definitions

Karma is the response of Nature or the reaction of Nature to our actions.

Nature means environment — with all energies involved.

Actions are physical, emotional, mental, and moral.

Reaction is an action against you.

Response is an action that benefits you.

For example, a crime you commit is in itself a punishment to yourself.

A *benevolent action* brings happiness to you.

Then why do people say, "Even if you do good, people do bad to you"? That is a very complicated statement. In our actions the most important point is not the nature of our action but the motive of our action. *Good appearance is not equal to goodness.* Bad appearance is not the proof of an inner corruption.

*Published in memory of my Teacher
Torkom Saraydarian
From a grateful student*

Table of Contents

	Introduction	9
1.	The Law of Cause and Effect	13
2.	Karma	37
3.	Karma and Omissions	47
4.	Karma as Opportunity	51
5.	Forgiveness and Karma	57
6.	Karma and Position	61
7.	Cause and Karma	71
8.	The Other Worlds and Karma	77
9.	Shared Karma	109
10.	Payment of Debts	113
11.	Willpower and Karma	117
12.	The Levels of Karma	119
13.	Facing Karma	137
14.	Reversing Karma	143
15.	Core Karma	151
16.	Building Your Bodies	153
17.	Consciousness and Karma	155
18.	Karma and Choice	165
19.	Karma and the Solar Angel	177
20.	The Law of Causelessness	185
21.	The Law of Inevitability	189

22.	The Law of Reincarnation	195
23.	Reincarnation	217
24.	The Immortal Spirit	243
25.	Birth, Death, and Reincarnation	257
26.	Self-Renunciation	299
27.	Building the Human Being	339
28.	The Soul and Its Vehicles	345
29.	Vehicles and Their Notes	349
30.	Reincarnation and Individuality	355
31.	Incarnation of the Monad	363
32.	Past Lives	373
33.	Resurrection	387
34.	Healing Through Approach	407

Index 417

About the Author 433

Introduction

Sometimes karma works in the following way. Suppose you went close to a porcupine and he projected ten needles into your body. Karma is like taking them out of your body, one by one, and releasing you from the pain that afflicts you.

The pain and anxieties you feel from the action of the karmic law have the aim of liberation from the pain of the "needles" you caused to yourself.

Another example is that you have fallen into a deep well, and Karma is the operation to rescue you from the mud, cold, insects, and death. No matter through what difficulties you pass, the operation of karma has one aim: to liberate you from your unfortunate condition. People look at the Law of Karma as punishment, but the real goal of karma is directed toward your liberation.

Karma is a friendly law in its essence. It protects you from total annihilation or condemnation. Suppose you owe $20,000 to someone, and if you cannot pay it in six months you will be put in prison. Karma makes you pay it in various ways, leading you into conditions in which you work and suffer hard to pay your debts. If you only think about how hard you are working, you think of karma as if it were retribution, but actually it is working in your favor to prevent you from eternal annihilation.

Karma protects people from falling into more complicated crimes. It guides people through their incarnations to discover Beauty, Goodness, Righteousness, Joy, Freedom, and even dedicate themselves to Striving and Service. It is a companion law with the Law of Compassion, leading to total liberation.

There is another point which we must consider. Karmic law develops our intellect, our love, and willpower. People who suffer more in their life learn more about the Law of Karma, and in their future incarnations they live, they work, they sacrifice to make others know about the Law of Karma and do all that they can to alleviate the suffering people brought upon themselves by their past actions.

Karma is explained as the Law of Cause and Effect. It can be better defined if we say that karma is a string of beads which are successively cause and effect. If we study these beads as cause and effect we are not far from the truth. Each effect has a cause, and an effect becomes a cause when it affects.

Any event is the effect of many causes, and any cause can be the result of an effect.

If we think ugly thoughts and with the intention to harm or if we nurture negative emotions and carry on activities that promote crime, violence, greed, and ego, we confront three kinds of reactions.

The first reaction is from the Law of Karma. An action on any level goes to the records of karma, and karmic law decides how and when to act in order to produce the best result for the one who, for example, committed a crime.

The second reaction is that every act touches the fire in space, fuses with it, and, if the action is in harmony with the Law of Compassion, amplifies its power. Or the fire damages the spiritual web which is serving the person as a path of ascent. Each of us expands our consciousness and moves on toward new achievements, building a path through our best aspirations, dreams, and labor. It is this path that is damaged by the fire because of our harmful actions.

The third reaction is the boomerang. When our actions are directed toward certain persons or groups with the intention to hurt them, we receive a strong blow which weakens us and makes us the target of dark forces. This blow is the arrow of our harmful thoughts, words, or actions which come back with increased fire and damage our aura. The Teaching says that people thus prevent their own progress by falling into the path of harmful actions.

• CHAPTER 1 •

The Law of Cause and Effect

In discussing the subject of cause and effect, certain ideas associate themselves with points of pressure in our psyche, and we feel depressed or angry. We rebel; we are confused and sometimes feel agitated. But these are good signs because unless you are agitated, angry, and confused to a certain degree, that which is eating you from within will not come out.

First, let us define the word *karma*. When the word *karma* is mentioned, people tend to get agitated. But karma is a universal law found in all religions, philosophies, and sciences. If you take beans and plant them, you do not harvest potatoes. Science knows that beans come from beans. We can synthesize what religions have said about karma and also add a few deeper esoteric ideas.

Karma is the *Law of Cause and Effect*. There is no effect without a cause; there is no child without a parent. Whatever you sow, you reap. This law applies not only to that which we see around us, but it also applies to our emotions, thoughts, actions, and words. Whatever cause we create, we will receive effects. If there is an effect, there must be a cause; if there is a cause, there will be an effect.

If humanity really understood this law, we would all be living on Venus. But we are in the pit of the solar system, and we will stay here until we burn ourselves or learn this law and liberate ourselves from pain, suffering, agony, war, and revolution.

From birth to death a man sows and then reaps what he sows. When a person thinks, he sends "thought seeds" into space. Whatever he speaks is a seed in space. Whatever emotions and reactions he has are seeds in space. Whatever actions he performs are seeds in space. These seeds are going to grow, and someday he must face their results.

For every action, there is an equal and opposite reaction in the physical, emotional, mental, and spiritual realms. How conscious are we going to be? What actions are we going to release, and what reactions can we expect in return?

This was the greatest Teaching of Lord Buddha. He wanted us to be conscious enough to know what caused that which is happening now. If one eliminates causes, he eliminates results — the effect or reaction. It is a wonderful law from which no one can escape.

In some remote areas of the earth, because they are more psychic and perhaps more spiritual, people do not use sophisticated names for the Law of Cause and Effect. They call it the *Law of the Echo*.

I used to go to the mountains and listen to my voice echoing back to me. Once when I was inside the Great Pyramid, I said, "OM," and waited. A few minutes later, I heard "OM" echoing back to me in different keys. The Egyptians were super scientists.

There is the superficial meaning to the word "echo," but there are deeper, esoteric meanings. In taking a physical action, the first echo is physical, the second echo is emotional, the third echo is mental, and the fourth echo is spiritual. This means that any action taken on any level echoes in all levels. There is no escape from this.

We come to the conclusion from this that the Universe, this life, is a conscious mechanism which works mathematically, psychologically, and scientifically.

As we develop and evolve, our echoes become clearer and purer. For example, we can do something very good physically, and pure echoes will result in the emotional, mental, intuitional, monadic, and divine levels. These echoes make up the harmony and symphony of our lives.

There is another quality of the echo in that it may repeat itself forever, until the ear can no longer hear it. You go to the mountain and shout; you may hear one echo, but if you are clever and sensitive, you will see that the echo is hitting other mountains and repeating the echo, even though you may not be able to perceive it. It is a continuous, perpetual motion in the Universe. This means that you will forever face the consequences of any action, thought, emotion, or word in the form of its echoes.

Karma in Sanskrit, means action, activity. But even in Sanskrit there is no reference to result and cause. This is because Sanskrit clairvoyantly and intuitively knows that there is no effect, but there is always a cause. The Western mind has a hard time understanding this. An effect is a minor cause. The effect that is created becomes a cause for another effect. So in essence, everything is a cause.

For example, a man is sick. His sickness is an effect, but because he was sick, he quit his job. His sickness has become the cause of his unemployment. He drank a bottle of whiskey and created a result—drunkenness. Because he was drunk, he had an accident. Because he had an accident, he was taken to the hospital. It is a continuous process.

The Great Ones say that we must strive every minute to become conscious of what it is we are doing physically, emotionally, and mentally in order to understand what causes we are going to produce.

The different names for karma are like facets of a diamond; they are different, but they each reveal another side of the same subject.

Karma is also called the *Law of Compensation*. "Compensation" means that every human being must be careful to compensate himself and others. His physical, emotional, and mental bodies, his friends, and so on must be compensated. Because his physical body works, it must be fed, dressed, and washed — compensated. He must take care of his emotional and mental bodies as well. The same holds true for the people with whom he relates. Compensation is the sensitive understanding that whatever is given to you must be returned. You are born with nothing and you will die with nothing.

When I was in a very remote area of Syria talking with some Dervishes, one of them referred to karma as the *Law of the Mirror*. Whatever a person's life is, that is what he is because he is reflecting in his life what he really is. If his face changes, his reflection in the mirror changes.

Emotional hang-ups and ways of living are exactly the reflection of what we have done before. Our physical, emotional, and mental conditions are an exact reflection of previous actions. Our life is a mirror reflecting what we are. To understand our life, we have only to look at the reflection. We go to the mirror and say, "My make-up is not so good," and we change it. If a person truly understands this, he can no longer complain about others because everything that happens in his life is a reflection of what he is.

We can use the mirror to change ourselves, but the problem is that we fall in love with what we see in the mirror. When this happens, there is no hope; this is the tragedy of the modern world. It has fallen in love with the mirror. It can be beautiful, but can we improve it? The more beautiful a person is, the more difficult it is to change.

We can change our lives by changing the reality of what we are and the mirror will reflect exactly how we have changed. The Law of the Mirror is a masterpiece explanation of karma.

What applies to an individual also applies to a nation and to humanity as a whole. Whatever is happening in national or global life is a reflection of mass consciousness. To change that reflection, we must change the reality, the object which is reflected.

Do you know anyone insane enough to stand in front of a mirror with a brush in his hand attempting to change his reflection, believing that by changing the reflection he will change himself? This is what we do day and night. We try to change the reflection instead of the source, instead of changing ourselves. In ancient monasteries, this was called the science of hypocrisy. You dress differently; you change your hairstyle, walk differently, change your voice, and so on, working on your reflection. The sad thing about this is that by applying a brush to the reflection in the mirror, it will eventually become impossible for you to see your real face in the mirror.

When you stand before the mirror, try to see exactly what you are. The "mirror" is your life, the way you are living, the conditions under which you are living, the condition of your physical, emotional, and mental health, the emotional turmoil and confusion of your life, the silliness, insanity, or sanity.

Karma is a battle between what you do and what you want to be. You want to be something, but you do exactly the opposite. You want freedom, but you try to be a slave. You want love, but you create those conditions in which everyone hates you. We all do these things unconsciously.

The battle between what you do and what you want to be is the true battle. You are in a karmic mess because both sides create karma. In doingness you create karma; in wanting to be you create karma. These two clash, and you become totally confused. In a few years, or in a lifetime, this confusion will express itself as insanity. Medical doctors, psychologists, and psychiatrists do not understand that they cannot heal an insane person because he makes himself that way. He is in conflict psychologically, inside and outside, between what he is doing and what he wants to be.

Eighty-five percent of what we do is opposed to what we want to be. We work against our own best interest, and yet we are so happy doing this. We all want happiness, health, prosperity, friendship, beauty, freedom, and so on, but we do not do what is necessary to bring these about. We must learn to take only those actions which are parallel with what we want to be. If there is conflict, there is karma.

A young man came to me and said he wanted to be healthy; then later he mentioned that he liked to take drugs. I explained to him that this was like cutting his own throat.

Another name for karma is the *Moving Scales*. A person is like a scale. Anything he puts in his nature will elevate or lower him. There are also echoes coming to him from previous actions, previous lives, like a tidal wave on its way. Five days or five hundred years later that tidal wave will hit him as he comes around the corner. We are learning these things so that in the future we can prevent the creation of the tidal wave.

We must question what it is we are putting on the scales. Is it hypocrisy, self-interest, ego, exploitation, fear, misuse, and exploitation of others? If this is what we are putting on the scales, that is what we will receive. If a person is treated in certain ways, it means that he acted in those ways in the past.

Karma is sometimes called the *Law of Self-Made Traps*. We build traps for ourselves, and the whole time we are very happy while we build them. We build physical, emotional, and mental traps with our speech, writings, and so on. We want to escape the trap, but the more we fight, the more trapped we become. Like a mouse in a trap, if we do not move, we live for a few more minutes. If we move, we immediately cut our throats.

How many traps have we built for ourselves? The person himself becomes a trap. Those who create traps in their lives become the most dangerous traps for others. When the trap becomes trapped in the traps of others, there is little hope of release. That is what we are doing to each other, trapping each other and becoming traps. If this continues, one trap trapped within hundreds of traps, what chance is there for escape?

When a person is trapped in his wrong doings, wrong words, wrong thinking, and wrong emotions, he becomes trapped by his own creations. Then he sees other people exploiting and manipulating, and he eventually becomes caught in their trap. In this process he tries to exploit and manipulate and becomes trapped in his courses of action. He loses his sanity, sense of direction, simplicity. When people talk to him, he misleads them and leads them into traps.

Insanity is contagious. Karma is also contagious. It is a very good sign if you realize that you are in a trap. When complaining about your health, happiness, personal relationships, and so on, it means that you have begun to understand that you are in a trap and that you want out. Most people do not make any effort to escape, but they complain. This is human music, karmic music!

Karma is also called the *Law of Payment*. Whatever you pay to Nature, Nature gives back to you. This is why it is important to be righteous with yourself and with others. If a person helps you with fifty dollars, you must pay that fifty dollars back. If he saves your life, you must save his life.

But we think we are smart when we do just the opposite. We think that by stealing and robbing from people, making more and more money off of them, that we are on the road to happiness. But one day we will find that a flood has come and taken everything that we built, including ourselves, because the tax must also be collected. It is more intelligent to be totally righteous.

We have five jewels that reveal our karma:

The first jewel is our physical condition. Our physical condition is the balance of actions we have taken against the laws of Nature and those actions taken in harmony with the laws of Nature.

There are two kinds of actions: actions that are in harmony with the laws of Nature, or with the Will of God, and actions that are against the laws of Nature. The balance between these two is exactly what you are.

For example, you have twenty dollars and you worked hard and made ten more dollars. You now have a total of thirty dollars. If you do something stupid and lose the money or give it away, you will have nothing.

Having nothing is not the worst condition. There is also being in debt. Every time you make a little money, you must pay the past debt instead of improving your life. You are paying the debt and not accumulating money in the savings. How much are you spending? How much are you receiving? Expenditures, in this symbolic language, are those things which break the laws of Nature.

A young man came to tell me that he had gotten married. "Congratulations," I said to him. Later, he told me that he had sex with his wife three times a day. "You will be an old man in five years," I told him. He did not understand what I meant, but three years later he had tuberculosis; he spent too much "money," too many resources. If you over spend the resources of the body, emotions, and mind, you act against the laws of Nature.

The second jewel is the condition of the emotional body. Our emotional body, or emotional conditions, are the result of our emotional reactions, imagination, and manipulative activities. From these the emotional body is constructed. Our emotional body is the result of our own emotional reactions, not the result of what people feel about us.

If a person reacts, he changes his emotional body. When he reacts, his emotional body is building, evaporating, agitating, and crystallizing. As soon as the emotional body changes, it crystallizes.

Let us say that I created a wave in the ocean, and that two minutes later that wave freezes, crystallizes. This is how we kill ourselves by reacting. The Tibetan Master, in speaking about these things, says that we must start developing divine indifference. When a person pities someone, he duplicates in himself the same body of emotions as the one he pities.

Reactions create certain formations in the emotional body when they crystallize in the aura. Most people's auras are like walking glass. Emotional-level crystallization means that the swimming pool of your emotional aura has become icy and no longer melts, except under extreme conditions. It takes a great shock to crack or melt that pool.

Imagination also builds the emotional body. We must begin to examine what kind of imagination we have. Every picture a person creates builds his emotional body, and two seconds later it crystallizes. This is how clairvoyants see what you are thinking and feeling.

The emotional body is also changed and built according to the manipulative techniques a person uses on others. No matter how much reasoning and logic a person uses to justify the manipulation of others, he is deceiving himself. In manipulating people, he is ruining his emotional nature, which will create heavy taxation and a very heavy echo which will hit him later like a wave. Manipulation is to use another for your own self-interest.

The process of crystallization is like the thickening of milk. When I was a child, I used to milk the cow. Ten minutes later, cream would form. One hour later, the cream would thicken to such an extent that it hardened. If the emotional aura hardens, it breaks or shatters at the slightest hit. One emotional shock can shatter a person to suicide.

Avoid manipulative techniques. Do not use the time, energy, position, money, knowledge, or beauty of other people for your self-interest. Also be very righteous with yourself.

The third jewel is the condition of the mental body. The state of the mental body, the development, expansion, and contraction of that body is the result of the thoughts we have. Nature gives us back exactly what we have given to Nature.

If a person thinks evil, evil forms in his mind. If he gives good thoughts, good is formed in his mind. Imagine how many evil thoughts we have had and what we are doing — ruining ourselves. And then we go to the doctor, psychiatrist, psychologist and complain.

We must make our thoughts pure and beautiful. They can seem sarcastic or square, very forceful, burning, or destructive, but the motive behind them must be good. Nature gives to us exactly what we give to Her. We may not receive it instantly, but the tidal wave will come.

The fourth jewel is the degree of development of the soul. The development of the soul is the result of three things:

a) the service we have rendered to others

b) the degree of our self-renunciation

c) the joy that we feel for the success and beauty of others

These three things make the soul bloom.

Service means to live, talk, act, and think in ways that increase the light and joy of others. Self-renunciation is freedom from ego, freedom from imposing your will upon others, freedom from imposing your fanaticism and traditions upon others. Self-renunciation is the exact opposite of manipulation. Feeling and experiencing joy in the success and beauty of others is a condition where jealousy cannot exist. When you begin to feel this joy, your flower opens.

Service, being able to serve, is a privilege. It is a gift from God. Our field of service is the result of sacrifices we have made for the world. If you have a field of service, it means that you demonstrated sacrifice in the past. If your field of service is great, it means that you graduated from the *Law of Sacrifice* in the past.

The field of service is one in which everyone strives toward Beauty, Goodness, Righteousness, Joy, Freedom, blooming, expanding toward light, toward Christ, toward God. If you want to be a server in the future, you must graduate from the Law of Sacrifice. You must prove that sacrifice so that the Great Supervisors of the Higher Worlds see and promote you. A great server has a history of sacrifice because Life cannot promote him until it knows that he is really sacrificial.

Christ proved His ability to sacrifice during the crucifixion for the cause of humanity. The Tibetan Master says that Christ won the official title of the Hierarch and is now serving on all Seven Rays. Can we be like Christ and do what He did?

Sacrifice leads to resurrection. Christ did not resurrect before the crucifixion. Every time a person has an expansion of consciousness, he has performed a sacrificial action just before. Every time a person feels joy, it is because he sacrificed something a few minutes before. If it is an echo, it could have been a sacrifice from days or lives before. A creative artist expands his aura and becomes more creative after an act of service and sacrifice. Progress is the result of sacrifice.

It is important to use common sense and apply the Teaching in beautiful ways instead of past life readings, channeling, mediumship, and so on. We are swimming in this sewage. A healthy man does not channel because God is already within him. Who is he going to channel? The Great Sage says, "A medium is a cave of disembodied liars." If a Master is saying this, who are we to oppose Him?

The field of service is the result of past sacrifice. If your field is increasing, you serve more people. It is a privilege, a gift given to you because of past sacrifices, because of self-renunciation, control, harmlessness, sacrificing your ego and feelings. This is a tremendous test for us.

Thanks to the treatment we are given by naughty people, we create those conditions that increase our field of service. Without them, we have no sacrifice. Because a person hurts you, you learn to control your passion. These are great opportunities for you to train yourself.

Karmic law is the Law of Justice, which nothing can deceive. Right is right; wrong is wrong. Even if what you are doing appears to be a comedy, the computer records that it is a sacrifice if it is sacrificial.

Joy is not a manifestation or an expression. It is an inner state of consciousness, of beingness. I may be crying on the outside, but my inner state of consciousness may be in tremendous joy. Joy is not an expression, manifestation, or result; it is a state of consciousness, beingness. Christ said to His disciples, "I give My joy to you," just before His crucifixion. He was telling them not to let the appearance of what was happening shake their faith.

The fifth jewel is that you are what you want to be. What you are is what you want to be, consciously or unconsciously. Face yourself and see what you are.

How We Increase and Multiply our Karma

Karma increases and greater complications result when you obey the urges and drives of your physical, emotional, and mental bodies and act under the command of these bodies. In the New Testament this is referred to as obeying the carnal body. If you follow these urges and drives, you will eventually find yourself trapped. When you use your urges and drives to trap others, you are creating a trap within a trap.

When we occupy ourselves with abhorrent vices, we create very complicated karma. Christ said that if we use slander, malice, gossip, and treason, we will pay a very heavy taxation. Treason is when you say to a person, "I love you," and then go behind his back and say, "He's nasty." Or you marry a nice woman and then sleep with other women.

When we disappoint or humiliate our spiritual Teacher, we create very complicated karma in our lives.

We create a tremendous amount of karma when we do not live in justice, observing the rights of others and our own rights. We must be righteous.

There were two cities in ancient Israel, Sodom and Gomorrah, where the people were living in immorality and insanity. Because the people were so degenerate, God decided to destroy the cities, so He sent His angels to burn them. Lot, who was a wise and good man, was sitting in front of his tent when the angels approached. They told him they were going to burn the cities because there were no righteous people living there. Lot pleaded with the angels and asked them to spare the cities if he could find ten righteous men. They agreed, but Lot was unable to find ten righteous men, so the cities were burned.

Righteousness was the virtue selected as a measure because it is the top principle. Because there were no righteous people in the cities, the Bible says, "Fire came from heaven and burned them into ashes." I have lived in areas on the other side of the Dead Sea in which there are mountains and mountains of ashes in which not a single thing grows.

Everyone has karma. Can anyone show me a person so holy, such a pure light, that he has no karma? We are human and make mistakes; mentally, emotionally, and physically we make mistakes. There is a point in consciousness when we stop creating karma; the five jewels which were previously discussed assist us in decreasing and annihilating karma.

Karma multiplies as a person approaches the more subtle levels. If he does something wrong physically, his karma is equivalent to four times four, or a karma of sixteen, speaking symbolically. If he commits an emotional wrong, it is equivalent to four times four times four, or a karma of sixty-four. If he commits a mental wrong, it is equivalent to the fourth power of four, or two hundred and fifty-six. If it is a psychic wrong, it becomes the fifth power of four, or one thousand twenty-four. Psychic karma is a blend of soul and personality, egoic karma, which is the blinded soul mixed with emotions, mind, urges, and drives.

Sometimes we find ourselves in family or personal situations in which the relationships are very strenuous. There are two choices for us to take in such situations. One is to develop divine indifference; the other is to leave and go. The latter option is a drastic measure, but sometimes if we do not go, we are moved anyway. Between the two, I would choose divine indifference. Let the annoying party go to heaven or hell; I will develop divine indifference because that person is the right one to help me learn and exercise divine indifference. It is an opportunity to detach and observe what is happening, why it is happening, how it is happening, what the results will be, and so on. If the person asks my opinion or advice, I would tell him without emotion that he is headed for disaster.

Spiritual life is steady discipline and building under difficult situations. We are unfolding and building higher bodies and mechanisms, which cannot develop in good conditions. The best conditions for the growth of the higher bodies and mechanisms are adverse ones, unfortunately. If one thinks about a difficult situation that he faced ten years ago, he will see that it was exactly that situation that made him develop, awaken, and unfold. Often we are not as grateful for these circumstances as we should be.

You multiply and increase your karma when you live a life of hypocrisy. If you are ugly, it is better for you to let people know you are ugly than to hide yourself. By hiding yourself, you mislead others. Do not pretend to be "holier than thou"; be what you are, if you can.

I feel grateful and happy if people aspire to make themselves more beautiful; this is natural. But a person should not disfigure himself or use make-up to cheat himself to try to appear beautiful. It is good to exercise and make the body more beautiful. There are also other natural measures to take that keep the body from aging. One way is eating the right foods that contain the proper nutrients, as well as relaxation and good sleep. Your cheeks will shine like a mirror.

Greed, jealousy, hatred, also joy, faith, hope, charity, and love change your face. A person is the exact replica of what he is inside. Why not find natural methods instead of spending money on chemicals that are taken from the internal organs of animals and women? Lord Buddha, Christ, and Krishna all taught us to be natural. To depart from what is natural is self-destructive.

Our karma increases and multiplies if we act under the pressure of our ego, vanity, and self-interest. When we think, speak, and act in tune with Beauty, Goodness, Righteousness, Joy, Freedom, Striving, and Sacrificial Service, we decrease and eventually dissolve our karma. Dissolution of karma is the application of these seven principles.

Beauty never builds karma. On the contrary, as a person works in beauty, his divinity manifests. *He* does not result in something; it is the Real Self that is expressed. Working for beauty decreases karma because karma is built by ugliness. Every ugly thing a person does creates karma; every beautiful thing he does destroys karma. The more beautiful a person becomes, the more he finishes his karma. It is a simple teaching to say, "Be more beautiful," but one must be physically beautiful, emotionally beautiful, mentally beautiful, have beautiful motives that are harmonious with divine principles. The same is true for Goodness, Righteousness, Joy, Freedom, Striving, and Sacrificial Service.

When I was seven years old, I was in my Father's pharmacy, which was built at the end of a dead-end street. At six o'clock my Father said, "It's time to close up." At this time all the shopkeepers would close and hurry home. My Father had bought a gift for my sisters, which was a bag out of which a spring-loaded goose would pop out when the bag was opened. I tested the trick many times, making sure it would work.

Just at the stroke of six as we were closing up, a man came to our door, very tired, saying, "I am very hungry. Please may I have a little something to eat?" My Father let the man in and prepared some food for him, and then said, "Take this food and go." He said, "It is very cold outside; may I please sit in here to eat it?" My Father looked at him, and then said, "All right, sit inside."

I sat down in front of the man, and watched him eat. He did not have any teeth and was taking a long time to eat the food. "The way he is going," I said to my Father, "it will take him three hours to finish his food." My Father told me to leave him alone and go play with the trick bag. As I was playing, we heard people screaming outside. My Father sprung to the door, opened it, and then quickly closed it, saying, "Thank You, my Lord."

An angry, large bull had gotten loose, and was killing everyone in the street. All those who closed promptly at six o'clock were killed. "Look," my Father said to me, "this poor man gave a great gift to us. A little bread and food saved our lives." By being hospitable to that man, we escaped.

My Father insisted that the man come home with us that evening, but the man hesitated because my Father was a professional man, and he was just a poor person. But my Father helped him into our car and we took him home with us. We may have certain karma, but one good act can save our lives.

Another time six of us were driving from Jerusalem to Amman. I was the middle passenger in the back seat. It was dark when we came to a place where there was supposed to be a bridge, but it had been totally washed out and the driver did not have time to stop the car. We plunged thirty feet down into the mud. As the water and mud began to enter the car, I said to my fellow travelers, "Come on, the mud is coming in. Let's get out of here." But no one moved. Though there was not a single scratch on any of us, all five of the other passengers were dead. When I asked my Sufi Teacher why I was not killed, he said, "You had savings in your bank account."

A poor old woman once came to my Father's pharmacy for medicine; he did not take her money and wrote "Paid" across the prescription. Then a poor man came in, and he did the same thing again. My Mother, who was at the pharmacy visiting my Father at the time said, "Who is going to pay?" My Father replied, "Whatever I give to these people will be returned in payment to our son." I came to the United States with no money; we now have two centers and many books published. I was really paid.

The Great Sage says that by visiting asylums, hospitals, and prisons, we will see the results of bad karma. Acts of Goodness, Beauty, Righteousness, Joy, and Freedom minimize karma. Christ advised us not to do bad things to others, even if they do bad things to us. By following this advice, we do not build karma.

Increase the joy of others. Do not make people sad, angry, irritated, or crazy for your own advantage. If you take the joy of others, you will never have joy; if you give joy, your joy will increase. Do not limit the freedom of others; if you limit freedom, you will not be free.

Karma increases and creates tidal waves on the shores of our higher bodies if we take people and situations for granted and use the psychology of exploitation. Do not take people and situations for granted, as if they belonged to you. Even if you sit under a tree and enjoy its fragrance, express your gratitude to the tree before you leave, and do something to help it if you can.

Karma multiplies if we change sexual partners frequently. This practice pollutes the aura. It also cracks a person's centers. Sex is natural; we need it. But we must use our mind, our judgment, and be righteous and clean about it. We also complicate our karma when we use sex to trap people.

This applies not only to sexual intercourse but also to sexual daydreaming, visualization, and imagination. They are actually more harmful than frequent physical sex with varied partners because we are committing those acts with our minds.

To trap people and manipulate them through sex is forbidden by all religions and codes of ethics. By doing this a person

    a. lies and pretends
    b. infects himself or others with various sicknesses
    c. fails to develop his love nature
    d. involves himself with complications and crime

These create heavy karma for the person which burdens his life, exhausts his time, and prevents him from working out his own spiritual and creative goals.

• CHAPTER 2 •

Karma

The Law of Karma is given to us not only to know that harmful actions will bring us painful events but also to help us discover how we can transform the inevitable wave of calamities by acting through wisdom and principles.

This mechanical law can be arrested and transformed by wisdom.

Any time of friction, opposition, animosity, or hostility is a moment of crisis, an opportunity when both sides, understanding the past, can stop and change the tension into friendship and mutual service. This is how karma can be stopped. Even if one side is destructively aggressive, the other side can "resist no evil," thus letting his karma be exhausted without making new karma. Of course, this is possible only for higher level Initiates who know the Law.

Such reasoning seems totally opposite to ordinary human logic. Self-defense is seen as a virtue in the world and a legal right, but in the Higher Worlds self-defense is a violation of the Law of Karma.

Those who do not know about the Law of Reincarnation will not understand the Law of Karma. It is thought that nonresistence encourages criminals, murderers, and exploitation. Truly it does not. Nonresistance gives an opportunity to the karmic laws to bring to their senses those who are aggressive in crimes. *What a power is necessary not to resist evil!*

The alchemical moment of transmutation is the moment in which you could kill an enemy but you choose to make him your friend. The alchemical moment of transmutation is the moment when you have an opportunity to slander, to kill, or to belittle a person but you do not. Any time your enemy involves you in his hatred and slander, you lose a precious moment of transmutation.

Enemies are agents of karma meeting with you for confrontation. You may change confrontation into compensation, into a moment in which you end the vicious circle of karmic occurrences.

Destruction of an enemy is the start of a new cycle of building a horrible karma. This is why, instead of having wars to end the problems of the world, one can use many powerful means to bring transmutation to the hearts of the people.

Resistance creates antagonistic power because it focuses the power. Nonresistance disperses it.

Wisdom, purity of heart, and understanding can transform your enemies and make them your friends. Of course, there are people who stay as enemies no matter how much goodwill you demonstrate toward them. Never give up. Be their friend and you will soon discover how much they have changed.

Karmic law brings together all those who are indebted to each other and gives them opportunity to cultivate a responsibility toward their Higher Self and toward others.

Karmic law gives place to the *Law of Conscience* and the sense of responsibility. As these predominate in our life, we stand above the karmic law and transform our past karma into experience and wisdom. In every crisis this opportunity is given to us.

People think that karma approaches us as punishment, sorrow, pain, and suffering. This is the half truth. The complete truth is that behind the appearance of karma is hidden the key of liberation — if this key is found and used in right the way through wisdom.

Pondering upon the Law of Karma releases many tensions accumulated in our psyche and consciousness.

People have many hatreds against those who have hurt them, slandered them, exercised malice and treason against them. They continuously carry grudges against those people. They cannot forgive them or forget what these people did to them. Such tensions accumulate and slowly destroy the creative forces in those who were attacked and slowly lead them into failure in various fields in their life. Also, their health suffers, and their relationship with other people slowly turns into negativity. Release from such tensions regenerates their whole being and field of labor.

One must go deeper into the Law of Karma and understand that the things people did to him was because he did similar things to others, in this life or in other lives. So the Law of Karma tolerated others to hurt him, or to "enlighten him," and put him on the right track of living.

Also, he must think that the people who caused him pain and suffering were actors under the command of karmic law, who may not even know why they caused pain or slandered him so deeply.

By thinking along these lines, you can minimize the tension and release those images from your mind — images you were holding with full hatred and anger, constantly wasting time and energy, and poisoning all your nature through a reaction against them charged with irritation.

Nothing would happen to you if you did not plant the seeds in the present and in the past. And if the things happening to you are in the nature of attacks, you have no reason to grieve because it is these attacks that will elevate you and lead you toward greater victories and achievement and call out of you more positive, creative forces into action.

But how to forgive yourself if you were the sower of the seeds of unhappiness that you are reaping now? The true approach to this problem is that it was not the *real, conscious You* who sowed those seeds but your personality who was not aware and awake. Your past lower self, activated by desires and blind urges and drives of the personality, did these things. Because you were more mechanical, you responded to the desires, malice, hatred, and fears of the environment and were used as tools by them.

Of course, you feel sorry for your past self that did many stupid things, but now you are not that self but an awakening one who knows how to live a better life, work hard, and joyfully pay the debts that your past self made.

Such a way of thinking will bring certain comfort and illumination if done consciously and carefully.

How to Overcome Karma

Karma can be overcome by two factors: one is repentance, the other is striving.

Repentance is a clear awareness of what you did wrong and a feeling of humiliation for your wrong deeds. It is also a readiness to compensate those to whom you did wrong.

In repentance you see where and how and why you did wrong and make a firm decision not to repeat those things you did wrong.

In repentance there is an attitude of understanding and sympathy toward those who did not tolerate your wrong doing.

In repentance there is also the attitude of asking forgiveness from those to whom you caused harm. In repentance you do not lie to yourself and to others.

A true repentance, we are told, can destroy a heavy karma, and frees you to build a new life upon a new consciousness.

Striving means to keep your spirit rising toward Beauty, Goodness, Righteousness, Joy, Freedom, Sacrificial Service, and continuous Striving. As you strive, the power of karma decreases and eventually you reach a stage when karma cannot hinder your advance in life.

Striving pulls your soul up from the three worlds and lets it enter into the peace and joy of eternal realms.

Often we think that karma is a blind law, like a machine which destroys anything that falls into it. *This is not true.* Karma adjusts itself by the following factors:

- Conditions or circumstances in which an action is taken
- Ignorance of action
- Forced action
- Possibility to avoid action
- Past blind forces urging the action
- Misunderstanding the result of the action
- Mechanical or unconscious action

- Repetition of recorded actions

All these factors on physical, emotional, and mental planes are taken under consideration by the very sophisticated computer of the karmic network.

Many actions that the mundane law condemns, the karmic law tolerates due to the nature of the above said factors. Manmade laws are not necessarily part of karmic laws.

There is another subtle point. Often people are forced to share family, group, or national actions, even against their own free will. Karma takes care of that problem too. Karma does not work on the principle of **justice** but on the principle of **righteousness**. This means that karma compensates all those who were engaged in actions not really within their own free will or intuition. Also, this means that the Law of Righteousness controls every action of karma.

There must be times when the load of the past karma is faced with heavy strain, stress, depression, grief, and shame. This is a period that brings deep enlightenment and a purification process if the person faces his karma with clear observation, acceptance, and with deep regret, and also with a decision not to fall into the same grooves again.

Karma can be met on different planes, such as physical, astral, and mental, and often on the three planes simultaneously, thereby creating a burning ground within the person.

During such periods of soul searching or facing one's own self in the submerging karmic dross, a man or woman must be left alone to go through such an internal conflict and purification process.

Artificial consolations do not help.

For example, when a person is facing the shock of his karma, he must not be told that

- it was not his mistake
- such a time of agony is like a bad dream which will pass away
- everyone has faults; do not consider public opinion
- he enjoyed doing the things he did, so what is wrong with it?

Rather, the struggling one must be left alone to come in contact with his Higher Self, or with his Teacher, and seek deeper enlightenment and purification. He must try to see the causes and find out where and when he took wrong action and why. Through such a procedure he will change the "poison" of karma into a cup of nectar. When the karmic flow releases itself, the person finds greater freedom and deeper sensitivity to cosmic shocks.[1]

There are three very important points:

1. The Law of Compassion or the pure Self or God is above Karmic Law.

---

1. For a full explanation of this topic, please see *Cosmic Shocks*.

2. No one can escape from the Law of Cause and Effect.

3. One can change his karma by striving and becoming a pure Self.

These points seem contradictory, but they are not.

1. When you are totally surrendered to God, He can do anything that He wants to do, irrespective of your past and present life.

2. You must pay for all that you did wrong physically, emotionally, and mentally as long as your consciousness operates in these realms.

3. When you are totally detached from the threefold personality and living as the Self, you have power to control the law or the reactions of your bodies and programmed events.

Karma operates like an object that is thrown up to the sky and falls down to earth. But when a person transcends his ignorance, he creates airplanes or satellites which transcend the law of gravity!

People think that the Law of Karma controls every stage of human development. This is not true. For every stage of evolution you have a specific law or a package of laws.

The same law is powerless on another stage of evolution. Laws are limited to certain areas and planes.

When we talk about the Law of Karma, we are aware that this law in time operates in a "limited" field which is the field in which the wheel of life and death continuously runs for millions of incarnations. But the miracle is that it is possible to operate beyond it!

• CHAPTER 3 •

Karma and Omissions

Karma is translated as *action*, and every time we speak about karma we speak about action. Karma is formed by our actions on physical, emotional, and mental planes.

But this is not the whole story. The neglected part of the story is that our karma is formed also by our inaction, negligence, denial, carelessness, inattentiveness, omission, or even stupidity.

When we are mentally, emotionally, and physically inactive toward a situation which needs handling, interference, response, or reaction, we create a great amount of karma.

Suppose a man is indifferent toward an increasing amount of germs around his house, increasing amount of crimes in his street, increasing amount of treason against his group or nation — what will happen to him?

When a person does not bring light into darkness, darkness swallows him. When a person does not disperse ignorance, ignorance overcomes him and destroys his future.

There was a little lake that belonged to our neighbor. I told him that some dangerous weeds had begun to grow in it. He was not interested in my words. One year later, the lake disappeared with the weeds. He spent so much money and time to clean the lake. During the cleaning, he passed away.

A doctor told a man to get rid of some poisonous insects in his yard. He neglected to do so and all his family was attacked and died.

Some nations rejoice when they see ignorance, crime, and corruption within their neighboring nations, but a few decades later through many ways and means, the neighbors become the greatest danger for their survival. If they were not ready to protect themselves, that neighbor would enslave them or even destroy them.

If your neighbor is in darkness, make it possible to educate him or else your nation will very soon be contaminated by that neighbor.

People speak about tolerance. The dark forces[1] are very intelligent to use this word on their own behalf. Tolerance does not mean to let people destroy your joy, health, and freedom, steal your bread, your home, your

---

1. For a full discussion of the ways of evil, please see *Battling Dark Forces, A Guide to Psychic Self-Defense.*

dignity, your honor, your rights. If you let them do it, you create an immense karma.

Negligence is responsible for the increase of crime and for the widespread of corruption and degeneration of our morality.

We allowed termites to enter and destroy our homes. We allowed people to destroy our principles, visions, the images of our worship until the sacredness evaporated from our lives.

Words like tolerance and patience are used by some who know how to use these terms against their true meaning. Tolerance can be exercised only when people's actions are controlled by Beauty, Goodness, Righteousness, Joy, Freedom, Striving, and Sacrificial Service.

Patience is the state of consciousness of a person who is equipped enough not to worry about the arrows released against him.

Patience is the state of consciousness of a person who wants to let evil die through its own efforts.

Patience is the state of consciousness of a person who knows that the Laws of Nature will bring him the future due to his striving and labor.

To be patient does not mean to wait until you die under the blows of evil.

People think that patience is measured by length of time. On the contrary, patience acts faster than the speed of light when it is needed.

Patience is used to equip yourself with full armor before you enter into the battle of light.

Enemies of mankind teach us the wrong idea about patience. They say, "Wait a little more, be patient," and during that period they destroy your foundation.

A misunderstood virtue is more destructive than a vice.

Thus, karma is created also by what you do not do. We build more karma by **not doing** things we should have done than by doing things we should not have done.

• CHAPTER 4 •

Karma as Opportunity

In studying the Law of Unity people will gradually turn their attention to group karma.

At the present, people talk about their individual karma and try to solve their own problems. But in the future, people will be intensely interested in the group karma and try to solve the group problems.

The health and happiness of humanity decisively affects the well-being of the planet as a whole, just as the striving of a man affects the well-being of his entire body. The widespread epidemics and diseases and slaughter going on around the planet deeply affect our planet. The condition of humanity, the increasing crime, the killings, the disturbances within the psyche of humanity such as fear, revenge, greed, all these testify that our planet is sick. We need to take extraordinary actions to do our best to slow down the destructions going on in the human psyche, in the planet, in the air, in the oceans, and in the morality of humanity.

The progress of technology and science has not been justified in giving us health and happiness.

The world is in a miserable condition. The money of the world, to the highest percentage, is used for wars, violence, and demoralizing pleasures.

How can humanity survive in such conditions?

Events are the effects of certain causes. When one is involved in such an event it is his *attitude* toward the event that is the effect of his past karma, not the event in which he is involved.

The same event occurring in the life of three persons is reacted to in three different ways:

1. One takes it as his karma and learns a lesson.
2. The second looks at the same event as the result of some causes which he wants to investigate.
3. The third one ignores the event entirely.

Here are three attitudes. It is the attitude that translates the motive of the event.

Our response or reaction, our attitude, is built by the forces which we put in motion in the past.

Events have collective causes, but our attitude toward any event is built up within us by our own hands.

These three people are like three surfers. The waves rise. One surfs and reaches the shore. Another one falls in the ocean but saves his life. The third perishes.

The skill, the muscles, the art of surfing correspond to their individual karma, but the rising waves are caused by a collective karma.

Sometimes when we are in a tense state of relationship with someone we justify continuing such a condition by thinking that "it is our karma."

But if your private, individual karma is favorable in every crisis, you will find an opportunity to heal, to transform, to lead instead of falling into the current of painful crises.

Pain and suffering come to people as the result of collective karma, but some people perish in pain and suffering. Some people use the situation as a great challenge to exercise their inner potentials. Some others entirely transform themselves, using the situation as a very rare opportunity.

The Karmic Lords work with human beings through the person's permanent atoms, the permanent recorders of his actions, feelings, and thoughts. They are the memory cells which, after the physical body has died, still continue to exist. When the person is taking incarnation, the permanent atoms create the forms according to the recordings.[1]

During one's life the Karmic Lords use these recordings to enact the karma of the man. Each permanent atom is a built-in system within us which records our life in all its aspects.

---

1. See also *The Science of Becoming Oneself*, Ch. XII, "The Chalice and the Seeds."

Another karmic informer is our Solar Angel,[2] Who is in direct contact with the Karmic Lords.

It must be realized that we move, live, and have all our being in an Eternal Presence. Nothing can be hidden whatsoever. All our lives are open books for that Great Presence.

Real privacy does not exist in Nature. The mundane sciences will very soon make any privacy impossible. The only privacy is to live a life in harmony with the Common Interest.

All qualities built into our bodies are the result of our good and creative thoughts, emotions, and actions. The recordings of good actions in the three planes accumulated in the permanent atoms turn into virtues and divine qualities in our three vehicles. As such recordings accumulate, the stream of joy releases itself from our Core and galvanizes all our systems.

People often cannot succeed in helping those whom they previously persecuted. This is a strange fact of observation. Their past karma stops them, unless they realize the magnitude of harm they caused them and feel deeply sorry for it.

This is why when a person is causing you certain damage do not do the same to him, so that later a chance is given to you to help him. Remember always that those who make malicious attacks on you are those who will need your help. Acting against them as they acted against you prevents the chance for you to help them in the future.

---

2. See also *The Solar Angel*.

People's harmful acts against someone break the natural ties that exist between them for a long time, until the karmic law makes them depend on those whom they hurt.

The Karmic Law may seem very complicated, but in reality it is very simple. The best way not to be involved with the Law is not to violate it. You do not violate the Karmic Law when you live a harmless life plus a life of service for others.

These two principles can almost certainly secure protection for you from the attacks of the Karmic Law.

A life lived in Beauty, Goodness, Righteousness, Joy, Freedom, Striving, and Sacrificial Service not only eliminates major parts of your past karma, but also enlightens you in such a degree that you do not build further karma.

To minimize a karma, and its force upon our life, we can increase our service to humanity. The more service we render, the more capital we have, and in the time when karmic bills are due we easily pay them.

Service and labor not only balance our karma but also create within us those powers by which we transform the karmic forces into creative forces and use the events produced by our past karma as resources of wisdom and courage.

When we face our karma consciously, we build our character, the attitude by which we overcome difficulties and hindrances and pave our way toward a new level of perfection.

The Karmic Law has one major purpose: to lead the human soul to his destination, which in the Ageless Wisdom is often called the *Mark*.

Stage after stage, the Karmic Law awakens in man the awareness of this Mark, which gradually absorbs the whole attention of the human being.

One can contemplate about the Mark, about the nature of the Mark. One can write and speak about the Mark, but until one experiences the Mark, being the Mark Itself, it remains a pleasant dream in our life.[3]

Experience[4] is not a physical, emotional, and mental response or reaction to an event, but a transformation process toward beingness.

Karmic Law eventually makes man achieve such a transformation.

---

3. See also *The Purpose of Life* for a full discussion of the true Purpose.
4. See also *The Ageless Wisdom*, Ch. 24, "Experience."

• CHAPTER 5 •

Forgiveness and Karma

We are taught that all our actions on all the planes of our being are registered in the karmic computer. If that is so, then what is the place of forgiveness?

The *first answer* is that by forgiving you do not involve yourself with the one who is creating bad karma for himself.

Second, by forgiving the person you give a chance to him not to continue his negative actions but instead to have a better attitude toward people.

When some people are forgiven they go back again to their former style of actions and worsen their life. This should not discourage people in forgiving them because though a person forgives another person, still the deeds of that person are in the computer.

Third, forgiveness builds a shield around you which prevents the negative thoughts of the forgiven person from penetrating into the sphere of your mental body and negatively programming you.

Fourth, the law says that "those who forgive will be forgiven." This means that every time we really forgive, we put savings into our bank, and we draw upon it at the time of our need.

Fifth, those who forgive cooperate with the Solar Angels of those who live a bad life. Their Solar Angels may use the forgiving person to influence the other with lofty thoughts.

Sixth, forgiveness creates tranquillity in our system, which prevents the buildup of irritation and *imperil.*

But we are advised that forgiveness should not make us sleep and prevent us from watching the person and not taking precautions for his possible misbehavior.

Every forgiver must develop also vigilance and closely observe the movements of the person he forgave.

Seventh, forgiveness draws you out of your self-interest, develops your love and compassion, and helps you to understand life and people better.

Eighth, forgiveness minimizes the taxation of your karmic deeds. You pay less karmic tax when you forgive.

Ninth, every time you feel angry and hateful toward a person who hurts you, you create a channel between him and you through which his malice flows into you and contaminates your aura. Many people became exactly like those whom they hated.

It is very wise to hand the problem over to the Karmic Lords, and know that They will handle the situation better than you.

• CHAPTER 6 •

Karma and Position

If karma does not let you go forward on the path of your evolution, you can be surrounded by an ocean of beauty, knowledge, and art but remain a sealed bottle in it. Such a karma prevents you from opening and assimilating the energy that will help you to progress on the path of your evolution.

You can have wonderful Teachers, the Teaching, but they never penetrate into your heart, and if at any time the Teaching or the Teacher contradicts or opposes your self-interest, you become a dark enemy against them. This implies that in the past you either tried to prevent people from enjoying the Teaching or you made their life miserable by persecuting them because of their Teaching. You are put, life after life, into circumstances in which you see in the mirror of your life what you did to others in the past.

There is also the possibility that, because of your vices, you are possessed by dark entities who use you against the Teaching or the Teachers.

In such occasions, your attitude is not the result of your past direct attack on the Teaching but, because of your corrupted life, you became an instrument in the hands of dark forces and allowed them to attack the Teaching, using you as their mechanism. Sometimes both cases are present, and this is what makes a person a traitor.

Some people think that when they do harmful things against people under hypnosis or under possession, they are not to be blamed or punished. This is not a correct conclusion. A person is punished for his past deeds, for associating himself with dark forces and serving them. When you fall into the hands of criminals whose purpose it is to stop your and others' evolution, this is a severe punishment in itself. If you are lying, stealing, killing, exploiting, hurting people in various ways, all these are really punishments for you. When you steal that thousand dollars, you are punishing yourself in committing that crime. You are trapping yourself in dire consequences.

Those who are in some way prevented from serving the Teaching and, through the Teaching, humanity, or in many ways persecute those who serve the Teaching, are those who because of their past are brought in to play such roles so that they eventually realize the facts and break the vicious circle of their lives. Often it takes a few lives to make people have such a breakthrough.

When we speak about the Teaching and the Teacher, many people think about religion. But in truth the Teaching is the Law of Life, the Law of Love, Compassion, Purity, Service, Unity. If this law is violated in any field, you become the enemy of the law and live a lawless life.

In violating the law for your own selfish ends, you make yourself the enemy of the law, and this is how you yourself punish yourself.

As a reward in life for your past service, a position is given to you in which you can truly serve people to refine their character and make them cultivate their virtues and unfold the divine potentials in themselves. Such a service is the reward given to you for your past beneficent actions or deeds.

In an ordination ceremony my Teacher told the candidates, "You are ready to vest yourself with the robe of responsibility and dedicated service. Such a life will be a source of spiritual prosperity in your lives. This is a gift for you, offered to you by life. Try to cherish this gift, and never let temptations and crises take this gift from your hands."

Karma blocks not only your roads leading to the fields of service and study but also blocks your understanding, the source of energy which would lead you to striving.

Do not waste your time with your vices, hatreds, jealousies, and slander, thus collecting enough wood to burn yourself.

This is why the Teaching says that if you follow the traitors life after life, you will see how painfully they pay their karmic debts.

Karma works in unexpected ways. For example, if you harmed someone in the past, you are put in a condition that you help him in this life or even you become his best servant or assistant. It is possible also that a position is given to you in the Teaching so that you serve, even if you do not believe in what you are doing.

One day my Teacher, pointing to a man who was the architect and treasurer of the monastery, said, "He built this monastery, and many others, but he never believed in the Teaching. He is faithful and clean in many matters, but he is not interested in the spiritual path. He does all these things to pay his karma of the past."

"Does he know about it?"

"Intuitively he knows, but his brain is not yet aware of it. My duty is to keep him in his position to help him to pay his karma, as long as he is faithful to his duties."

"Can't his presence in the monastery deteriorate our thoughtforms of the Teaching and weaken our dedication?"

"It may, and if some standards are affected by him it is good, as it will reveal to us those whom we cannot entrust with more responsible jobs. And also if some are affected by him, they will start an inner fight between doubt and dedication, and through such a battle only the true dedication can be won and expressed. In reality he is not a dangerous fellow because in his heart he knows that he is paying his past bills in this life."

"Then why is he not punished in other ways? This is like a vacation for him."

"It seems that he worked against the Teaching in the past and, without conscious intention, profited from it. Maybe he paid a heavy karma in the past, and in this life he is almost ready to pay his last bill and to have a chance to come again to the Teaching."

I know well that my Teacher spoke the facts because I saw in my life how slowly and miraculously I was initiated into the Teaching, in spite of many difficulties and in spite of many traps on my path. The greatest gift in our life is to be in the Teaching and to remain in it in spite of all kinds of problems and difficulties because the Teaching is the straight path leading us to health, happiness, prosperity, and to sacrificial service. Also the Teaching is the Light of your Real Self, which you cannot avoid in the long run.

Some people, after many lives, realize the damage they did to others and come back to pay for their damage. Some people come back to destroy the walls they built between people in the past. Some people come back to change the laws which they made in the past for their selfish intentions.

Once I heard someone saying to a lawmaker:

"You make these laws and burden people to please your immediate motives, but it is your children and your children's children who will suffer because of these laws."

"Well, if they do not like them, let them change the laws again."

"I believe that you yourself will come back painfully to change the laws you made in the past. It will be good for you if you do not delay doing it because the longer you wait, the more painful will be your efforts to change your own laws."

It is man that does things and undoes them again. The process of undoing is the chance to change and is the chance to pay your bills

One day my Teacher told a graduating student who was going to work in a school teaching teenagers, "I am giving this certificate to you for your graduation to make you realize the importance of your office. Often we are shorter than our office. Be careful that because of your ego, vanity, and self-interest you do not hurt your office and that for which it stands. Even if many vices and weaknesses want you to violate your office, fight courageously and always hold your office higher than your personality interests."

He spoke these words so powerfully that for some fifty years I have not forgotten them, and many times I have realized how people destroy the glory of their office for their pleasures, greed, jealousy, and so on.

Karmically, an office is more important than your self-interest and pleasures. An office is a standard and is established as a center of service. For example, fatherhood, motherhood, and leadership are offices, formed by the highest standards possible.

The position a teacher has is an office. The offices in the army, in the government are centers for higher principles. A judge is a higher office. Karmically, even if you hurt yourself, you must not hurt your office.

Karma is more severe to those who betray their office than to those who hurt themselves. Karma highly rewards those who, even having many weaknesses, protect and uplift their office at the expense of their lives.

A person elected into office must fit to the office and with his conduct, thoughts, words, and actions represent that office.

The office is the expression of certain standards, principles, duties, and responsibilities. The "officer" must try to embody the spirit of his office. In trying to honor his office, a person can even transform his life.

Many people do not feel ready to represent a high office, but once they dedicate their life and sincerely and honestly try to represent the spirit of their office, a miraculous inner change takes place. It is as if the person feels he is overshadowed by his inner Light, by some superhuman entity.

Commitment to the job of a high office is the shortest path to transform your nature and to build a beautiful karma for your future.

People will slowly understand that a part of space is the most intricate computer ever conceived in the brain of man.

The recordings of our karma are automatic. Each action, each word, each emotion, and each thought sends electrical waves to the computer and is recorded there.

These recordings in cycles condition the life of the person according to their contents.

Karma remains in the computer, and in every birth the person is born and raised under the invisible control of karma. Karma is a continuous process, and we can say that man builds his future through the life he lives, he feels, he talks, he thinks. Once the Law of Karma is understood, people will live in love, in respect, and will help each other to have the best life.

The Law of Karma was given by the Ancients. *Whatever you sow you will reap.* This law must be taught to everyone in the world, from kindergarten to university levels. The better we understand the law, the better will life be on earth.

The Law of Karma is the law of action and the corresponding reaction. Life on this planet is built on this law. One can use this law and prepare for himself a life of bliss, or ignore it and prepare a life of suffering and pain.

If we read history carefully, we will see how this law acts not only individually but also on national and global levels.

A life lived with selfishness, ego, exploitation, separation, murder, injustice, and so on will bring a life of unhappiness, pain, and suffering. Life lived in harmlessness, love, joy, service, righteousness, goodness, beauty will create a kind of life which will give all opportunities to be mental, spiritual giants. The life of the planet is the expression of how we lived as individuals and nations in the past.

It is interesting that some of our universities have special projects, in various fields, but none of them have a project to discover the causes of all the suffering, pain, wars, natural calamities, crimes, and widespread corruption. It will be interesting to see what the result will be of such a research, given all the means we have in our hands at the present.

Can humanity not decide to turn this planet into a planet of joy?

We have all kinds of technology. What is lacking is the technology of right human relations and right relations with the Universe and with its Source.

• **Chapter 7** •

Cause and Karma

We learn in the Ageless Wisdom that a cause comes into existence only through its opposites, and with its opposites it creates an effect. This law is applicable in all the seven fields of human endeavor,[1] not just in science and philosophy.

People think about cause, forgetting its opposite which makes a cause be causal. These causal activities in the world come into being by their opposites, which then create effects. The opposites are not antagonistic to each other but are positive and negative cables that make your battery function as a cause and produce effects.

---

1. Politics, Education, Communication and Philosophy, Arts, Science, Religion, and Finance.

When the Teaching speaks about going beyond the pairs of opposites, it refers to a state of beingness in which this triangle no longer limits the freedom of the emancipated human soul.

The Teaching indicates that the Great Bear with its opposites, the Pleiades, created seven solar systems. This was the effect. We know so little about this effect. The Tibetan Master suggests that when a Rishi from the Great Bear forms a triangle with the Pleiades and the Planetary Logos, then the secrets of karma will start to unfold.

The karma of the Solar Logos is hidden in the One Who uses these mighty constellations as vehicles of His threefold personality.

The karma of people is the result of the law of this triangle.

In the human being we have a similar triangle. We have the Great Bear, the seven centers in the head; the Pleiades, the seven centers in the etheric body; and the effect of these, the seven solar systems and the 777 incarnations resulting from our karma.

The Tibetan Master speaking about the 777 incarnations says that, "At the termination of the 777 incarnations, a man passes through the door of initiation and enters upon a brief synthesising process, or a final period in which he garners the fruits of the experience in the two first halls, and transmutes knowledge into wisdom, transforms the shadow of things seen into the energy of that which is, and achieves the final liberation from all the lower forms which seek to hold him prisoner...."[2]

The unfoldment of the petals are related to the series of incarnations that the human soul goes through, gathering experiences and wisdom.

For example, we are told that we need 700 incarnations to activate the lowest petals of our Chalice. Then we have 70 incarnations which develop the second tier of petals, the love petals. Then we have 7 incarnations which are related to the sacrifice petals.[3] The Tibetan Master says that "the two outer rings of petals are stimulated in a new and special sense through the conscious act of the probationary disciple.... the mental body becomes active, and two of the will [sacrifice] petals are co-ordinated, and one 'awakes' vitality and unfolds."[4]

When we talk about national karma, we must consider the various elements that incarnated in that nation, and the reasons why they incarnated.

Nations are not composed of homogeneous elements. They are like rivers into which many streams unite and form an apparent whole, which in reality is a mixture of many human elements.

Every nation is formed, for example, of those who are enemies to each other on three levels — physical, emotional, mental — as well as of elements that play their part in negotiations between them and those who fan

---

2. Alice A. Bailey, *A Treatise on Cosmic Fire*, p. 829.
3. For more information on the Chalice and petals, please see *The Subconscious Mind and the Chalice*.
4. Alice A. Bailey, *A Treatise on Cosmic Fire*, p. 828.

the fires of separatism. Every nation has this, and humanity is an example of it. So a national karma is the result of two antagonistic forces, and two interfering elements. The same is true for humanity.

What brings salvation or freedom from such a complex is the fifth factor. This fifth factor is the factor of spirit. I am not referring to religions, dogmas, and doctrines. The fifth factor is one that uses all these four elements toward a purpose, which then provides the point of accomplishment of the purpose of life for all these four elements.

And what is that factor? It is the realization of the purpose of our individual life.

It is not the karma that must run our life, but it is the purpose of our life that must run the life of the planet.

Cause and effect seem to us a duality, but in reality this law is based on a trinity. We have a cause which cannot produce an effect without its opposite.

For example, energy as a cause cannot produce an effect without matter. Willpower as a cause cannot produce an effect without vehicles. An idea cannot produce an effect without mental substance. So we have a trinity. We have cause, substance, and the effect.

Our karma is the cause of our future. Future is the effect of our karma working through what we do, feel, and think. Without these, karma does not exist.

To make karma nonexistent, we must go beyond our thoughts, emotions, and actions. This is what it means to enter into Nirvana.

It is not only things that we do to others or for others that create karma, but it is also things that we do not do to others and for others.

When we are all involved with our self-interest and do not care to illuminate our neighbors or bring prosperity into their life, they eventually attack us by weapons of darkness and poverty. And we blame them for their deeds!

Karma is the result of action and also the result of inaction.

Many nations create karma by choosing apparent neutrality toward demanding needs.

My whole labor is the result of my research. My research is in the field of laws and principles that manifest as relationship between people, groups, and nations; as relationship between physical, emotional, and mental life with the Purpose of life. I assume that life is leading us to an ultimate Purpose, as every seed is led to its ultimate purpose of unfoldment.

I try to study the laws, the principles, and the process by which a labor is accomplished.

• CHAPTER 8 •

The Other Worlds and Karma

What are the Other Worlds?[1] We have this earth, our globe. Around it there is an electromagnetic field called the etheric body of our globe. What does this electromagnetic field do? It receives energies from the solar

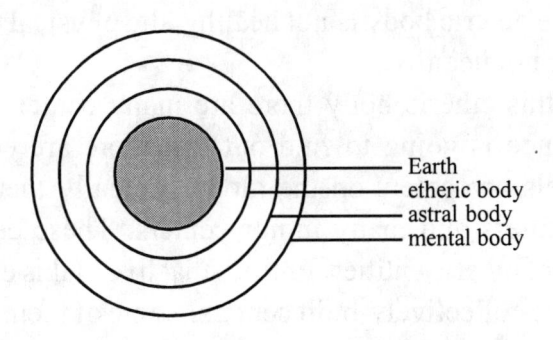

- Earth
- etheric body
- astral body
- mental body

---

1. Much detailed information on this topic is available in *Other Worlds*.

system and other galaxies and refines them and adjusts them and gives them to the planetary body. In the sun we have lots of energies which create growth, which create progress, even create wisdom, intellect, love, and light. All these come from the sun. The etheric body is the reception center of our planet. The same is true for your etheric body. Your etheric body receives energy and transmits it to the physical body. If you do not have an etheric body, you do not have the energy transmission system.

All of us have an etheric body. The Great Teacher, talking about the etheric body, says that "in the future people will know that most of the sicknesses of the physical body are the result of a disturbance in the etheric body." The etheric body is very important for you, for the planet, and for every living form. Even a leaf has an etheric body. For example, when Kerlian photography brought us the electromagnetic field of the leaves we saw that some of them were healthy, some of them were not. When the etheric body is not healthy, the physical counterpart is not healthy.

In this etheric body there are many centers. One day science is going to find out that there are energy whirlpools or centers on the globe. Actually there are seven centers and many minor centers. These centers are built of etheric entities. Entities that live in this etheric sphere are collectively-built centers. Some of them build the head center. Others build the sacral center. Others build the solar plexus center. These are all centers, but these etheric centers are formed of small lives in the etheric body of the planet.

In the etheric plane there are lots of human beings. When people leave their physical body, some go directly there. Those who commit suicide or those who suddenly die or are suddenly killed, mostly they go to the etheric plane. A very important thing to know is that a part of the population in the etheric plane is also formed of aborted children. That is very bad news for those who commit abortion. These children are stuck there for maybe seventy, eighty, ninety years.

Karma is the energy and the law which decides what will be the result of your actions, emotions, and thoughts. It is a very complicated law, and it is the first program in the computer of the Universe. It is a big program, and it is very minutely detailed. It is very developed, and it does not miss any point. If your thoughts, emotions, and actions combined do not exceed in light, love, and beauty, let us say five or ten points, when you leave your body you go to the etheric plane. What do you do there? You are really stuck there. You cannot do anything. We can do nothing in the etheric body, in the emotional body, in the mental body that we did not start in the physical plane. Any work that you started in the physical plane you can continue in the Other Worlds if you are awake to a certain degree.

Karma causes disturbances in three energies. If you disturb the love principle, light principle, and beauty principle, you are bound to come back. Imagine how many millions of times you acted against love. Immediately when you feel hatred, you are against love. Immediately when you are separative or selfish or have different vices that are against love, you are bound to come back because you disturbed the Law of the Universe which is the Law of Light, Love, and Beauty.

This planet is a very big school. God created this school so that we become perfect. How to be perfect? It is by seeing the results of our actions, emotions, and thoughts. We will never develop if we do not see the result of our actions. The Other Worlds is like a mirror, and in this mirror we can see exactly how we lived in the physical plane. In general, people cannot change anything in the Other Worlds. They cannot start anything new there, except sometimes they are awakened one second and see the results of what they did while on earth.

There are five kinds of people who travel. There are those who go all the way to the mental plane and come back like a cocoon; they are not conscious of what is happening. Maybe eighty percent of humanity is in that level. They die and they are dead. There is no consciousness at all. They go to the etheric plane, to the emotional plane, and to the mental plane, and the law sends them back to earth so that they awaken on earth. If you awaken in the physical plane two percent, you will be awake in the Other Worlds two percent. It depends on your life in the physical plane. You cannot be illuminated in the Other Worlds. You cannot be a Master in the Other Worlds. You cannot continue your evolution in the Other Worlds. Your evolution is carried on only on the physical plane.

The second kind of people are those people who are able to awaken momentarily in these planes while they are travelling in the Other Worlds. What they see in their moments of awakeness is the result of their actions, of their thoughts, of their speech. That is what hell is. For example, you did an action and you are so happy, but in the etheric plane you see how many laws you disturbed and how many people you harmed. You do not see it here. For example you shoot an arrow and that arrow goes through the fields. How many insects did it kill, how may flowers were cut? How many plants did it destroy? Eventually it reaches somewhere and you think that it is over. But your words, your actions, and your thoughts continually do their damage if they are destructive or harmful. An awakened person sees the effects of his actions in the Other Worlds.

Conscious living is to know what will be the result of what you are doing. It is so important, but people are hardly living a conscious life. They just live automatically, do things, feel things, think things without knowing what will be the result of their actions. The result of their actions will disturb many beings, many laws, many principles, many standards, but they feel that they were just speaking a little lie or slightly cheating someone. The lie that you speak here goes to the Other Worlds as if it were a truth and fantastically grows there; it becomes a monster. When it reaches the mental plane, the law hits it back and you are exposed in some way in pain and suffering.

The third kind of people are awakened people. They are seventy percent awake. Immediately when they sleep or die, they are in the etheric plane, in the astral plane, and in the mental plane. What happens to them? They visit the etheric plane and learn tremendous sciences there — the science of cause and effect, causes of things that are happening, and the effects of the things that happened. This is science. Science is to find the cause and the effect and program your life in such a way that you are able to be a cause instead of being an effect.

An awakened soul also goes to the astral plane and learns tremendous things there. The astral world is a very superior university where laws and principles and activities are going on, and you cannot benefit if you are sleeping there. If you are in the airplane and traveling in sleep, you come back without seeing or experiencing anything.

An awakened soul also enters into the mental plane and sees the Ashrams, the groups, fantastic scientists, sees how the laws of the Universe are working, the cause of everything that came into being, how they became effects starting from one little leaf, to the insects, to the baboons, to the man, to the Universes.

A man who is awakened in the Other Worlds makes his trip and comes back as a genius because he learns much in his journey. If he stays on any plane of the Other Worlds thirty years, that thirty years is equal to three thousand years on the physical plane. The learning on higher planes is very fast. For example, you have a dream. You say it is nine-thirty and you sleep. You awaken at nine thirty-two. You slept two minutes but in two minutes you were dreaming something that may be a ten-hour event. There is no time and space there. The etheric plane time is faster than the physical plane, but the emotional plane time is faster than the etheric plane, and the mental plane time is faster than the emotional plane. If your dream is in the mental plane, you cover approximately three hundred years in your dream, but if you are in the emotional plane, you cover a dream of thirty years. If you are in the etheric plane, you cover a dream for ten years. These figures are symbolic. As you go higher, your speed goes higher and annihilation of time occurs. Still there is time, but when you are in higher planes the time is almost nil.

The fourth kind of people are those people who go beyond or into the Higher Worlds and do not come back. Their karma is paid, their obligations and responsibilities are paid. They clean their hands and they say goodbye to the nursery of the planet. They do not come back anymore to the nursery because it does not contribute to their evolution. They need other planets, other universities, other galaxies to go to and learn to actualize "O Self-revealing One, reveal Thyself in me."

All these schools help you slowly to realize and actualize the God *that you are*. You are not this body. You will see forty, fifty years later that they will dump you, burn you. It has an end, and then you will come again as a baby.

The fifth kind of people are those people who go to the Higher Worlds and for a special mission they come back. But it is not karma that is bringing them; it is Their mission bringing them back.

There are three things that bring you back. They are karma, mission, and responsibility. *Karma* is that you are forced to come and you cannot escape. *Mission* is that you think about people on earth and say, "Let me go once more and shed a big light for them. Let me go once more and be an example for them. Let me go back and save them from a disaster." For example, in Atlantean times when the earth was shaking and fire was coming and the whole Atlantis was breaking into pieces, a Great One came and collected some people and took them to the Himalayas. He should no longer have come, but because of His love and responsibility, and because of the mission given by Higher Forces, He came back.

For example, you are in the Higher Worlds resting. You are in Universal, Cosmic duties and responsibilities. Then the Boss says to you, "Go down. Build a ship, and save these few million people from the deluge and take them to the Himalayas." This is a mission.

A mission is given to you by Higher Powers. *Responsibility* is one that you feel. The Law of Karma makes you to reap whatever you sowed.

When you are in the physical plane, you make three kinds of mistakes. The church translates them as sins. We call it karma. Karma means action which always produces reaction. The three kinds of mistakes are mistakes in thinking, mistakes in feeling and speech, and mistakes in actions. There is nothing that moves without thought, speech-feeling, and action. When I am talking, this talk is going everywhere and creating some results in the Universe. When you receive some results, you also create some causes. For example I say, "Do not steal anymore," and you say, "I am not." You become a cause yourself by obeying that rule, and you never steal again. You become a cause. You take the effect and understand the effect and change it into a cause, and you become a source of a new cause. And by the new cause you change your life.

On the planet you have thoughts, emotions, actions. All these form human relations. How do we communicate with each other? It is with these three things. If your actions are making karma, you pay the karma. You see the results of the karma in the etheric plane. When this etheric plane is really polluted, you have "earthquakes and cataclysms." This is because the electromagnetic sphere of your body becomes so shaky and so rejective, so disturbed in transforming and circulating the energies of Nature, that you create friction between you and the Nature. That is how sickness comes. If one million people are like that, that place is earthquake-prone. Escape from there. For example, in Sodom and Gomorrah three men came and said, "We are going to burn Sodom and Gomorrah." They were asked, "Why?" "It is because there are no righteous men here."

What does "righteous man" mean? People take this religiously, but we must take it scientifically. A righteous man is one who is in harmony with the laws of

Nature. An unrighteous man is a man who has friction with the laws of Nature. He is creating friction between the laws of Nature and himself. So the Great Ones come and say, "We are going to burn the city with earthquakes and cataclysms and floods." At this time we have had lots of them. So the Teaching says, "We send you floods; we send you fires; we send you earthquakes. But you never awaken. You continue to do the same things that you were doing: doping, living and laying, cheating each other, stealing from each other, and so on." The etheric body is a very sensitive mechanism.

The Great Sage says, "If you are clairvoyant and see a man who is in action, watch his etheric body. You will see tremendous changes with every second of feeling, thinking, imagination, and visualization which totally change the color and formation and circulation of his aura and etheric body." Most of our sickness and health depend on the etheric body and aura.

Our action is perceived in the etheric plane. If you did not really see the result of your actions on the physical plane, you will have a great opportunity to see the results on the etheric plane if you have seeing eyes. You become a super psychiatrist, a super psychologist because you really see what is happening in your aura. This makes you a great scientist because you see how some physical, emotional, and mental energies are operating in your aura.

All our life is the reflection of our aura. Our aura shows what will happen to us in the future. For example, I may think badly about you. That is an action, and thousands of atoms and cells in your bodies are disturbed and you do not go to work the next day because you feel weak. The job suffered. Somebody who was coming there to replace you had an accident. Because he had an accident the boss lost ten thousand dollars, and because he had to pay the ten thousand dollars he was so mad that he went and hurt another man. When he hurt the man, many lawyers started to make money by lying. The money was transferred to their children, and they lived with that money that was brought by the lawyers' lies. All the money was gained by lies. There was no reality in it. Now you can see this on the etheric plane before it manifests in life. You become such a great scientist, but you have to develop a seeing eye.

One of the greatest purposes of your life is not to make money, is not to eat, drink, and so on. These are all fine. You need them because you have bodies. The greatest purpose of your life at least for awhile is to see and to be awake. As soon as you are on the etheric plane, you can see what is happening there as a consequence of your actions. The same is true on the astral plane and the mental plane. You have to be awake to see on the planes the effects of your actions, emotions, and thoughts. But when you die, the results of your life affect the etheric plane.

How does one become awakened? When you say on the physical plane, "I am always awake," you are not. You are really sleeping because the physical body is controlling you, the emotional body is controlling you, or the mental body is controlling you. You are a puppet of your physical, emotional, and mental energies and currents and actions and relations. You are not awake. When you awaken ten percent on the physical plane, on higher planes you will be awake ten percent.

When emotionally you are hating, you are violating the Law of Love. For example, a queen hates another queen, and she manipulates her king eventually to make war against that queen because she is jealous of that queen. Eventually the war occurs and things get out of hand. On the emotional plane one day when the queen dies she will see the effects of her jealousy, lies, hatred, anger, fear, exploitation, revenge. When the queen incarnates she will be more instructed and she will say, "You know, I saw the terrible results of my actions on the emotional plane. Now I do not want to live with jealousy and live destructively."

On the physical plane millions of people know what a beautiful man you are, but inside you know that you are cheating, you are lying, you are jealous, you are hating, you have fear, you have mixed emotions, these kinds of things. But nobody is seeing these vices. People are seeing how beautifully you are dressed, how sweet your words are, and so on, but when you enter into the emotional plane you are totally naked. People living in the emotional plane see in your emotional body what you did in the past. That is awful. That is another hell. You cannot hide yourself anymore. For example, a man has lots of wounds in his body, lots of cuts in his body, lots of damage in his body, and he is dressing very well and nobody can see the wounds. But get naked and everybody sees your body. The emotional body is totally revealed to inhabitants of the emotional plane, and that is a terrible revelation for many.

In the Armenian Church there is a prayer. I did not understand that prayer for a long time. Finally I understood it. It says, "God, give me a long life so that I will have a chance to renounce and clean my life before I die." A man is eighty and he is praying, "Give me ten years more so that in the next ten years I clean my account, I clean my house, and I tell people that I lied, I stole, I did this and this, millions of things." In these ten years' time you do everything possible to clean and go to the Other Worlds with as little luggage as you can.

In your life you appear different than you are, but in your thoughts you hate, you are separative, you are full of ego, vanity. You are greedy, you have bad motives and bad plans. Everything that you have in the mental plane will be appearing to you in the mental plane when you pass away. But if you are asleep, you are going to transit through them and come back without increasing your consciousness and expanding yourself, without benefitting from your past. It is a loss of time for you to die and come back, except that it is a punishment for you because you are getting slower and slower in your evolution.

If you are in the first or second category, you do not see anything in the Other Worlds. But if sometimes for one minute, two minutes your Guide awakens you, you see the results of your actions. Sometimes it is your

Solar Angel who takes you up, protects you, and brings you back to your duties and responsibilities here on earth. If you are an advanced person, you are born from very beautiful parents and in conditions that evoke and call out all your hidden talents.

When you awaken in the Other Worlds for one second or more, you cannot change anything there; you see so clearly what the effects are of what you did on earth that when you come back you never repeat them. You change your life. Some people die and come back after their Solar Angel awakens them in the Other Worlds for one or two minutes, and they see the mess that they created in the past. When they come back, they are so afraid of doing the same things that they automatically reject them.

Karma acts everywhere, but actions in the Other Worlds do not create karma because the life there is the result of your karma. You cannot create new karma there unless you are awakened; you are just an automaton. Your karma was created on earth. That is why you came again and again back to earth to understand and solve your karma, to correct your karma, to pay your karma. In the Other Worlds you have the result of your karma. You cannot make new karma because you are living there as the result of your earthly karma. You do not have free will there.

You cannot create karma in the Other Worlds. If you are awakened you can create karma which affects not only the Other Worlds but also your physical life.

The Law of Karma helps to adjust, harmonize, and erase the continuing causes of misfortune. Cooperation with karma is the best way to overcome your past karma.

The Law of Karma is for our ultimate good because it removes our manmade obstacles on our road and paves the way toward perfection.

It is our karma that creates our relationships with people, with the Teaching, and with the Teachers. If we met Teachers in the past, we will accept their Teaching and the Teachers when we meet them again.

Also, when we find our enemies and traitors, we will be very careful to solve our karma and try to make them our friends and co-workers.

We created many personalities and will create more in coming ages. They are the results of our karma and the effects of the moments of awakeness.

Each personality automatically takes form to fit in different needs and obligations until we consciously create and use our personalities for the Plan of the Soul and Hierarchy.

The expansion of consciousness in the Subtle World is almost an impossibility. Helena Roerich says that "whatever is not realized here on Earth will not be realized in the Subtle World."[2]

She says also "... in earthly life we must sow the seeds of aspiration which in the Subtle World can be transmuted into knowledge."[3]

---

2. Agni Yoga Society, *Letters of Helena Roerich*, Vol. I, p. 376.
3. *Ibid.*, p. 376.

"... Only the earthly existence provides the foundation for our further perfection and conscious existence in the Subtle World."[4]

"The Subtle, or astral, world is the world of effects...."[5]

"It is impossible to outlive vices in the Subtle World...because only on Earth can we receive new impulses of energy and regenerate or transmute these into their higher manifestations. But in the Subtle World with the help of Guides one can realize the harmfulness of passions not yet outlived and can impress this knowledge upon the subtle centers to such an extent that in the new earthly rebirth it will be easier to conquer the attraction to this or that vice."[6]

"...For the transmutation and sublimation of our energies — passions — we need our earthly, physical laboratory, in which are united and transmuted the elements of all worlds."[7]

"... [When] man crosses into the Subtle World with all his vices and virtues, he indeed preserves his character in full. 'Ulcers of the spirit are carried over into the Subtle World if they are not gotten rid of on earth.'"[8]

Sowing is here; reaping is there.

---

4. *Ibid.*, p. 262.
5. Agni Yoga Society, *Letters of Helena Roerich*, Vol. II, p. 53.
6. *Ibid.*, p. 498.
7. *Ibid.*, p. 498.
8. *Ibid.*, p. 480.

Most of the problems of humanity can be solved by educating people about the Law of Karma and about the Law of Reincarnation. When people are enlightened by these two laws, the personal, national, and international crimes will disappear.

Of course these two laws must be taught in all departments of Nature, and especially in medicine, to make it a truly potent factor to change the life on the planet.

Q&A

Question: *What is the difference between responsibility and mission?*

ANSWER: Responsibility is an action which you decide to perform for the good of all concerned. A mission is given to you by a higher authority.

Question: *When we return for a mission, is it possible to create new karma?*

ANSWER: Yes, you do because you "consciously" act on the physical plane. Sometimes you use your wisdom gained in the Other Worlds. Sometimes you become trapped by different influences and do not put your experience or wisdom into action. Sometimes the subjective life affects you so negatively that during your life you show your unhappiness and irritation.

Question: *When you have gone past the wheel of karma and you do not have to come back but you come back for a mission, are you in any danger of creating karma or are you past that?*

ANSWER: You may be free from karma if you are in tune with the Universe and so purified that you never do anything that is against the laws.

Question: *What is the principle that governs the amount of time that you spend in between incarnations?*

ANSWER: The amount of time is determined by the intensity of your actions carried on upon the physical plane. The lower-than-average people come back very soon. The intelligent people who create lots of karma stay in the Other Worlds for a long time. Very advanced people stay a very short time in the Other Worlds or a long time if they do not decide to come back soon.

Question: *If the etheric plane absorbs energy from the sun, and the etheric plane is being populated by the actions of criminals and from suicides and abortions, then it must be getting more and more densely populated or it must be expanding. It must then be interfering with the energy that is coming in.*

ANSWER: That is true. The energy that comes and goes through the etheric body to the planet can be very polluted. If it is too polluted, the planet starts to decay. Some planets totally disappear when the etheric body is totally polluted. The planet enters into chaos.

How are we going to create a nice planet? When all of humanity see the results of what they are doing and decide to come together and establish a beautiful planet that is a paradise. We can do it. This planet is such a beautiful sphere in the ocean of space. We can make it beautiful, a wonderful university for our future progress.

> **Question:** *How can some go out to the mental plane and be asleep and yet others on the etheric plane are awake enough to know their actions?*

ANSWER: In the etheric plane you are always awake because the etheric brain is there. When you get out from your physical brain, you are in your etheric brain, so it works there except when you suddenly die. Suddenly a rocket comes and kills you, and you went to sleep there. Most of the inhabitants are awake. The mental plane is too far from the physical plane, so they are all asleep there if they are not conscious.

> **Question:** *Is it true that the difficulties of the etheric plane make you intelligent?*

ANSWER: No, because people there do not learn from difficulties. They see but do not learn. It is the same as when you take a criminal who killed a person and put him in prison. Then you release him and he kills ten more persons. He is not learning because prison does not teach him. The etheric plane does not teach you either. The astral plane teaches you. The mental plane teaches you. The etheric plane is a whirlpool of energies where you go and rotate upon your own axis. You are in very bad shape there, especially if you are a criminal. If you kill somebody, when you die and go to the etheric plane you will continue killing that man everyday, every minute, so that eventually it becomes like a nightmare for you. That is the hell they are talking about.

> **Question:** *How can we change certain patterns in our brain so that we do not follow them anymore?*

ANSWER: If we want to change certain patterns in our subtle bodies before we die, we can use the visualization process. For example, visualization affects the etheric and mental planes. A visualized action changes the etheric patterns. A visualization on geometrical forms and sound creates changes in the mental substance.[9]

Imagination affects the astral plane. Imagination is related to pleasure and pain.

Daydreaming affects lower sub-planes of the astral and etheric planes, which in turn affect the physical body.

---

9. See the visualization excercises in *Mental Exercises* and *The Art of Visualization*. Many exercises and visualizations can be found also in *New Dimensions in Healing* and *Thought and the Glory of Thinking*.

You can use the visualization technique, intelligently visualizing that which you want to be. Many disciples use visualization to improve their life, overcome limitations, and secure a better birth for the future.

Question: *Do people actually land in parts of the Other Worlds innocently?*

ANSWER: Yes, both if they are very primitive, or highly enlightened. If they are primitive the Law of Karma brings them back to incarnation to allow them to progress.

Question: *Can people continue their physical lifestyle in the Other Worlds?*

ANSWER: Exactly. For example, when you are going to the astral plane and you are half-awakened and you were a shoemaker in the past and you awakened one minute, you continue your shoe making business there. You buy a place and build because in the astral plane whatever you imagine is instantaneously built. The Great Sage says that "sometimes We go to the astral plane and amuse ourselves, looking at how people are busy building houses, businesses, and are occupied with money. They do not need anything. They are building houses but they are souls and do not need houses. But the impression of the physical life is so impressed on them that they do not have alternatives. They are the slaves of their past. That is why students of wisdom must daily think that this life is transient and that they are Sparks, they are energy waves, they are circuits. That is what the advanced Teaching says.

Question: *If you develop compassion and identify with the interest of humanity as a whole, is that the moment you transcend karma?*

ANSWER: Let us say, you create less karma. Because of your compassion, you create a sense of responsibility in yourself. Compassion turns into responsibility and responsibility makes you engage in various works. If the compassion does not turn into responsibility, it is not compassion. Compassion says to you, "What is going to happen to this earth?" and you say, "I am emancipated from it now. I do not care at all. Let it go hell." Then you say, "No, I must come back," and you become a scientist, you become an artist, you become a composer, you become something great and shine your light and become something greater and they crucify you again. You go back again and say, "Bad boy, why did you go there," because they crucified you and for a few centuries you think, you digest that. Three centuries later you say, "No matter what they did, I will go back." That is what the Avatars are doing, coming back, coming back. Why are They coming? Christ is coming back. Was He not fed up with us? We will crucify Him again! And how!

Question: *How do you learn to be awake on the astral and mental planes?*

ANSWER: It is through meditation and living a conscious life. Most of us are not living a conscious life. Conscious life means living according to our principles and knowing what we are doing, what we are talking about, what we are thinking, and what their effect will be. If you know the effect and the cause, you are awake.

For example, you suddenly start gossiping and slandering and creating a mess. Then some people say to you, "Shame on you! Do not do that," but it is gone. Already you did it. Why did you do it? It is because you were asleep. Most of us are sleeping. Most of the actions that we are doing are the actions of sleepwalkers. You have never seen sleepwalkers. I have seen them. In our house we had a girl who at night would get up and cook and clean everything and put the food in the refrigerator and then go back to sleep. If you would tell her in the morning what she did, she did not know it. That is what we are, sleepwalkers.

Question: *You say some stay seventy, eighty, ninety years in the etheric plane. How do they make a breakthrough to get out of there?*

ANSWER: The Law of Karma sends them back for another round. And when they come back, they must come to the Teaching. They must read the Teaching. They must start meditation. They must start discipline. Your salvation is not bound to anyone. Your salvation must come from inside you. You must say, "Today I am going to sit and read this book and think about it, and then do some discipline, eat less, drink less, have sex less, and so on. Slowly, slowly you gain control over yourself and, as you gain control over yourself, you awaken more and more and more because control and awakeness are related to each other. Every one of us is helped by certain people. Nature provides opportunities — but you must catch them.

The mantram that we use often can be explained as follows:

> *Lead us, O Lord,*
> *from darkness to Light* (from the physical etheric plane to intelligent living),
> *From the unreal to the Real* (from astral glamor to reality),
> *From death to Immortality* (from the mental plane to the Chalice),
> *From chaos to Beauty* (from physical, astral, mental planes to the Intuitional Plane).

Question: *Did you say that karma is not created in the Subtle Worlds?*

ANSWER: That is true. The Other Worlds, for the majority of people, is the world of effect. Causes cannot be created in the Other Worlds except when one is conscious there. We reap in the Other Worlds what we sowed in this physical world. But when an awakened consciousness is operating in the Other Worlds, he can create causes but not a karma for which he can be responsible. All those who are awakened do not create karma that binds them.

There are two kinds of causes and two kinds of effects. One cause does not create karma, but the other cause creates karma. When you sacrifice your life for others, you do not create karma. You create beneficent effects.

When you hate and hurt people you create karma. Karma means action. One action is in harmony with the laws and principles of the Universe; one is not. The one that is not creates karma.

There is also a condition in which individual karma is not created. That happens when a Great One sends a "projection" for a certain mission. Whatever the projection does is not recorded as karma for "him."

People generally live in a dream-like state. They do not have "free will" to act as they want because all the causes of their actions are generated by their life on the physical plane. They reincarnate to clean their karma. In the Other Worlds karma cannot be paid off.

In the Other Worlds we see the result of our actions committed in the corresponding plane in the physical body. The majority of our actions are reflected in the etheric plane. The majority of our emotional actions can be viewed in the lower or higher astral planes. The majority of our mental actions can be seen in the lower or higher mental planes, but in truth all these actions are fused in each other but are emphasized in the corresponding planes.

It is interesting also that if we are *awake* on the physical plane we are awake on the etheric plane. If we are awake on the astral plane while in incarnation, we have lucid sight in the astral plane. The same is true for the mental plane, which is rare.

One of the goals of human destiny is to make man *awake* in all planes. The awakening process can also be called the initiation process.

Question: *How does karma come into being?*

ANSWER: Karma is the reaction of the laws and principles of the Universe. Whenever the laws and principles are violated, karma comes into being. There are three major kinds of violations: violation against Light, violation against Love, and violation against Beauty and Unity. Also karma can be paid through Love, through Light, and through Beauty and Unity.

The less karma you have, the more chance is given to you to have moments of awakeness in the Other Worlds. A moment of awakeness does not create effects in the Other Worlds. If the memory of the moment of awakeness is kept in your consciousness, after you incarnate it may create tremendous changes in your physical-plane life.

Question: *Can you give some examples?*

ANSWER: Yes. A moment of awakeness and understanding of the Law of Karma in the Other Worlds gives you a sense of immortality, gives you a sense of infinity, gives you a sense of balance between matter and spirit, gives you a better direction in life, gives you purpose and dedication, gives you power over your habits, and creates a new image. Such changes come slowly after you incarnate because your higher mind subjectively affects your thoughts and decisions. Such new changes offer new possibilities for you to have moments of awakeness in the Other Worlds while you are asleep.

Meditation also prepares you to be awake in the Other Worlds, both when you are in the physical and out of the physical body.

Question: *Do the moments of awakeness in the Other Worlds cause changes in our self-image?*

ANSWER: Yes, it does while in incarnation. The self-image created in the Other Worlds in a moment of awakening becomes an unconscious image in our life that pressures us to change or adjust our self-image in the physical plane.

An awakened moment in the Other Worlds can be a source of continuous inspiration and a cause of aspiration for us while on earth.

Question: *Can you give us an example?*

ANSWER: Yes. Suppose you lived all your life in the slums, but you helped people. Because of that a man wanted to reward you and took you to a party of noble people in a magnificent palace. After you return you do not fit in the slums anymore. You must change your life. Or, when you see the consequences of your physical life in the Other Worlds, you are very careful how to live in the physical plane.

The experiences gained in a moment of awakeness in the Other Worlds may change all your life from mechanicalness to conscious livingness.

The more awakened moments you have in the Other Worlds while out of your body, the more lucid dreams you will have while in your physical body.

Question: *Is it possible that people refuse the understanding caused by a moment of awakeness in the Other Worlds when they incarnate?*

ANSWER: Of course, some people knowingly will disobey the law, principle, or advice because the lure of the lower life traps them, and using various logic they disobey the voice of their inner being. We call such people "those who work against their own good."

You know that there is individual karma, family karma, group karma, national karma, global karma, and so on. Helena Roerich says that "...when we finish one round of karma for a certain cycle, we start a new round on other planes and worlds...."[10]

Question: *Do you think that we must teach the Law of Karma in our schools?*

ANSWER: Yes, if you can. I feel that in coming centuries, the Law of Karma will be taught in all elementary schools, in colleges, and also in universities. I even feel

---

10. Agni Yoga Society, *Letters of Helena Roerich*, Vol. II, p. 29.

that a proper school will be called the "Law of Karma" where advanced people will study the Law of Karma in all its possible dimensions.

It would be very useful if the teachers compile every reference to karma from the Teaching and prepare on a gradient scale a course which must be given to the students from the elementary school to the university level. Such a course will eliminate eighty percent of the crime and awaken people to cooperate with the Law of the Common Good.

What can be the topics of the course?

1. The definition of the Law of Karma
2. The function of the Law and practical examples
3. The significance that it brings in our life
4. How it leads us to harmlessness
5. How it releases our mind from self-created problems and hindrances
6. How it deepens our understanding of our duties, responsibilities, and obligations
7. How it serves others
8. How karma may lead us to freedom, to service, to the understanding and application of the Law
9. How karma leads us to higher states of consciousness

10. How denial of opportunities creates a dark karma
11. Karma in family, group, and national relationships
12. Karma in international relationships
13. How disastrous it is to try to escape karma
14. How disastrous it is to fight against karma by might and armies
15. How important it is to cultivate consciousness to handle one's own karma and be ready to solve the karma
16. Karma and the Subtle Worlds
17. Karma and incarnations
18. Group karma
19. National karma
20. International karma
21. How to help ourselves dissolve our karma
22. Doing good and karma
23. Karma and fear or fearlessness

You may add another one hundred topics onto this list.

Fear of God — referred to in many scriptures — should be the fear of karma.

God and fear cannot agree with each other. God is all compassion, forgiveness, and no one must fear Him but rather the Law of Karma. The Law of Karma is created eventually to teach humanity how to surpass that law or how to spiritualize themselves and be in highest harmony with the Life.[11]

---

11. See also *One Hundred Names of God.*

• CHAPTER 9 •

Shared Karma

It is important to bear in mind that for an enlightened human being there is not "my karma," "his karma." It is one karma. And whatever we do to improve the life of the planet is good for our karma and for the whole karma.

We share every minute the karma of others, and every other human being does the same. We improve the life conditions with our right actions; others do the same. We increase the misery of the world with our wrong actions, and others do the same.

Once we understand that the karma of the world is shared by all of us, then each of us will do our best to improve the life of the planet as far as we can.

The oneness of karma teaches us that we cannot get rid of our enemies by trying to annihilate them. We can understand that we share their karma, and they share our karma; and through long ages of experiences we learn to understand them, educate them, and to serve those principles that will make the planet a better place to live for all of us.

We share also our family and group karma. If a group is dedicated to the highest principles, it turns into a center of cleansing of the karma of the world in the physical, emotional, and mental realms. Such a group advances closer to those who consciously use the karma of the world to bring out the best that exists in the heart of humanity.

This teaches us that we must gain control over all our actions to minimize the karma of the world and increase cooperation, goodwill, right human relations, and unity.

It is important that we impress these ideas upon our children in all schools, as the true world citizenship can emerge from such a training.

People often are afraid of the term *"world citizenship."* World citizenship does not mean to lose our identity, our particular religion, nationality, color, race, sex, and so on. But it does mean the development of *right human relations*. This is all it is. Right human relationship is the cure for most of our pain and suffering and problems. It is a science, and advanced human beings can translate that science and make it applicable in all domains of life.

If we want to alleviate the suffering of the planet, the first lesson we must teach to all the children in the world will be the science of right human relations with all its details and practicality. This will be a science that will clean the pollutions on earth and the animosity between nations and people. It will pave the way for universal cooperation.

The science of right human relationship is the practical dissolution of the accumulated karma of the ages. Every human being who tries to live by the principles of right human relations eliminates a part of the dark karma of humanity, thus rendering a great service to humanity.

At this time in history when the world is becoming a world community, it is imperative that people develop a new constitution for the world, and that new constitution will be written on the foundation of right human relationship.

The science of right human relations will be a science that eventually will reveal not only the unity of mankind but also the Purpose of life on this planet and the role that the Law of Karma plays to help people reach to that Purpose.

• Chapter 10 •

Payment of Debts

There is a law in our life which can be called "the payment of debts." If anyone receives from you

1. Any offering
2. Any labor unpaid
3. Any help given physically, emotionally, mentally

the person is indebted to you.
Similarly if anyone

1. Harmed you physically, emotionally, mentally
2. Slandered you
3. Limited your spiritual progress

4. Embarrassed you
5. Humiliated you

he or she is indebted to you.

Those who received advice, wisdom, encouragement, upliftment, direction, healing, protection, from you will be indebted to you.

Equally, those who harmed you, slandered you, deceived you will be indebted to you.

The more they harmed you, the more they will be indebted to you. The more they insulted and slandered you, the more debt they will have to pay. This is why we are advised not to worry about all the things that we offered to people. They are money in the bank for you, which will be available for you on the crossroads of life.

This is why you must also not grieve over the treason and slander of others. They will pay for them one hundred percent more in the future.

Our greatest helpers in this life are those who hurt us in the past, or those who are indebted to us for our past service. If you deny your Teacher, Father, and Mother, you will sacrifice your life for them in the future.

The best way to be the slave of someone in the future is to slander him or her. The best way to be indebted to others is to receive many blessings, but not be grateful for them. Life operates upon such laws.

One of the laws that is not discussed in books is the *Law of Recognition*. People subtly are hit by this law when they refuse to recognize the beauty in others, the service of others, and, urged by their self-interest and stupidity, they refuse to recognize and appreciate those who help them.

It is a great transgression to have a light around you and deny it. It is a great crime to have a beauty around you and slander it. It is a great crime to have a big fruit tree, full of fruit, and try to cut it, or to let it go dry.

When you do not respond to values, it means you are contaminated by jealousy. Envy of the value of others turns you against them. This is the most pitiful state of consciousness when you, as a frustrated person, stand against your own Soul, who stands for values. Denying the values of others is a denial of the source of life within you.

• CHAPTER 11 •

Willpower and Karma

When we talk about joy, we must not forget that joy can be sustained only by a well-developed willpower.

Willpower is just like a wind which sustains the sails of joy and pushes the boat of life forward.

Willpower is like a shield which prevents disturbing factors to enter into our aura.

Willpower is like a spring in a lake which keeps it clean forever.

What does disciplined willpower mean?

It means the ability to control the automatic reactions of the three bodies to outer stimuli. It is cessation of automatism.

This power of the will is an accumulated quality. Every time we conquer an obstacle; solve a problem constructively and selflessly; overcome a difficulty; dissolve an animosity; control a habit; are able to reject being in a glamor, vanity, or ego; are able not to be operated by our push buttons and subconscious blind urges and drives; are able to refuse to fall into the traps of our five senses and pleasures; are able to survive after lengthy and painful tests of labor and hostility; are able to transcend our level of consciousness and beingness, we prove that we are using our willpower.

All these victories accumulate and create a pressure which evokes the willpower of our inner divinity.

As our willpower increases, our joy increases because joy is the awareness of invincibility, everlastingness, and indestructibility.

Those who have no willpower will escape the marathon race carried on through tests and temptations, difficulties and hostilities, dangers and attacks.

Those who cannot survive after their failures, mistakes, and humiliations escape from the race.

Those who cannot stand on their feet after the fierce warning of their Teachers cannot run the race.

Those who kneel in front of the Golden Bull and separative pursuits cannot run the race.

The marathon race of world service and perfection can be run only by those who develop their willpower.

• CHAPTER 12 •

The Levels of Karma

Karma is a Sanskrit word meaning action, which is a combination of both cause and effect. There is no effect without a cause, and a cause can only be called a cause if it produces effects. Cause and effect follow each other as night follows day and day follows night. This process is called karma, the Law of Cause and Effect, or the *Law of Action and Reaction.*

This Law operates on all levels. It operates on the physical as well as on the emotional and mental fields. Actually, these three fields are one field of the Law of Karma. A physical action can have a mental reaction; a mental action can have an emotional reaction or even a physical reaction, and so on.

We are living in space. Space is not a vacuum. It is full of electromagnetic energies and forces. Every time we move a finger, we put into operation certain forces. Every time we have any emotional or mental activity, we affect the energy field in which we live and move. All our actions, on all levels, create electrical charges in space. Even when we sing, talk, or dance, we project electrical charges which create certain actions and reactions in the energy field of space.

The Law of Karma is also the *Law of Absolute Justice*. It is translated by the saying: "Whatever you sow, you will reap." The reaction we create in this energy field is equal to our action. Sometimes this action has a triple charge — physical, emotional, and mental together. Sometimes it is a one-or two-level charge. Sometimes its voltage is of a higher frequency, sometimes a lower. Whatever the situation is, the law does not change; we receive what we give.

The Law of Karma transcends the limitations of our time equations. The triple reaction to action — physical, emotional, and mental — can reach us at various times. For example, the physical reaction to an action may come two thousand years later. The reaction in our emotional nature may come a few centuries before that, and the reaction in our mental nature may come in fifteen years or even immediately. It may also happen that all three of these reactions come to our personality in one package. The law is that no one can escape the consequences of his actions.

If an action is a good action, it brings those reactions that open our way toward greater joy, greater beauty, greater goodness, greater harmony, greater mastery, and greater knowledge. If an action is a bad action, it brings greater difficulties and problems on our life's path so that eventually we learn to take right actions.

A right action is an action which is harmonious with the intent of the Greater Life in which we are living as cells, just as the right action of a cell in our body is an action that contributes to the survival of the body for a given period of time.

The words we speak, the feelings and thoughts we have, and the actions we perform physically are all registered forever in our energy field not as words and letters but as electrical impulses. These impulses may travel quickly or slowly. After a certain distance they turn back with a different charge and eventually reach the source of origination.

The originating source may be on a higher or lower level, which makes a difference in the process of response. The reactions are always conditioned in accordance with the updated responses of the originating source, which may increase the impact, modify it, or absorb it easily.

Ancient Sages told us that we cannot escape our karma, that whatever we are doing at the present moment we are doing to ourselves as well as to others. There is no moment in our lives in which we do not act; we are always in action, even if we are in a state of inaction. This means that man is a continual action-producing energy source, whether he is asleep or awake, dead or alive.

All that we have ever done will reach us one day on another shore as echoes of our former songs. It is even more accurate to say that we will be the sum total of our echoes. All reactions produced by former actions will create a new personality. This personality will be the condensation of all reactions. This is why we can say that in the future we will be what we feel, think, and do at the moving time which we call the present.

In the light of such knowledge, it is possible to plan our future life as we want it to be. Exactly as we create plans for a huge building, so we can plan our life for the future and live according to the requirements of that plan. It is difficult but not impossible to change our present karma if we use the fire of the spirit and put our psychic energy into action.

People sometimes think that karma is only individual. This thinking is a result of a lack of observation. Humanity is a total unit in which each person is a cell. We have the karma of each cell and the collective karma of all cells. This means that we affect each other by the kind of life we live on all levels. Also, we are responsible not only for our own actions but for the actions of others as well because often others act the way we cause them to act.

There is individual karma, national karma, and global karma. We can no longer say, "Let that nation live the way it lives; let us care only for our own nation." This was the outcome of our ignorance in past ages. In the future, we will be aware that the individual is affected by the greater whole. Hence, the more educated nations have a serious responsibility to work for the welfare, progress, and prosperity of other nations. It is like saying that the mouth, the eyes, the hands, or the feet must take care of other sections of the body if the whole person is to be healthy.

The new morality will be built on the foundation of karma.

Each of us pays the karma of humanity as well as our own karma. Here let us remind ourselves that we are talking about good and bad karma. We share all the good that is produced by others and by humanity as a whole. The striving and achievements of each person help others to strive more toward perfection and toward greater achievements. All our good deeds, good thoughts, and feelings of love and gratitude form a raincloud of blessings for all humanity. It is from such accumulations that individuals and groups secure their inspirations and visions and step onto a higher path of evolution. Thus when we speak of karma, we mean a greater computer system built by webs of electrical and magnetic energies, a huge superhuman computer which is righteous for all individual, group, national, and global karma.

Not a single word, thought, or impression from action is lost in space. They are all in the computer. In esoteric books, we read that the operators of this computer are Solar Beings Who are far more advanced than man can imagine.

Karma is not only balanced through negative and positive actions, but it can also be paid or finished through heroic actions and great sacrificial deeds. The Great Sage says: "Energy and will are the rulers of karma. He who renounces self, he who strives for the Common Good, who is devoted in battle, joyous in labor, acquires momentarily the Arhat's enlightenment, which makes him lord of his karma."[1]

The purpose of the Law of Karma is to teach us how to renounce the self, which is the axis that keeps the wheel of karma turning. Once the self is renounced, man becomes the lord, or let us say the master, of his karma.

There are two main approaches to karma:

1. When karma controls you
2. When you control your karma

Control of karma is achieved when all separative motives and actions are eliminated from one's own being and one's whole life is dedicated to the Common Good.

It is also possible that "...one can take upon oneself the collective karma."[2] Such is the case of great Avatars Who come and take upon Their shoulders the very heavy karma of humanity, the collective karma of great masses of people. They pay the consequences consciously, willingly, and joyously.

---

1. Agni Yoga Society, *Agni Yoga*, para. 127.
2. *Ibid.*, para. 417.

Karma is not a frozen picture; it is a fluid, an ever-changing and adapting flow of energy currents. We can always modify it or cause minor or major changes in it according to our power of sacrifice and our will to serve the Common Good. Most of our karma cannot be changed unless we realize the consequences of our actions and take the necessary steps to modify them. This is why great Teachers always advise us to review our actions, feelings, and thoughts daily. Once we notice the motives of all our manifestations and their consequent effects upon others, we can take the first step in the process of mastering our karma either by paying it or increasing our credit.

Good deeds, good words, positive emotions, right thinking, right spiritual aspiration and striving — all these create a savings account in our karmic bank. Then, any time a previous karmic debt presents an unpaid bill, our bank automatically pays it out of the account, and we escape from a grave danger.

I remember a time in 1944 when several friends were going to Jerusalem by car. Suddenly the car skidded off a bridge and plunged twenty feet to the ground. Three people were sitting in the back seat. The one in the middle moved himself to check if any part of his body was damaged or hurt. He felt alright and told his friends on each side of him to jump out. Hearing no answer, he managed to get himself out of the car. To his shock and horror, he realized that both of his companions were dead.

This is an example of drawing from the savings account and escaping from a real danger.

We all have had the experience at some time that we were able to escape real danger in a few seconds. The reverse can also happen. When there was a big earthquake in Los Angeles, a family, afraid that aftershocks would destroy the city, decided to move to another state. As they were driving in their big van, they had a fatal accident, and the whole family was killed.

The Great Sage says, "If karma be diverted, it will react against thee. The travail of the spirit is the one ladder of the shortest way. The suffering of a decade is crowded into a day in the lives of the chosen ones."[3]

There is no escape from our karma, and the best way to face our karma is to have a savings account of good karma.

The process of paying our karma is purificatory; it purifies our personality, cleanses our debts, and gives us a new chance to proceed on the path of greater enlightenment and joy. In many scriptures, pain and suffering are called the "gifts of God" or "the messengers of God who bring good news" — meaning the news of releasing us from the deeds of our past which were not in harmony with the Divine intent. In the Orient, one sometimes hears the following expression, "You can depend on that person because he passed through pain and suffering without losing his head."

---

3. Agni Yoga Society, *Leaves of Morya's Garden*, Vol. I, para. 232.

Is it possible for people to hurt us in spite of the fact that we do not deserve it, or to help us without our being worthy of it? The answer is that if people intentionally hurt us, they may be operating under the influence of dark forces in order to limit our service, to prevent us from applying our usefulness to a great task, or to stop us from carrying out a great service which we are trying to render to humanity. The damage they inflict on us goes to our credit; at a later time, this credit can protect us from a still greater attack. On the other hand, when we receive help from somebody, it goes directly to our debit. It puts greater responsibility on our shoulders if we do not pay it back in a form of service or help given to others, or help given to the same person who helped us.

It may happen that some people help us indirectly. For example, although the music given to us by Beethoven, the electrical light given to us by Edison, or a Teaching given to us by Christ is given to humanity as a whole or to an individual nation, all of us share the benefits. These are examples of group karma or the karma of humanity in which we all share to a greater or lesser degree. We may use the help given to us by performing creative activities of our own and dedicating them to the human welfare.

It is almost impossible to know whether it is our karma or not when someone hurts us or helps us directly. The only indication that can be applied for our clearer understanding is that when we are hurt without karma, we recover very soon and the damage done turns into profit. It opens greater opportunities for us to bloom; it helps our evolution or turns into an asset for us.

When we receive direct help without karma, it does not give inner satisfaction but turns into a burden on our shoulders. Also, we do not appreciate the help wholeheartedly if it is not the result of our karma. For example, if somebody just gives us money, we may feel good, but when we earn it through our own labor, it gives us greater joy and satisfaction.

One of the best ways to avoid any attack is by a firm and sincere dedication to the service of humanity and to living a life of goodwill.

I remember when there was an epidemic of cholera in the town where we used to live. At that time my Father was working in the hospital. Daily, under his supervision, they put thirty or forty people into lime and buried them. Once I asked, "Father, aren't you afraid that you will catch cholera?"

"No," he said, "because I have dedicated my life to serving these people, nothing will happen to me." And nothing did happen to him. He lived a long life. My Father had *faith*. Faith means, esoterically, to sense or perceive something intuitively that is not yet reflected on or translated by the mental plane. But it is there and we know it.

Karma that is disciplinary is formed by reactions to actions that break the Law of Love. Any action against the Law of Love will bring violent reactions in due time. This phenomenon can be traced throughout the history of humanity.

Two very important factors which contribute to our karmic account are criticism and nosiness. Criticism interferes with the karma of others and creates violent reactions. When we criticize, we force and try to impose our will upon others. If we succeed in making them act the way we want them to, their mistakes are added onto our account. Criticism is mostly the result of our pride, vanity, and jealousy. We hide these vices within us and present ourselves as superior human beings.

Criticism strengthens the personality faults of the one who is criticized and makes him defensive. It breaks the bonds between people. A teacher or leader should analyze an event or an expression and call the attention of the students to a higher standard only if he thinks that they are ready for that level. He should never focus the attention of his students on their guilts and faults, especially if he sees good motives in their hearts.

One who criticizes eventually develops in himself the same qualities which he criticizes in others. The best way to remove a fault in the life of another person, if he is ready and wants to get rid of it, is to develop his consciousness to such a degree that he himself sees his own limitations and removes them. Attention should be focused on his virtues, not on the things that can be criticized. When a teacher analyzes the situation, he should do it in a way that it does not belittle the person or focus attention on his faults. He should remind him of the vision and encourage him to strive for it, pulling himself from the lower level.

In analyzing a situation, always use light and love-energy. When we criticize, we are using the force of our vanity, pride, jealousy, and hidden motives. When these forces are put in motion, they will create violent reactions or karma.

The Teacher says: "Yet, brother of old, why are you so sure that you are right and that your point of view is necessarily correct? It may be that your slant on life and your interpretation of a situation needs readjustment and that your motives and attitudes could be more elevated or purer. And even if they are — for you — the highest and the best that you can achieve at any given time, then pursue your way and leave your brother to pursue his. 'Better a man's own dharma, than the dharma of another.' Thus does the *Bhagavad Gita* express this truth, telling the disciple to mind his own business.

"...Groups of disciples are groups of free and independent souls who submerge their personal interests in service and who seek that inner linking which will fuse the group into an instrument for the service of humanity and of the Hierarchy. Continue with your own soul discipline and leave your brothers to continue theirs."[4]

---

4. Alice A. Bailey, *Discipleship in the New Age*, Vol. I, pp. 48-49.

The next factor is nosiness. The Teaching always emphasizes: *mind your own business* and do not interfere in the privacy of others because nosiness creates karma. When we are nosy, we involve ourselves with other people and their glamors, weaknesses, and illusions and develop some kind of mechanism of censorship upon them. This is, again, an imposition of our will upon others.

Everyone must learn his own lessons and must conduct his private life the way he wants. The way he lives should be his own experimentation.

Nosiness is different from criticism. It is a way to collect information about others which can be used later against them, or it is a way to use their failures or errors for one's own personal benefit. Sometimes this is called psychological exploitation. The Great Sage says, "I know nothing worse than to cross the neighbor's path."[5]

When great Teachers emphasized the law of love, actually they were giving us the key to health, prosperity, joy, understanding, and unity. The Great Teacher speaking about this says, "Love is the response to contact and this — in the human being — means understanding, inclusiveness and identification. Wisdom connotes skill in action as the result of developed love and the light of understanding; it is awareness of requirements and ability to bring together into a fused relationship the need and that which will meet it. Service is essentially a scientific mode of expressing love-wisdom under the

---

5. Agni Yoga Society, *Community*, para. 74.

influence of one or other of the seven rays, according to the soul ray of the serving disciple."[6]

It is very probable that the violation of love not only produces all our social, economic, and political problems, with their negative consequences on our well-being, but also directly affects our health. Restoration of the health and harmony in our social life all over the world can be accomplished only through love as defined by this great Sage.

Love is the fastest and safest way to pay karmic debts. Love creates triple interest in our bank account and never produces negative karma. We know, of course, that many distorted people are also talented enough to use their hatred and poisons under the label of love.

Greater love is proved through greater sacrifices, greater self-renunciation, and greater humility. The greatest joy comes the moment we do our utmost to help humanity because that moment is a moment of contact with the intent of the Solar Purpose. Only through such moments do we pay off our enormous negative karma and remove the burden from our shoulders. This is why there is such great joy.

Some people see great suffering, calamity, blood, pain, and misery in pictures of the Crucifixion. But that moment was one of greatest bliss and beauty for the Christ because He was divine enough to give all that He was for the salvation of the world. The recordings of the Crucifixion in the New Testament are not in accord with reality.

---

6. Alice A. Baily, *Esoteric Astrology*, p. 494.

Never before had He been in such glorious ecstasy as He was on the cross, bleeding for His love of humanity.

The same sacrificial spirit can be found in the hearts of all true leaders and saviors, in all religions and races. Their lives were demonstrations of the ways and means to free humanity from its man-made prisons and miseries.

Karma teaches us how to be changeless in the midst of change. This seems very strange, but if we observe carefully, the greatest lesson that we must learn is to be changeless in a changing world. The Changeless One is the innermost essence of the Self. It is the True Self.

Karma teaches gradually that attraction brings repulsion, accumulation brings distribution, and power ends in weakness. Karma makes us wise enough to find ways through the jungles of change to the summit of changelessness.

"The Indweller of the body is never born, nor does It die. It is not true that, having no existence, It comes into being; nor having been in existence, It again ceases to be. It is the unborn, the eternal, the changeless, the Self...."[7]

We will not be able to reach such a state of changelessness as long as we are caught in the courts of karma. Only payment will release us onto the path of the True Self. Every wrong deed, on any level, is a withdrawal from our True Self, an escape from our Self. Identification with matter and those forces which, in their whirlwinds of

---

7. *The Bhagavad Gita* 2:20, tr. by author.

operation, will not allow us to find our heads is a separation from the Self.

In the school of life we learn all this, and the curriculum of that school is nothing else but the dissemination of karma.

What role does forgiveness play in karma? First of all, forgiveness means a total giving of ourselves for others. It is an act of laying down all that we are and have to meet the need of a greater whole. Forgiving someone does not erase his debts in the karmic records, but it helps to cut our emotional or mental connections with the physical, emotional, and mental force field related to him. Also, forgiveness can be an act of love on our part.

The forgiven one must never forgive himself until he pays his karma in the best way that he can, unless the other person takes the forgiven one's karma upon his shoulders. After such a forgiveness, with the assumption of another's karma, we are under a greater watch, and transgressions will cost us double or triple.

Forgiveness on our part prevents us from increasing our negative karma. If a person has done bad things to us, we can do good things to him. Only through such an activity can we protect ourselves from the trap confronting us to make negative karma. Such an escape is possible, but difficult.

Forgiveness is an act of real love. Really to love means to put ourselves in such a condition that the other person will be able to reach or strive toward his highest possibilities. In love, we increase our positive karma or our savings.

Karma teaches us another very interesting lesson. It teaches that all that we are is the result of our labor. If we are talented, it is because we worked hard to unfold ourselves. If we are geniuses, it means we have worked very, very hard throughout many incarnations and have, at last, reached such a stage of radioactivity and beauty. Thus, nothing is gained in the Universe without labor.

This explains the justice of creation and the differences between people everywhere. We are the result of our own hard labor. Nobody can make us creative if we do not work hard to unfold ourselves. The condition of progress and success is not the accumulation of matter nor the result of imposing our will upon others. It is unfoldment; it is a process of blooming and a process of transfiguration.

The greatest lesson that we can learn from the Law of Karma is to work hard because only through labor and striving can we transcend our limitations and surpass ourselves.

• CHAPTER 13 •

Facing Karma

It is inevitable that every moment we face the waves of our past karma. The Great Sage says, "The stream of karma rushes like a torrent, and consciousness may transform this tide into a repeated sacred flow of beauty."[1]

Transformation takes place when we realize the message of the karma and face ourselves in sincerity, in reality, and factuality.

Seeing the causes and the results of our karma, we shift our consciousness and create causes which will both expand our consciousness and provide great opportunities for us to serve. In this process we will release great beauty and potentials hidden within us

---

1. Agni Yoga Society, *Hierarchy*, para. 25.

instead of fighting against the Law of Karma and inviting upon ourselves pain, suffering, and limitations.

Shifting our consciousness toward the realm of Beauty, Goodness, Righteousness, Joy, Freedom, Striving, and Sacrificial Service will protect us from falling into the torrents of karma.

It is a fact that all beauty manifests when one overcomes his karmic limitations and uses his karmic experiences to live a life of sacrificial service. Innumerable are the beauties that a person can create by living a sacrificial life. All beauty experienced in this world is the gift of those who were able consciously to handle the torrents of karma, expressing through individuals, groups, and humanity.

Facing karma with a new consciousness and making an effort to free humanity from the karmic torrents creates heroes in all fields of human life. Beauty is born the moment when a person offers himself to free people from their cages and reveal to them the freedom of new dimensions.

Karmic Law is there to move our Divinity in activity. The more our Divinity manifests, the more beauty comes into being.

Many people fight against their karma as if the greatest injustice were done toward them. They fight against their karma because they do not use their consciousness or understand their karmic conditions.

Not everyone lives his life consciously. That is why karma is there. As our consciousness expands we face less karma, and we try to teach others to create less karma.

As our consciousness expands we learn the secrets of the law and use the same law to create beauty. All Beauty, Goodness, Righteousness, Joy, Freedom, Striving toward perfection, and Sacrificial Service are the gifts of those who were in the torrents of karma, and now they change these torrents into the flow of beauty, planting seeds of beauty and letting the law fertilize, nourish, and multiply beauty for everyone all over the world. Every beauty is the result of victory over karma.

Nothing can be gained without breaking the limitation of karma and without knowing the causes of limitation.

The more one controls his actions on all levels to remain above the karmic harvest, the more he becomes sensitive to the energy of the Cosmic Magnet. The Cosmic Magnet inspires man to live in beauty. Every contact with the Cosmic Magnet, every step taken with the energy of the Cosmic Magnet creates beauty in our beingness, in our life expressions, in our creative actions. Thus the Cosmic Magnet transfers our life to a level in which the "torrent" of karma does not control our life but reflects the achievement actualized in the current of the Cosmic Magnet.

All past karma illuminated by the rays of the Cosmic Magnet transforms into beauty, into paintings, drama, poems, music, but above all into life — a life that manifests the wisdom of the karmic law.

We must learn how to handle the powerful currents of karma in order to change the pain into bliss, ignorance into light, weakness into power. Every great achievement is gained by achieving victory over our karma. Karma limits our life and may for ages chain us to the wheel of unreality. To break the limitation and to free ourselves from the mechanicalness of unreality need great power, decisiveness, and striving. All these are gained when we intelligently face our karma and understand the hidden message of the karmic law.

To be ready to face the karmic consequences of our past deeds requires the spirit of a hero, a hero who is ready to surge above the karmic waves.

Every time I see a skillful surfer I think about those who can create beauty on the waves of karma, standing above them and advancing because of them.

We must not face our karma with depression, fear, anger but try to learn how to withdraw ourselves toward higher planes, toward our Core and, observing the waves of karma like a surfer, not to be drowned in those waves.

All that we learn in the world is nothing else but the art of how to meet our karma and transcend it through creating bridges and steps of beauty.

The karmic law helps us to be causes instead of being results. As long as we do not live a conscious life, are not aware of the Law of Cause and Effect, we live as results. The karmic law awakens us and gives us an opportunity to be causes.

A cause unites with the flow of karma and creates a life which is in harmony with the Cosmic Magnet.

My Teacher used to say, "Try to see who is controlling you or to whom you are the slave or who you are serving."

It is very powerful to see the causes which are using us, manipulating us, and exploiting us. Free people are very few, and they are the ones who are the hope and the future of humanity.

• CHAPTER 14 •

Reversing Karma

People wonder why they were born in a certain family, why they became members of a particular group or organization, why they were born in a certain nation. They wonder why they feel that they stand alone no matter where they are and do not feel any affiliation with anybody, any group, any nation.

Two kinds of karma bring people together:

1. Karma which is built by *harmful actions* toward each other
2. Karma which is built *through service and cooperation*

Groups can be the result of these two kinds of karma.

Harmful action can be divided into many parts:
1. Physical harm
2. Emotional harm
3. Mental harm
4. Actions that prevent the spiritual progress of others

These kinds of activities pull people together to work out their karma — to pay or receive the bills or checks for their past deeds.

Karma as a result of service or cooperative action for good can also be divided into categories:
1. Service related to the physical plane
2. Service related to the emotional field
3. Service related to the spiritual needs of people
4. Cooperative work to enlighten, to protect, to lead people

Such actions create a very powerful personality or spiritual ties between people, and life after life it brings them together in group formation to render greater service for humanity and the Divine Plan.

Another factor which brings people together is devotion directed to the same Teacher or to the same Teaching. This creates very strong ties between people, and for centuries and many incarnations this tie continues with advancing mutual benefit. For example, those who are in Ashrams for a long time followed the same Teacher, the same principles, or the same Teaching.

Karma formed by hatred, crime, and harmful actions brings many parties together. Usually people do to others as others did to them. We can see this in families, groups, and nations. Wars and conflicts among nations originate from past causes. And sometimes on battlefields the cause is dissolved if the nations are led by Sages to reverse the karma.

The reversing of karma is a very interesting fact. Christ gave the clue to this when He said, "Pray for those who do harm to you." Buddha said something similar: "Hatred cannot be dissolved by hatred, but hatred can be dissolved by love." These can work in group, family, and individual cases too. Because of the wisdom gained from the Teaching, people do not exercise "an eye for an eye" method but use love, understanding, and power so as not to allow the formation of similar karma.

Karma created by service and cooperation creates those groups who are born together, life after life, in order to bring enlightenment and beauty to humanity all over the world.

Often they act in groups in one location. Sometimes they are scattered all over the world as individuals and groups. In the seven fields of human endeavor you see the result of their united cooperative labor. It is such individuals and groups that lead humanity from chaos to beauty.

As people advance in service and cooperation, they go closer to the source of their light, their Ashrams. Gradually, because of their service and cooperation, they build a karma that leads them directly into Ashrams and into the ashramic activities. It is at this stage that they turn into sources of inspiration and impressions for those who are engaged in building karma through service and cooperation.

The greatest victory of our life is to be a part of a group that serves the highest good of all humanity.

Karma not only creates positive or negative groupings but also creates those conditions in which certain people feel aloof, detached, indifferent, within or outside of any group. The Teaching says that these people lived in the past only for themselves without trying to help or harm others, and karma gave them what they wanted.

Does such a condition continue indefinitely? The Teaching says that it can, and it cannot. *It can* if the individual continuously isolates himself and forms a tumor in the body of humanity. On judgment day he is operated on and thrown into the forces of chaos. *It cannot* because the pain and the pressure of aloneness reach such a degree that he eventually relates himself to people through harmful actions or through cooperation.

The same law works in astral and mental worlds. People are divided into these three camps. In the higher mental world all groups are engaged in cooperative work.

In the lower mental plane there are divisions because parties do not yet see the causes of their differences.

In the higher astral plane there are groups for pleasures, ecstasy, and love. In the lower astral planes there are oppositions.

Lonely people often are seen in etheric planes. Aloofness creates an energy field around them which repels the attraction of higher realms. Their ego and vanity build a wall around them, and this wall becomes the cause of their future suffering and their breakthrough.

Usually these lonely people who make a breakthrough go directly to higher levels of the mental plane if they accumulated much knowledge and wisdom to be used for the common good of humanity.

People think that karma can be changed only if the bill is paid. This sounds right, but the payment of a bill can take many forms. For example, you killed me in one of my lives. We meet again in another life to get even — which means I have an innate urge to kill you. But instead, I kill within you the urge, the tendency, to commit crimes. I enlighten you and annihilate your obsession or possession — thus gaining great merit.

There is no higher action than the action that reverses karma. That is why Christ said, "Love your enemies." But these words are mistranslated. To have an enemy means to reverse the karma by enlightening your enemy, by cultivating in him greater virtues, and eventually bringing his consciousness to the level where he will pay his own karma by heroic sacrifices for you to fulfill the Law of Righteousness. The greatest friendship is built between people who reversed their karma. Their friendship will never end.

Do good for others that do evil to you. All progress and merit are gained by our actions, on all levels, by our good karma. All our suffering and pain, failures and defeats came upon us as the result of our past bad karma.

One day in a study group our Teacher addressed the students, "All your knowledge, information, positions, possessions, and your certificates will not benefit you if you do not have the power of discrimination between what is good for your future and what is bad for your future. It is this distinction that will enable you to be aware and alert every minute of your life to choose the path of the good:

- the good for you
- the good for others
- the good for all sentient beings

"It is this discrimination and choice of good that will decide the level you achieved on the path of your evolution. Once the path of good is chosen, all your virtues and achievements will cooperate with you to lead you to the highest bliss.

"But if you choose the wrong path, all your education and knowledge and positions will not help to bring you back into light and into the path of joy and bliss."

Then he spoke about how we must develop discrimination in all that we do, say, feel, and think.

The first thing we must learn and teach is karma. Once we learn about it we must choose the *action* that liberates us, expands our consciousness, and opens an unlimited contact with the Universe.

• CHAPTER 15 •

Core Karma

There are two main divisions of karma: one is cause and effect, the effect of your life; the other is the karma of the Lord, His Purpose, His motive. This needs a little explanation. The Lord has a Purpose — and everything that is against that Purpose is destined to vanish sooner or later. This karma is related to your spirit. This law takes your soul toward harmony with the law, and age after age your spirit develops and radiates those beauties which are in the Purpose. This karma can never be broken, but everything against it slowly degenerates and vanishes.

The life we know in the world is the closest of these two karmas. Actually the first karma exists only because of the Lord's karma — the Lord's Purpose. The energies, principles, and laws of this karma try to clean the karma of the earth, creating *the effect* of causes. The effect is a cleansing process, that eventually annihilates what the bad cause created and disciplines the creator of the cause to strengthen his life in harmony with the Purpose.

We see now that in the greater existence of the Will of God there is the karma of individual man and the karma of humanity. This karma is beaten age after age by the forces of the Purpose of the Lord, eventually to synchronize and harmonize with the Will of God.

This dual karma exists in man himself. His Core represents the Lord's karma, but anything other than the Core creates earthly karma — acting against the will of God, of the Lord's karma, and these two forces clash until the worldly karma is cleaned.

We can say that earthly karma and the Core karma are always in a conflict when man creates a cause which will produce an effect against the Lord's karma.

The discipline that a man must pass is how to live in order that his life's actions do not create any effect that is against the harmony of the Core karma because every such effect will eventually be annihilated by the Core karma.

The karma of the Lord has in itself two parts. One part is the world's karma; the other part is the karma that initiates one into creating an assistance to the Lord's Core karma. His Core karma is the synthesis of past experiences and visions unified in one Purpose.

• CHAPTER 16 •

Building Your Bodies

It is a metaphysical fact that we recreate ourselves in each life. We create our mental body by the way we think. We create an emotional apparatus by the way we feel or the way we project our emotions. We create our physical body by the way we act. Our actualization built the body that we have. If it is not healthy, it is because we did not have health-producing actualization.

To have a beautiful, creative mind and a healthy mind, we must think lofty thoughts, interchange lofty thoughts, write about great ideas, and leave our mind open to all new inspirations and impressions without crystallization. This will create a mind in the future we will be delighted with and can use for the service of others.

To have an emotional apparatus that is up-to-date, all our feelings and emotions must be colored and mixed with the highest love and compassion. This will create that emotional mirror which will reflect in our life higher visions from the Intuitional and Monadic Planes.

To have a healthy, dynamic body, which has great endurance and energy, we must harmonize all our activities with the Common Good, with the common interest, and not allow any action which is based on self-interest, greed, hatred, and exploitation. These four are called four destructive viruses of our protective net.

A life lived upon these principles will control the fires of the body, mind, and spirit and create the ideal man.

The fires of matter will accumulate in the pranic triangle.[1] This is a triangle of fire with the fire of mind at the bottom of the scale. This combined fire will climb to the top of the head and create spiritual radiance, mixing with the fires of spirit. All the aura of man will be a shield and an atmosphere in which *centers*, senses, and glands will operate at their optimum, bestowing health, stability, creativity, and endurance.

This is how, in a nut shell, a future leader for humanity is created.

The life you live in the three planes builds your future bodies and decides the field where you can best serve humanity.

---

1. See *New Dimensions in Healing*, Ch. 5, "Three Centers of Prana."

• CHAPTER 17 •

Consciousness and Karma

Consciousness continues to exist even if the mental body dissolves when one enters the Intuitional Plane. Also, when one brings back his mental body at the time of incarnation, the consciousness remains the same, even though the brain cannot register it for many reasons. If the consciousness remains the same, then why is it that one cannot remember his past life when he incarnates?

The Teachers say that one can remember only when the seven etheric centers in the head are kindled. As man passes away to the astral and mental planes, the impressions from the worldly life slowly vanish and only a faint impression remains. This faint memory registered in the consciousness cannot make an impression on the brain without the fire of higher centers. This fire brings the memory to the surface and impresses the brain.

Those who remember their past lives accurately have kindled centers through which spatial fire circulates and makes the continuity of events in the consciousness possible. It is this fire that preserves all accumulated memories within the consciousness and within space and associates them in proper sequence.

We have the same consciousness in the physical, emotional, and mental planes. First, they seem to be different consciousnesses, but as our evolution advances we realize that they are parts of our one consciousness.

It is easier to carry up to the subtle planes our earthly consciousness than it is to carry down the subtle consciousness to our earthly consciousness. The reason is that as we go to the subtle planes we have more freedom from matter and flesh, but as we go down our consciousness mixes with matter and flesh, and the recordings do not keep their clarity and purity.

The unification of consciousness is achieved only when the human soul enables himself to work on the Intuitional Plane. There, the lighted area of the mental body, the field of consciousness, is withdrawn to the Intuitional Plane and the human soul can see all that was impressed on it throughout many incarnations. At this stage, the human soul realizes that his field of consciousness, throughout ages, was nothing else but his own sphere of light.

On the Intuitional Plane, this sphere of light is no longer called the consciousness but the field of awareness. The human soul is aware of all that impresses his field of awareness. Impressions reach this field from the etheric, astral, mental, and intuitional worlds.

The difference between consciousness and awareness is that consciousness is duality; it is created by the intelligence ray of the Inner Guide and the human soul. As the human soul advances, the Inner Guide withdraws Its beam of light, and only the light of the human soul shines on the mental plane. When the boundaries of the Intuitional Plane are crossed, this light is withdrawn to the Intuitional Plane and is the field of light of the human soul only. It then has no duality but is a unified whole in which things are understood not because of conflict, comparison, measurement, or logic but directly, as they stand.

Another difference is that consciousness changes when the physical, emotional, and mental bodies undergo change, crises, or tension. The consciousness is influenced by all that happens in the three lower worlds. But awareness stays the same even if the three lower bodies go through many changes.

It is in the awareness field that all memories are — if one wants to remember.

Beyond the Intuitional Plane, man comes into contact with the Universe not through the awareness field but through *beingness* or identification. The consciousness field turns into the awareness fields and the awareness field melts away in the advancing human soul, who realizes that it was he who was conscious, or aware. Instead of looking at things through mirrors, he sees himself face-to-face. Thus, the human soul travels from states of multiplicity to oneness.

Those who develop a certain amount of awareness can remember their past lives. Awareness is developed only when the fire of the human soul charges the head centers and connects the mental consciousness to intuitional awareness and links the physical brain, the etheric brain, and the Mental Permanent Atom with the Intuitional Permanent Atom.

Awareness starts when the twelve-petaled Chalice[1] begins to unfold and the Solar Angel pulls the jewel, the human soul, up to the Intuitional Plane.

The Law of Karma plays a great role on the path of advancement. No step forward can be taken without balancing the waves of karma. On each step we pay for the things we did wrong. On each step we are protected by the things we did right.

Right and wrong things are not judged by human measures. Right things are those electrical waves of karma which pave the wave for our spiritual unfoldment. Wrong things are those electrical waves which slow our evolution and waste our time and energy.

The karmic force-waves expand in space. And when they hit certain strata in the spheres they bounce back to the originator. There are white and black waves.

---

1. See the *Subconcious Mind and the Chalice*.

Sometimes they come back together; sometimes they come back separately. These waves are the waves caused by our deeds, emotions, and thoughts. All of these have their shades. White ones travel faster and go greater distances, but black waves bounce back in relatively short distances. These waves not only come to our physical existence but also to the subtle existence when we are on the astral or mental planes.

Man advances by producing less black waves and more white waves.

One can increase in wisdom by living more in light, love, and service. Such a life radiates a great amount of white waves and balances or even destroys many dark waves. White waves come to our rescue in our darkest hours and protect us.

In the mechanics of space, not a single ray of love, light, or service is lost. These bring a great amount of energy to man and enlighten his mind, especially in times of need.

Dark waves function as hindrances. They delay our progress and cause great expenditures of energy. We advance through the white waves, and sometimes they surround us like a shield to protect us from incoming hostile rays.

As the human soul progresses he passes through waves of dark and white karma. On each step he is tested, and when he passes the test his consciousness expands and shoots up seeds of awareness into the Intuitional Plane.

To have intuitional awareness, one must clear himself of dark waves of karma. This is why we are told that we must not increase our burdens as we try to climb the mountain of our beingness.

The Teaching reveals that karma can be changed or even destroyed by thought and psychic energy. It is possible to fight and destroy the dark waves of karma through the lightning of our thoughts, to avoid being handicapped by wrongs we did in the past by paying our debts with light and service to others. Such a purification process by the energy of thought paves the way toward greater expansion of consciousness and awareness. But when the dark waves are destroyed, one must be extremely careful not to produce dark waves again because any new dark wave revives the elements of the dead waves and creates a chaotic state on the path of man. This is why man must not turn back into his old vices.

Purity on the path of ascent is the shield of the traveler. With purity of thought one must strive to build a sensitive antenna. Antennas of the mind are not a figment of imagination. Every true thinker has an antenna which penetrates into different levels and transmits thoughts of different magnitudes. The Teaching says that Great Ones have sevenfold antennas which draw ideas and thoughts from many dimensions.

It is very beneficial to spread your antenna before you engage in any creative labor. Just visualize a beam of light of extreme sensitivity extending into space from your brain, transmitting creative thoughts to your consciousness. Gradually you can learn to project your antenna into different locations and pick up different layers of thought from various stations of light.

As we advance it will be possible to tune in with various stations and transmit to our consciousness the information and knowledge we want. Thus it will be possible for an electrical engineer to receive information about philosophy or about any subject he needs. These various stations are the forty-nine Ashrams of the Hierarchy, Whose members are far more advanced in knowledge and power than average humanity.

Not only our consciousness but also our thoughts change in different conditions. Outer and inner conditions have a great effect on our consciousness and thinking. We think differently in the mountains, near lakes, or rivers. We think differently in the cities, in restaurants, or in bazaars. We think differently when we are at a party or when we are alone.

One must find the best conditions in which he can have the best thoughts. Of course, one cannot stay long in such a condition, but with willpower, one can occasionally create such conditions and touch lofty thoughts.

Consciousness expands and functions more clearly in an area which has no conflicting waves of thought clashing with each other.

Higher and purer thoughts originate from an expanding consciousness.

In the future it will be possible to get immediate assistance from such sources. For example, in surgery a surgeon can evoke the help of those doctors who are in the Ashrams and have far advanced knowledge about a surgery of any kind.

It is very interesting to note that karma often interferes. On certain occasions it blocks our consciousness, and on certain occasions it enlightens our consciousness. For example, if an intelligent man is going to fail because of his karma, he misses an important point in his plan and because of that point he fails. On the other hand, when the future of the success seems dark, he is inspired to take a certain step which brings total, surprising success to him.

This is also seen in different occasions. For example, if because of his karma a man is going to die, he does something wrong and he passes away. On the other hand, if he is not going to die, even in very dangerous conditions he receives help.

Sometimes it even happens that the Inner Guide, knowing the man will pass away or will fall into a great difficulty, inspires the man to make certain arrangements for his work or possessions. Being healthy, the man never thinks about his death, but he makes the arrangements anyway "for the future" and passes away in a few days.

The awareness of the Inner Guide is sometimes not registered upon the consciousness of man due to his preoccupation, dreams, and level of consciousness.

It is necessary to observe the behavior of people in order to find out if they are unconsciously following the plan of the Inner Guide without noticing any difference in their own behavior. A keen observer can distinguish between the operation of the Inner Guide and the operation of the human consciousness, both of which are working through the personality.

Very often our future is reflected upon the mirrors of our higher bodies, but our consciousness is not yet trained to reach them and translate them to us. Sometimes the karma is hidden from our consciousness so that we do not follow a path against it.

For example, if a man knows that he is going to die half an hour later in an accident because of his karma, he will not drive his car and he will try to escape. But if his karma wants him to be alive, either he is not hurt in the accident, or he arrives upon the accident a few minutes late.

One of my Teachers a long time ago knew that he was going to pass away on a certain date. A few days before the date he fell ill. My Father took his medical bag and hurried to his home.

My Teacher was waiting for the right time to leave his body. In spite of all the advice and pleas of my Father, he refused to take any medicine or an injection. A few hours later he raised his right hand and held the hand of an invisible visitor he said was Jesus, and he passed away.

There are many other cases such as this in which one works consciously with the Law of Karma. King Akbar used to do very dangerous things. Once when he was asked why he was risking his life, he replied, "Nothing will happen to me if I am protected by God. If not, let it happen."

It is possible to expand our consciousness in such a degree that we become aware of our karma and cooperate with it in full measure. It is also possible that once we reach a state of knowing our karma, if absolutely necessary, we can change our karma through our fiery thoughts.

People often think that karma cannot be changed, but the reality is that it can be changed through fiery thoughts, and through transmuting our consciousness. Such a change is introduced or induced not because of fear, not because of personal interest, but because of a dire need for sacrificial service. This does not mean to break the law — but to meet the law in a different way.

At the time of great cataclysms, one can see how karma programs every detail for every man. Often those who know about the hour and location of the cataclysm cannot utter a word to those who are karmically going to perish. This is one of the tests of an Initiate. They cannot interfere with the law. Sometimes they are even ordered to stay at the location of natural cataclysm so as not to make people follow them and escape their own karma. The majority of people, even if warned, are too busy to heed the warnings. Their consciousness is blocked by their deeds.

It is through expansion of consciousness that one will be capable of cooperating with the laws of Nature. The decisive factor in your karma is not what you know, is not what you have, but what you did and what you are.

Very soon instructions will be given to humanity on how to build the antennas of thought and consciousness and thus expand the horizons of humanity.

• CHAPTER 18 •

Karma and Choice

"Karma is but the condition of the choice."[1]

In all actions, feelings, and thoughts we choose between those which are supportive for our evolution, and those which create karma. Wrong actions on these levels create karma. We can choose wrong actions, and we have the power to choose right actions.

Most of the time our actions are mechanical, but they create effects, and effects turn into karma.

Often our mechanical actions for the present are ones which are repeated conscious actions from the past. They were repeated so many times that they became automatic. Nevertheless, they built karma because of their effect. Causes produce effects. Effects turn into causes and then run along with our daily lives, conditioning our relationships.

---
1. Agni Yoga Society, *Leaves of Morya's Garden*, Vol. I, para. 266.

People also speak about actions that are forced upon us by obsession or possession. Are we responsible for such actions? We are indirectly because we provided conditions in our life which attracted obsession or possession. This is why the Teacher says, "...naught happens by accident."[2]

Some attacks we receive are not because of our karma. They come to us when we dedicate ourselves to the Path. Dark forces[3] may create various obstacles to prevent us from proceeding on the Path, but the Hierarchy of Light eliminates them.

We learn much from such attacks and use our knowledge to protect others who are having similar attacks.

Sometimes our striving toward beauty and light creates physical, emotional, and mental problems. Such kinds of troubles or problems are not attacks of dark forces but the result of our past karma. In the past we may have collected certain trash in our nature that demands cleaning when our spiritual forces become active.

Obstacles arising from our karmic records are soon paid, and the path is open for us once again.

The Great Sage says, "Karma will overtake one, but its quality may be altered by a voluntary sacrifice to unknown people."[4]

---

2. *Ibid.*, para. 233.
3. See also *Battling Dark Forces, A Guide to Psychic Self-Defense*.
4. Agni Yoga Society, *Leaves of Morya's Garden*, Vol. II, p. 14, para. 12.

The expression "unknown people" is very significant. People sacrifice for the members of their family or close friends. This can be considered the safest sacrifice because a person serving close ones has the possibility of serving himself. Identification with close ones makes them part of himself.

Often we are given dreams and visions to warn us or to encourage us. But they are given in such a way that they do not violate our karma. We use our free will and decide to see the depth of the vision and dream and act accordingly. Or we ignore the warning and the encouragement.

Our Solar Angel, or our Higher Self, does not violate our karma but hints, suggests, and gives certain warnings. We may use such occasions consequently to bring out the best of our karma.

The Great Sage says, "Remember, guidance is on condition that karma be not infringed upon."[5]

Advanced disciples are workers who do not give direct advice or impose their will, information, or knowledge upon others. Even in their highest moments of discussion they remain detached from their ideas and opinions. They are deeply aware of the level of consciousness of the people and let them be free to decide according to their own karma.

A true Teacher teaches the ways and means of discovering wisdom and how to bloom. The rest is left to the

---

5. *Ibid.*, p. 145, para. 11.

student. But it is true that inspirations are given to the degree of the student's consciousness.

Whenever we create karma, it is under the *law of dates* that decides when karma will manifest. Not every action meets immediately its reaction, or not every cause immediately meets with effects. The law of dates inherent in karma decides the time. Sometimes karma is met five lives later or is met in three months or instantaneously. To know the dates of manifestation of karma is beyond our ability as it is entered into the computer which processes the group, national, global, and Cosmic karma — together with our individual karma related to the rest.

There is the opinion that our karma is final and nothing can change it. This is a superstition. We can change our karma. We can improve it, even totally erase it by actions that are sacrificial, heroic, all-inclusive. Even in a dire situation a bad karma can appear as a feathered friend if you lead a sacrificial and intelligent life.

We must consider our karma as a chemical compound. It is possible to change its chemistry using chemicals that change it, dissolve it, or render it totally beneficial.

Chemicals are not only physical elements. They are also heroic actions, sacrifice, devotion, dedication, lofty thoughts, unconditional love, spatial ideas, and supreme striving. Such chemicals have power to change the compound of our karma.

The human soul is immortal only if he is one with the Intuition. The soul in Intuition is immortal.

When the soul in the mental plane fuses with the buddhic substance, it radiates a light which is called *Taijasi* in Sanskrit. This is what illumination is. But it is an illumination, not beingness, until the mental soul is assimilated into the Buddhic Plane. There starts his conscious immortality. *Taijasi* can be defined as the light of the Intuition, striving through the mental body.

People think that we face our karma when we leave our body. This is not true. We pay for our past karma when we incarnate again on the physical plane. After we die we enjoy the result of our sacrifices. The Teaching says that after death the soul receives only the reward for the unmerited sufferings endured during its last past existence.[6]

"The whole punishment after death, even for the materialist, consists therefore in the absence of any reward and the utter loss of the consciousness of one's bliss and rest."[7]

Karma has also a very uncommon meaning. Often we think that what we do, what our nation or humanity does becomes our karma. But such a conclusion is not complete. Because of the Purpose of the Solar Lord our karma is to advance forever on the path of our Cosmic destiny. This is the most essential karma. Every one of us

---

6. See *Other Worlds*.
7. Blavatsky, *Studies in Occultism*, p. 204.

confronts and no one can really escape such a karma. It is our work and labor to meet the Purpose of the Solar Lord. The Great Sage says, "Eternal, indefatigable is the labor of ascent! This eternal motion is your karma!"[8]

This motion is directed by the currents of will, a will that is synchronized with the Will of the Cosmic Magnet. Then all advance under this karma. Those who try to reject such a karma fall into the chaos of self-denial.

Our own created karma turns upon us — sooner or later. Also, when we violate the karma of others we create pain and suffering for ourselves. But the karma impressed upon each Spark cannot be rejected without due consequences. Such a karma is the foundation of striving, evolution, eternal and infinite progress of improvement and actualization. The striving to attain that which is predestined is also our karma.

People think that they can easily be part of a spiritual or esoteric group, a group that is formed to help people, to lead them on the path of improvement. But such a thought is not true. To be a part of a spiritual group depends on your individual karmic debts. If your personal karma is not at least seventy percent clear, you cannot participate in spiritual work and be part of a spiritual group.

However, you can penetrate into a group to manipulate it for your personal interest, to slander the group, or to be an agent of destruction and ugliness. But you cannot be a valid member of that group as far as your soul is

---

8. Agni Yoga Society, *Infinity*, Vol. I, para. 20.

concerned. Such people know in their hearts that they are not real members, but they are there for certain personal interests. They do not benefit from the discipline and the Teaching of the group. Though they study, the Teaching does not penetrate into their skin.

Most of such people know the reality, and because of their lack of commitment they are window shoppers or gophers.

What prevents them from being a real part of the group is their karma. Their karma prevents them from being a committed member. Such people sooner or later leave the spiritual group in peace or create confusion. But after they leave the group, their personal karma heavily descends on them.

In a sense, group members ease the karma of each member by sharing it. When the sharing stops, the full pressure of personal karma descends on the individual. Those who are in the spiritual group but are not committed and are not meeting their responsibilities and duties, are thrown out by their karma, sometimes falling into pain and suffering.

Whenever one promises to be a part of a striving group, that person is expected by the group Soul to cooperate with the striving people. But when he does not strive, the group Soul throws him out to face his personal karma.

Thus to be a part of an advancing and serving group requires a certain degree of understanding, intelligence, purity of heart, and willingness to commit and sacrifice. These qualities cannot be ours if our karma is still heavy on our shoulders.

One must release himself from his own karma to a high percentage to be able to participate in group service and group striving.

Q&A

Question: *You said that the crystallizations of the emotional body can only be broken through the shock of striking or intense heat. If there is no one to do this for you, how can you do it for yourself?*

ANSWER: If your time has come that you must have a transformation, a person will come into your life and do it for you.

Question: *How do you feel about organ transplants?*

ANSWER: Very sincerely, I am against them. It is a most obnoxious way to make money, and it works against karma. Let the person die so that he returns with a nice body. Patching the heart with a baboon heart is criminal. Karma will beat him so badly. God gave us organs to take care of and to use.[9]

Question: *What about blood transfusions?*

---

9. See "Organ Transplants" in *Other Worlds*, ch. 14.

ANSWER: The Great Sage advises us, as much as possible, not to take blood from another person. The best policy is not to be sick.

Question: *Can you talk about the Akashic Records?*

ANSWER: The Akashic Records[10] are the television set of Sanat Kumara and the Kumaras. They watch it continually. In *The Legend of Shamballa* it says that Sanat Kumara watches in His mirror everything that is happening on earth.

The Akashic Records are the records, the film of everything that has happened. For example, a man dies in an accident and says, "God, why did You allow this? I am a nice man!" God says, "Come here, you silly bug, and watch your records." He sees what he has done in the past, and so he says, "My goodness, please excuse me." It is self-recognition, the meeting of yourself that shows you the righteousness of Life. Life is systematized justice.

If we hesitate to make the right decision, our karma goes crazy. One wrong decision can cost you one life or many lives. In making a decision, it is important to know what decision you are making. When you fail to make a life decision, you fall into karmic complications. You must be sharp to make the right decision by cultivating straight-knowledge or Intuition. You feel in your heart what the right time is, what must be done, and so on. If you

---

10. See "Akasha" in *Other Worlds*, ch. 31.

make things hang on or depend on you, you are doing the worst thing with karma. Every minute you are late will cost you "one year" of punishment.

Straight-knowledge and Intuition are cultivated by regular, continuous, and rhythmic meditation. Without them, you will make wrong choices. It is also important to be sincere with yourself. When you are sincere, your choices will instinctively be the right ones because the higher forces will work for you. Even if, by chance, your decision is wrong, you will find yourself on the right path. The Chinese say that the wrong path becomes the right path for a good person.

If we hang on others and manipulate them under the guise of loving them, we create the worst karma. This is totally self-interested and dangerous.

Question: *If we realize that somebody is manipulating us, is it right to break off?*

ANSWER: You do not need to break off. You can tell them, "I don't like your attitude. Why are you doing this? It is no good for you and I do not want to be sapped. Like a leech, you are sticking to me and sucking my blood, saying that you love me. What kind of love is this?" There are millions of relationships like this, where people hang onto each other. The bottom line is hypocrisy, self-interest, and ego. This does not work. Karma knows these things, and it will beat you.

Do not hang onto others; stand on your own feet and examine your life. Fact is fact; reality is reality.

Question: *Is divine indifference the same as non-attachment?*

ANSWER: Non-attachment is one step forward; you cut everything and forget it. Divine indifference is watching the situation like an eagle, without involvement.

• CHAPTER 19 •

Karma and the Solar Angel

The karma of a person and the plan of the Solar Angel do not conflict because the Solar Angel bases Its plans on the karmic records of the person and the potentials that he demonstrates. But it so happens that due to various influences, a person may do unexpected things which create conflict with the plan of the Solar Angel, and he may fail to fulfill the plan.

The plan of the Solar Angel is to help you overcome past vices and wickedness and help you develop your potentials. It is always the plan of the Solar Angel to prepare you in such a way that you take part consciously in the Divine Plan. Let us remember that the Solar Angel is a member of the Hierarchy and cooperates with the Hierarchical Plan.

When disciples are accepted, they are mostly under the control of the Hierarchy, which acts as the collective Solar Angel for humanity.

The Hierarchy may prepare a disciple to perform sacrificial deeds and die. But such a disciple is always conscious, whether he is in or out of body. After he dies, he does not succumb to the lower hells, as do suicides, but procedeeds to higher planes, with greater enlightenment. Sometimes a disciple sacrifices all his time and energy with self-forgetfulness to help others, but in doing so he does not slow down his own spiritual progress. When he dies, special Teachers take care of him, teach him, and help him assimilate in just a few years all that he would have learned and assimilated in the life span that he sacrificed for humanity. Total righteousness exists in the Higher Worlds, and you are paid back for a "cup of water given to a thirsty soul."

Sometimes fanatics appear like heroes or disciples. The difference is that they are following the direction of obsessors or possessors, or following the dictates of their glamors and illusions. Most fanatics do not have continuity of consciousness.

The Hierarchy presents the Plan to disciples, and leaves them free to engage with the Plan. The Hierarchy even leaves them free to choose how they will exercise their ingenuity.

Those entities which are totally dedicated to genocide, terrorism, and destruction are those people whose Solar Angels have left them. Such people can be very vicious and bestial. In human history there is evidence of people obsessed with such entities. These are people who butchered others and tried to destroy whole cultures or civilizations.

There are two kinds of people who do not have Solar Angels:

1. Those who in previous manvantaras achieved individualization by the power of the Divine Spark within them
2. Those who were endowed with Solar Angels on this globe, but lost them

Some people who do not have Solar Angels came to this planet from space to continue their education. They demonstrate a strong mentality with great intellectual powers. They are materialists who use separatism and factions. They are scattered throughout all nations and work with selfishness and separatism. They create the crises necessary to awaken the thinking of average people. They do not belong to a single religion or nation but are from all nationalities. They are recognized by their selfishness, cunning intellect, power of manipulation, materialism, and totalitarian attitudes. Sometimes they are born into families among those who have Solar Angels.

Those who have lost their Solar Angels are primarily destructive people. If a chance is given to them, they would burn the world and enjoy its destruction. Fortunately, these people are rare. A contemporary example is Hitler and his seven evil co-workers. Hitler was not possessed by a disembodied human being but by a member of the Dark Lodge.

You read in mythology and legend about people who denounce their souls and make a pact with Satan. There is some truth in this. When a human being becomes totally inhuman and loses his Solar Angel, he becomes an agent of the dark forces and uses his intellect, knowledge, and resources to bring destruction to earth.

Those people who evolved without Solar Angels and eventually individualized, or developed "I" consciousness or ego consciousness, were inhabitants of other or previous solar systems. Their Spark very slowly unfolds itself with the help of great Masters Who act as Solar Angels for a large mass of people. Through Their methods, the focus of consciousness of people was eventually drawn into the lower mental plane, where "I" consciousness developed, and they realized that they were separate, thinking human beings.

To undergo further evolution, these people came to earth to develop their love nature. If they fail to overcome their separatism and materialism by cultivating inclusiveness and spirituality, they will be counted as failures in the next manvantara. Who knows what destiny awaits them.

Sometimes Soulless people develop their love nature through the experience of incessant pain, suffering, isolation, revolution, war, and destruction, unless they take deliberate action to develop their heart nature and compassion.

Those who developed without Solar Angels and are now living on this earth are those who attach fanatically to teachers, ministers, or leaders, sometimes with total blindness. The reason for this is that they use their teachers and leaders as "solar angels" of sorts. These people are usually fanatical devotees. Of course, one can highly respect his teacher and follow the wisdom imparted by his teacher and still have a Solar Angel, but there are oceans of difference between these two kinds of devotees:

- One is exclusive; the other is inclusive.
- One separates; the other synthesizes.
- One obeys blindly; the other obeys consciously and with his free will.
- One destroys for the sake of his beliefs; the other tries to understand the beliefs of others and find beauty in them.
- One is materialistic and totalitarian; the other is idealistic, practical, and purely democratic.
- One collects and stores; the other distributes and shares.

I was once asked what happens when a man without a Solar Angel marries a woman who has a Solar Angel. Do their children have Solar Angels or not? The answer is that any soul which has a Solar Angel is born with It. The soul that does not have a Solar Angel is born without one. If two people who do not have Solar Angels marry one another, they tend to attract children without Solar Angels. If by chance they have a child who has a Solar Angel, their life will not be easy with that child. The child will eventually leave them, after making numerous attempts to open their heart qualities and inclusiveness. It is also possible for two people who have Solar Angels to have a child that does not have one. These parents will have similar problems; the child will eventually leave them to join those who do not have Solar Angels.

People without Solar Angels have a very strong tendency and urge to be together for protection. They go into business together and share various interests.

Fortunately, people without Solar Angels are not a single nation; they are in all nations, in all churches, in all organizations — pursuing the same goals: materialism, totalitarianism and separatism.

It is very rather than grouping.

It is important to remember that all those who strive can reach perfection. Those who do not have Solar Angels can achieve the Fourth Initiation and beyond, just as people who have Solar Angels can. It is also possible for a person who has a Solar Angel to fail to reach the Fourth Initiation, or Arhathood. The path toward perfection is open to all men.

People without Solar Angels must unfold their heart, cultivate compassion, inclusiveness and intuition. People with Solar Angels must cultivate reasoning, logic, practicality, and other mental qualities, and strive toward perfection.

Both types of people eventually meet on the Intuitional Plane as brothers. Both of them at this stage do not have Solar Angels, and both of them are in the Light Supernal.

People who do not have Solar Angels think that they are the Solar Angel for the personality, which is comprised of billions of lives divided into the mental, astral, etheric and physical planes. These billions of lives must proceed on the path of their evolution through the light shed upon them by the human soul itself.

A person who does not have a Solar Angel has a hard time understanding the subjective dialogue which goes on between a human soul and its Solar Angel. Such people have a different psychology, and do not experience the intervention of a Solar Angel.

The intervention of the Solar Angel is very subtle. It is not direct or imposed, but because of the very presence of the Solar Angel, with all Its glory, beauty and wisdom, the person, no matter what he does, at some level measures himself by the standards of the Solar Angel, and thus feels happy or guilty. He feels guilty if he does not meet the standards of the Solar Angel. He feels happy when he cooperates with the standards of his Solar Angel. There is always a dialogue or inner connection between the two poles.

In the case of those who do not have a Solar Angel, they do right or wrong without having an inner reaction or response. To explain this further, those who do not have a Solar Angel have an orphan psychology. They feel as if there is no one to whom they belong. They do not experience an inner pressure to which they complain or rejoice. They create substitutes. Their wives or husbands carry a heavy load of their complaints, and are forced to rejoice with them in the smallest success they have. And if they do not find any substitute, they sink into deep depression.

If they are average, they always need someone to tell them what to do. They need constant encouragement to move forward. If they are advanced, they are totally indifferent to praise or rebuke. This is why they can donate ten million dollars without the joy of giving, or commit a serious crime and feel as if nothing has happened. You cannot scold these people. No matter how deeply you try to insult them, they do not feel the slightest impression on their skin. All of this does not mean that they are bad people, merely that they are different than those who have Solar Angels.

People without Solar Angels often act like little children; dependency is very high in them. This is why those who do not have Solar Angels often rule, manipulate and exploit those who do. In a sense, an average person who does not have a Solar Angel is more immature than an average person who does. They have a cunning mind, and find ways to cheat those who have Solar Angels and manipulate them, and by so doing, help awaken them to progress.

• CHAPTER 20 •

The Law of Causelessness

Much emphasis is placed on the Law of Cause and Effect, but very little is said regarding the **Law of Causelessness** mentioned in the *Lotus Sutra*.

The Law of Causelessness transcends the Law of Cause and Effect. This law operates from Higher Realms within all worlds, alongside the Law of Cause and Effect. The foundation of this Law is **Compassion**.

The Law of Compassion functions beyond the Law of Cause and Effect. This is sometimes hinted at in Christian literature in references made to grace. Also, in the *Koran*, it is found in the idea that "God can do anything that He wants."

According to the Law of Causelessness, a person can attain instantaneous enlightenment. A wicked person can enter the path of liberation; a person can become a Buddha or a Christ.

Certain people also are programmed to do what they do; their good or bad deeds are not related to them, and they neither decrease nor increase in merit. They play their part in the drama of life, appearing in different roles or non-roles, and their future is not conditioned by their past — because the past was merely acting.

Even if a person is loaded with past karma he can turn into a saint instantaneously if that is what "God wants."

The "wanting of God" is not the result of any move that a person may take toward freedom. This "wanting" is not conditioned by any human attitude. It is the action of "God," the action of the Law of Causelessness. Thus, a new chance is given to anyone to whom "God wants to give that chance."

The existence of this law supports the idea that "God" is independent and that "He" is not even controlled by "His" own laws. In a deeper sense, since an individual being essentially is divine, he is potentially above any limitations created by his past deeds. Potentially he has the Law of Causelessness in him. Potentially he has the power of grace, the power of compassion, and potentially he can negate the Law of Cause and Effect.

The Almighty One is within him, or is his Self. It is only a matter of how to activate that Self.

While most of life proceeds under the Law of Cause and Effect, there are those who are not subject to it. For example, those who

1. operate as Selves
2. are programmed to live the way they live
3. have already paid all their past karma

• **CHAPTER 21** •

The Law of Inevitability

The Law of Inevitability can be detected by those who observe how certain things in life run their course no matter what people do, desire, or think. It is as if everything is programmed in the way it should run.

This law acts or operates based on our past actions, desires, thoughts, and future dreams, using them as a collective cause to create a live drama or comedy through which the person goes in spite of all his efforts to quit the show.

This can be seen in various human relationships, job conditions, politics, the economy, and other fields of human endeavor. An iron hand leads the show, and pain, suffering, joy, all your efforts to escape become part of the preset drama.

Under the Law of Inevitability, this happens to all of us who live under the physical, emotional, and mental spheres. This law is subsidiary to the Law of Karma. Karma has tolerance, and it allows good causes to interfere and change the result. But the Law of Inevitability has no tolerance. Things go on and finish their cycles, and events do not change their course. The suggestions and help given by outsiders do not make any difference.

But the Law of Karma allows the higher energies let loose by the person to change the events.

These two laws cooperate with each other within the physical, emotional, and lower mental spheres. The Law of Inevitability stops at the border of the lower mind, but the Law of Karma goes beyond it.

To break the Law of Inevitability one must learn how to surpass physical, emotional, and mental planes and function in the higher mind or in the Intuitional Plane. How can we do this practically?

1. Try to observe how mechanically all is going on around you.

2. Try to see the flow of the mechanical current passing through many different forms, events, relationships — but never changing its specific kind of flow. In simple words, see how the same actors play different dramas in different dresses and roles.

3. Try to see how you are involved in the events and are taking part in them mechanically.

Once the power of clear observation is dominant in your mind, then it will be easy for you to break the vicious circle and penetrate into the higher mind and into the Intuitional Plane.

The higher mind begins to operate when you think in terms of being a cause or think in terms of causes, for example, seeing the real cause of a particular experience or event.

The Intuitional Plane is reached when you contemplate and try to reach a level where you do not relate events to yourself but take them as ripples on the ocean of life.

Intuitional level awareness does not try to change the causes of events but tries to create an alternate state of living, dramatically different from the mechanical one, not part of it but interwoven in it. Once such a condition is established

1. Mechanical events become raw materials to be used for an advancing spiritual life — as a source of experience

2. The intuitional current begins to expand the consciousness of man to such a degree that the person escapes suddenly from the circle of the mechanical flow and achieves the power to stop it

Contemplation is a state of expansion of consciousness toward the Intuitional Plane with a deep expectancy to receive light and guidance from the Intuitional Plane. Intuitional light does not give formulated and ready-made advice but makes you realize how to find the ways and means to weaken and dissolve your programming and make yourself free.

The Law of Inevitability runs also by the power of hypnotic suggestion and self-induced programming. Events are made so strong by such programming that often it is very difficult to break them lose.[1]

Such circuits are collective chains of many self-induced programs and post-hypnotic suggestions. Often they run for a long time no matter what you are taught, advised, or forced to do. They are like whirlpools in the vast ocean of your life. They are controlled by the Law of Inevitability.

Education, discipline, heavy effort to change oneself build only artificial barriers to these circuits. Sometimes people feel convinced that the person has changed the course of his life, but the circuit operates as if underground, and occasionally hits the surface and destroys all that was built artificially.

This is why certain educators feel disappointed after doing everything possible to change a person, only to realize that actually nothing was changed in him!

To be free from this Law of Inevitability, the circuits must be dissolved. And that is not an easy task. Through long hours of discussion with the victim and watching the pattern in his life, one can slowly detect the

---

1. See also the *Subconscious Mind and the Chalice* and the *Mystery of Self-Image* on programming.

chains of events and advise the person to use the ruby-laser beam of the Self to destroy those circuits. This beam cannot be used until one is close to his Transformation Initiation. Until then, things go according to the inner programming.

• CHAPTER 22 •

The Law of Reincarnation

These words are going to be very simple, but simplicity does not mean we can understand them and put them into practice. The most important thing in life is not only to know the Teaching but also really to assimilate the Teaching and live accordingly.

Whenever the Great Ones give us a law, give us instructions and ways to live a better life, immediately that law descends into the brain consciousness. Sometimes it descends into the marketplace and becomes so ridiculous that you think it is not right to talk about it. People have taken the concept of reincarnation and used it to make a few dollars for their pockets, and now one hesitates to talk about these kinds of advanced Teachings.

I want to make reincarnation so clear to you that you will not be trapped by those who speak about reincarnation or who read your past lives. You can do that for two or three dollars and then flip out. There are many nice people who do this, and I like them as persons, but it is not good to take supreme doctrines and make them into caricatures. There is a great danger in it. Eventually something which does not sound true to your Intuition, you reject. People now are very expert in taking real things and making them so unreal that your Intuition says, "I am not going to believe that."

The Teaching of Reincarnation

To understand the Law of Reincarnation, we must talk a little about the human composition: what a man is. For example, you have a body and you make your body function. When I say to my body, "Do this, do like this, look like this, do like that, do this or that," it means I am using my body. And because I am using my body, I am not the body. Sometimes it happens that your body uses you. In either case there is duality. You use the body or are used. Your body says, "I want to eat these things. I want to drink these things. I want to eat this poison. I want to do all these things," and you allow your body to do these things or even control you, forcing on you its own free will. This means that you are not your body, and either you are controlling your body or your body is controlling you.

What is the purpose of having a body? The purpose of having a body is to put you in contact with the physical world so that you can perform your duties, your responsibilities, on the physical plane. The body must be healthy, happy, energetic. If you misuse the body, it will create problems for you. The first thing to do is to make your body happy, healthy, and really dynamic so that you use the body according to the purpose for which that body was given to you. It is very simple, but we forget that and we let the body control us. When the body is controlling you, you are lost. If you are controlling the body, you are found. You exist.

The same thing applies to our emotional life. If we are controlling our emotions, it means that the emotional body, the emotional nature, is not us. It is something — a device or mechanism — which we are using.

People differ on how they are using their emotional body. Sometimes our emotions use us, and when our emotions use us, we really do not exist as independent drivers or owners of the body. You are always going to think in terms of owning these bodies and using them for the right purposes. If you start using your physical body in the right way, you will very soon realize you are not your physical body. Many people think about this, talk about this, but they do not know about it. Sometimes walk and say, "My body is walking. I want him to walk. Okay, I want my body to stop. I want my body to lie down and sleep." If you start doing these very simple exercises, you will see that there is a little cleavage between you and the body and the body is slowly, slowly becoming the body, not the *owner* of the body. If you really develop this, you will gain your independence from your body.

Let us say your body wants to drink a bottle of whiskey. Now, create a cleavage between your body and self. Say, "Body, I know you want it, but I am not going to let you do that." If you continue like this, you will see that there is a cleavage between you and the body and you are identifying as the owner of the body, not the body. If you are climbing and the body says, "I do not want to climb," you say, "Look, I want you to climb." If you make him climb, you are seeing that you have power over the body.

These are very simple exercises, but they create that division between you and the body. It is not an unhealthy division. It is a healthy division because whenever you are lost in your body, the body is controlling you. Whenever you are lost in your emotions, the emotions are controlling you. Therefore you are going to come back again and say to your emotions, "My emotional mechanism, I do not want you to hate." Most of you, when you start hating, continue hating. You continue to be jealous. You continue to be in fear, in anger, in anxiety. This means that your emotional body is not under your control yet. How are you going to control your emotional body? It is just as you control your body. For example, say, "Look, I am your boss and you are not going to hate now because hatred will burn you, my mechanism. Hatred will create lots of disorders in the mechanism of you, the emotional body. I want you not to hate." When your emotional body starts obeying you, you are becoming the owner of your emotional mechanism instead of being owned by your own mechanism.

Whenever you are owned by the mechanism, you are under its control, but when you own it, discipline it, and really refine and unfold it, then you have a great mechanism in your hands which you are not only using on the physical plane, but you also will be able to use on the emotional plane. You will slowly realize that your physical life is only a portion of that great life about which you do not yet have any idea.

You are slowly, slowly withdrawing your identification and becoming the boss of your bodies. Many, many centuries, millions and millions of years ago when the Divine Spark within us came down and down and identified with the physical body, we eventually lost our memory of what we were before. We became the body. We are going to reverse that process and slowly detach ourselves from the bodies with which we have identified ourselves.

Then we come to our mental body. The mental mechanism is also a body. What is that mechanism? You will have these experiences later if you follow these instructions. The mental body relates us to the mental plane — ideas, revelations, concepts, thoughtforms, higher inspiration, higher knowledge. It is the mental body which relates us to higher levels. We understand the world better because we have a physical mechanism which says, "This wood is hard," an emotional mechanism which says, "This is hatred or love." We have a mental mechanism which says, "This is right and this is wrong. This is square and this is flat." When you start disciplining your mental body and you have a worry or anxiety, you have something repeating in your mind continuously. If you try to stop it and control your mind through meditation, concentration, contemplation, eventually you will see that your mental body will start forming. When your mental body starts forming, you have a mental body in your hand: you have a "car." The next step is to use your mental body in your mental travels, in your mental contacts.

When you learn to use the computer, it becomes a better instrument in your hand. The computer is not you, and your physical, emotional, and mental bodies are computers in your hands which you are going to learn and use the best way possible for your own spiritual purpose and interest.

If you do these exercises, you will slowly, slowly realize you are not the body, you are not the emotions, you are not the mind. Then the question will come, "What am I now?"

Then you are going to search. Most of us do not know what we are. We think we are the emotions. We have faint ideas that we are the body. Sometimes we are our minds. But whenever you are identified with something which is not you, you are becoming something which is not you. Whenever you lose yourself in something which you are not, you start working exactly the opposite of when you were yourself. If you ywere the body you would work this way and that way, but if you are the soul, the owner of the body, you will work differently.

This is a supreme Teaching which was given to us from the Hierarchy, from great Sages, those who had experiences. They say that the Doctrine of Reincarnation is the Doctrine of Hope and Responsibility.

What is hope? The man who is you and is controlling your physical, emotional, and mental planes is trying for one thing — to be perfect physically, emotionally, mentally, and to fulfill or learn the lessons which you were sent to this world to learn. As long as you are identified with your bodies you cannot do that. Immediately when you are free from the control of your bodies, you start thinking about who you are and what your purpose is. You start thinking, "It is not my purpose to be the body, to be emotions, to be mind. They are mechanisms which I am using."

You ask, "What is my real purpose being here?" Now you realize suddenly, intuitively you feel that your purpose here is to be perfect. As Christ said, "Be perfect as your Father in Heaven is perfect." Then you become 90 years old and you see that you are a cabbage, not perfect. Still you are hating, still you want this and that, still you have mental, emotional problems. You say, "Why didn't I do anything in this life?" Another life is given to you as a chance to come and work out your perfection.

For example, you go to your computer and you learn a little, tomorrow you learn a little more, the next day you learn a little more, and eventually you learn everything which is possible. Then you do not need to come to the school anymore where you learn how to use your bodies and what your purpose in life is and how you can perfect yourself according to that purpose.

A child came to school and was told, "You are going to learn your ABCs." He learned his ABCs, and when the school was over the boy went home and repeated ABCDEFG. Then the next day (next life) he came and learned how to read and compose phrases. He went home and the next day came and learned something else, next time something else. Eventually in "seventy-seven days" he finished the class. That is just like us. There are numbers of incarnations in which we must finish the class and graduate with honors. If you graduate with honors, you do not need to go to that class anymore.

Astronomically, astrologically people think how beautifully God ornamented all the heavens with little stars and galaxies and solar systems. People never asked about the purpose of these until a great Sage talked about it. He said, "This whole creation, all the little lives and the greater lives, are going to the university, to school, to perfect themselves." Actually this whole creation is created so that we learn our lessons, we graduate from schools, from one school to another school, so that eventually we reach the purpose of our life. What is the purpose of our life? It is to be as perfect as our Father in Heaven is perfect. This is a symbolic saying. The words are not important. It is what it says that is important. Your whole life must be a process of perfection, improvement: physical improvement, emotional improvement, mental improvement. Then a day will come when you have such great power over your physical, emotional, and mental bodies that you will say, "Now I want to take this jacket off and leave it here and go away."

Some great Teachers do this. Actually I saw many, many Teachers who were doing it. One time something very bad happened. Three or four Hindus lay down under a tree, slept, and left their bodies. They were going to the stars. They were going to bring great wisdom, great formulas of science, great psychological secrets, philosophical depths. Some soldiers, seeing that they were lying there, shot them — thinking they were dead. This happens.

There was another great man called Damodar. One day H.P. Blavatsky was in Bombay and fell down, hurting her knees. Damodar and Colonel Olcott were several thousand miles away. Suddenly, Damodar felt that something had happened and told Colonel Olcott he was going to go to sleep and go and see what had happened. In one minute he went and came back and said, "She hurt her knees." Then, fifteen minutes later a telegram came to them announcing that Blavatsky had really broken her knees.

If somebody wants to do these things, there should be some kind of science, some kind of knowledge to do them. What is that knowledge? The first step of that knowledge is to control your body and purify your body. As long as our bodies are not purified, not controlled, they will control us, and when they control us they will attach in such a way that will never be free to see our destination.

Your present bodies are nothing else but the result of how you thought in the past, how you felt in the past, and what actions you took in the past. It is a doctrine, a beautiful Teaching that does not lead you to destruction, to stupidity, but it is a doctrine which teaches you to sublimate, to refine, to unfold yourself, and eventually understand the Purpose of God and live accordingly.

For example, we say that God is really righteous. Can anyone say that God is not righteous? He knows everything He is doing. Then you go to the hospital and some babies are born, for example, with Down's syndrome. Some babies are born really geniuses. Why is God doing that? You can hear many, many people saying, "God is no good. I wanted a beautiful boy and look what happened." You can see your bodies. Some of us are healthy; some of us are not healthy. Some of us are emotionally criminal: we hate, we are jealous, we gossip and slander. Some people do not like these things. They like beauty, love, right human relationships. There is a big difference between us. Then some of us have very sharp minds, creative minds, beautiful minds which can assimilate problems, understand them, solve them. Some of us do not have all these things. Why is that? Why did God not create everyone equal? Is He guilty? Well, some people think He is guilty because one man was born into a family of kings and queens and another was born in the New York jungles. What is the difference? The difference is that whatever you sow, you reap. Whatever life you live now, exactly your life will be in the future. If you are killing other people, you will be killed in the next life or even in this life. If you are cheating people now, they will cheat you. If you are misleading people, you will be misled. If you are making people crazy, you will be born just like that. Christ says, "If you plant figs, you cannot expect plums." Fig are figs. Plums are plums. How come? That is the law!

Omar Khayyam went to a mosque and in the mosque they were saying, "God creates man the way He wants. Some people are created mentally defective, some people are created smart, some rich, some poor." That is what they believed. To show the error of these ideas, Omar Khayyam, when at the mosque, saw the most beautiful rugs. He folded them and put them under his arm and slowly snuck out. Then he went home and found lots of sheiks sitting there. They said, "Why did you steal these things?" Omar answered, "Do not blame me. God created me as I am, so I did whatever I am. So if you are blaming me that I am a thief, blame Him because He created me as a thief."

Those who do not believe in reincarnation are caught in such kinds of problems for which they do not have explanations: Why are you a thief and I am a really good man? What is the difference? Why did God create me like this? Well, God did not create you like that. God gave you free will. He created you and said, "Go and work at whatever you like. Whatever you sow you will reap." This is it. If you are criminal, criminal things will hit you. If you are crazy, crazy people will teach you. That is the difference. According to our physical, emotional, and mental activities we create our future bodies and the future conditions of our life. For example, maybe you are a criminal, doing things secretly, destroying people, cheating them. And because the government is not catching you, you are so happy and you enjoy your money. Wait until the crop comes next life. Next life you will find yourself in a bad condition. The Great Sage, talking about these things says, "If you want to know how the past affects the present, go to asylums and hospitals. All that suffering, all that misery is the result of how they lived."

There is a little story which is very interesting. There was a man who was very bad to his wife. "Do not do this, do not go there, do not read this, do not meditate, and so on." Eventually he died. He was born again in a place that was like a dungeon. There was a witch there and continuously the witch said, "Do not move right, do not move left, do not think this, do not feel that." The man was in such pain and suffering that one day he fell on his knees and said, "God, why did You create me like this? What did I do to You?" A voice came and said, "Open your eyes and you will see what you did in the past. Notice what you were doing to your wife in the past. That is what is coming to you because it is a great law."

This is also Christian law, Judaic law, Hindu law, Buddhist law, and Islamic law. What is that law? Whatever you sow, you will reap. Buddha, speaking about this says, "Your physical, emotional, mental deeds will follow you as the wheels follow the hoof of the horse that pulls it." This gives us a little sense of caution.

This happens on computers today. With a push of a button, the police can find out all about your past. It is right in the computer. What about the Creator? He has a computer which can read your bones, your thoughts and emotions, what you were thinking, feeling, and doing.

The best way to handle the Law of Reincarnation is to live a good life — physically a good life, emotionally faithful and beautiful, mentally a good life so that in the future you prepare nice bodies for yourself and do not get sick and go to the hospital every day. This is a must.

The Teaching of Reincarnation says that when you die you leave your physical body and start living with your emotional body. Then your emotional body dies and you go to the mental plane. When the time comes you slowly come back to the emotional, etheric, and finally, the physical plane and become another baby. You are recycled. If you are a good boy, good girl, you come to parents who will love you and cherish you and do everything possible to make you unfold and bloom like flowers. But if you were a bad boy, bad girl, fanatical, ugly, narrow-minded, you will come to parents who do exactly what you were doing in the past. You will find parents blind like you, forceful like you. If you are born in a family which is using drugs and you were using drugs in the past, you will be so sick of seeing people using drugs in the past that eventually you will say, "I hate these things." You will start finding a new way of thinking to strengthen your path toward Infinity.

Three Kinds of Reincarnation

According to the doctrine, to the Great Teachers, reincarnation happens in three ways. First, it is automatic. You go and automatically come back when the times are ripe, when the computer makes the cycles and says "print," and you are printed again.

Second, there is the reincarnation in which you know what is happening. It is so beautiful. If you build the continuity of consciousness in your mind, if you build the Antahkarana esoterically speaking, if you become aware of what is happening after you are asleep consciously, you will see that you will die but you are conscious. You will withdraw from your body consciously and will start seeing things as they are. A great chance will be given to you after you die in two or three days to see exactly what you did in the past in your video film. The film will play in your eyes and you will see it. Wow, you were doing this, you were doing that. You were killing your husband, your wife, your children, your neighbors, destroying other people for your silly interests, with your gossip, malice, and hatred. You will see all these things and you will ask, "Why did I do these things?" Then you will go forward. When you come back you will slowly, slowly forget what you saw about your past life, but only instincts will remain. This time, if you are seeing a bottle of whiskey you will hesitate a little to drink it. If you are lucky a Teacher will say, "Do not do it anymore." If you have an inclination to kill a man like in the past, the impression you receive from your videotape will tell you, "Do not do that," and that is what happens. If you really analyze it, you will see that every time you do a wrong, you know it is wrong. You know it is wrong but you do it anyway. Or, you are worrying about doing or not doing, or you do it and feel so regretful at the end. You feel so sorry, and that is what leads to repentance. "I am not going to do that anymore." Why do you not want to do it? Why is that instinct in you to do things the right way? There is a push in you, subconscious urges and drives which make you to do exactly what you did again. But if you meet good Teachers, good parents, good friends, they will tell you, "Do not do it," and that is a great help for you because you are going right and left and someone holds you and says, "Go right," and it saves your soul. See how beautiful it is to see your life and where you are going and how you are going?

The third kind of reincarnation is if you reach a certain level of spiritual unfoldment you either come here or you do not come here. You say, "I finished my school. I can go down just to teach people and illuminate them, but for myself I do not need it."

So, let us summarize the three kinds of reincarnation:

1. The first one is that you automatically come back. The time runs, kicks you, and you come back and are born.

2. The second one is that you know where you are going, why you are going. You even choose your parents and situations. It is so beautiful to be intelligent and conscious.

3. The third one is that you do not need any reincarnation, but you come voluntarily because of a great service you are going to do.

Q&A

Question: *If you come voluntarily, does that improve your karma even if you do not need it?*

ANSWER: For example, Elijah came voluntarily. Christ said, "Do you know John the Baptist? He was Elijah. He came back."[1]

Question: *What level of an Initiate do you have to be to have that choice?*

ANSWER: It does not matter what initiation it is because it is a complicated matter. The first thing is to know that you are not the body. Do you really have experience that you are not the body? I was sleeping one day. I oozed out and saw my body lying there. Now I know that I am not my body. If you are not having these experiences, all your

---

1. See for example: Matthew 11:11; John 9:34; Romans 9:10–13. These are all about reincarnation.

prayers and religions are false because you are not maturing. You do not have the experience. Have the experience that you are not the body. Some religions say you are the body. You are not the body! You are the driver of the car. The car can be changed. You can change the car many times. How many cars have you owned since you have been driving cars? The car is not you. You are driving the car. That is what you are going to realize and know experimentally: "I am not the car."

Can you make your body do things which it does not want to do? That is striving. Your body says, "I want to be lazy." The house is a mess. "I do not want to clean it." There is a chance for you to realize that you can give an order to your body and say, "Hey, no matter what, I want you to clean this mess." There you are experimenting. When you are angry, when you are jealous, when you are hateful, when you are really excited, stop it. Can you? If you stop it, you are making your emotional body begin to form. But if you are identified, then it does not form. Mentally, if you have vanity, pride, "I know everything, I am right in everything," you are lost. You are really lost and you do not know about that. Control your vanity, control your ignorance, and say, "I am looking from this side to that side and I am seeing a mountain and I thought only one mountain exists. Well, turn three hundred sixty degrees and you will see what else exists. "This is what I believe." Wait a minute. There are billions of people who believe different things. Look, examine them, listen to them. Go to this church, go to that church, to that temple, to that mosque. Search!

A woman told me the other day she was saved. I said, "I am so glad you are saved." Two minutes later she was telling me she was divorcing her husband." "Why?" "He is the most obnoxious person." "How come you are saved?" You cannot just pronounce being saved with your words. Lip service does not work. You are going to be true. If you are saved, you are an angel and you will prove you are an angel.

Question: *Is it necessarily a sign of advancement or higher consciousness for one person to be born into wealth and royalty and another person to be born into a small town?*

ANSWER: If they are coming consciously knowing what they are doing it is wonderful, but if they are unconscious and the life is controlling them, the computer is controlling them, the computer is righteous. God is righteous. Do not blame anyone if you have sickness, if you are poor, if you are stupid. Blame yourself. God never does these things to you. It is a humiliation, an insult to God to say, "God created me stupid." They brought a little boy to Christ and asked, "My Lord, this boy was blind when he was born. Who sinned to make this boy blind? He or his parents?" — referring to the former life. It is you who makes you blind. Chances are always given. You go back to your slums. A chance is given to you, a book is given to you, a lecture is given to you. You understand it. You are opening your mind or you are closed, thinking you know everything, everything will be all right with you, but you are ignorant.

A few days ago a lady came and asked, "Can I read your past lives?" I answered, "I do not need my past lives read. My past lives are exactly the copy of what I am now. I think I was beautiful in past lives." **The Teaching says that no one must try to know his past lives unless he is a Fourth Degree Initiate and his consciousness works in the Intuitional Plane.** This is exactly as it is. But if you go to a past life reader, it is just like throwing one penny into the ocean and "seeing" what it is. It is like a snake, like a flower. "In the past you were like a snake." Because the water is reflecting, moving, it is a snake now. "No, no, wait a minute. It is a ball; it is a scorpion." Well, that is how they cheat you in reading your past lives.

One day the Sage Teacher by mistake saw the Akashic records of a man. He was so regretful that He saw them without permission, and He said, "I will never do it again." A **Sixth Degree Initiate** is not permitted to enter into your privacy. It is a total secret. The computer is sealed in a diskette and that diskette can only be read by the Karmic Lords.[2]

Question: What relation does karma have with reincarnation?

ANSWER: Karma conditions reincarnation. According to the way you live, that way you will incarnate. Again, there are three kinds of reincarnation. One incarnation is that you are sloppy, in inertia, you are just like potatoes. Why is that? In past lives you did so many dirty things that the

---

2. See *Other Worlds*, Ch. 31, "Akasha."

life sent you to experience what you did to others. Second, you are energetic, you are a businessman, you are a good man. Because you did good to others, now you are good. Then there is a superior man. He is born intelligent, is emotionally pure and loving, physically dynamite. How did he become this way? It is because he sacrificed in his past lives to make people energetic, smart, beautiful, intelligent, creative. Whatever you sow, you reap.

Question: *With the three kinds of incarnation, where would the concept of the soul coming into service fall?*

ANSWER: Even if they are coming from the stars, they follow the same routine. Some of them are totally ignorant. They are sent here to be punished in this smoggy environment. Sometimes they come to bring us science and revelations and they know it. The third group occasionally comes to bring great mental revolutions. For example, in the 15th, 16th centuries these people came from Jupiter and Venus.

But, look at this comedy: A man who is totally trash thinks that he came from Venus. He says, "I am Venusian." He does not know how to comb his hair yet. This is how they destroy the wisdom. Intelligent people think you are a nut to believe these things. We are ashamed sometimes by the people who are doing these stupid things. They say, "That leader is also talking about the same things." He is not. It is a science, a philosophy. It has solemnity, beauty. People destroy this great concept by their stupidity.

A medium came to me. I asked him, "What do you do?" He told me about different procedures he follows. I said, "You are glamored. You do not know what you are doing." He answered, "No, the man is talking in me." "But what is he saying?" Three years later he was in an asylum.

I am not against contacting higher worlds. A masterpiece book, *Other Worlds*, is here ready for you to read. But do you know what you are doing? A telephone call comes. "Hello." "Give me fifty dollars." "Okay, I will send it to you," but you do not ask, "Who are you?"

Mediumism, psychism, these kinds of things are wrong. They lead you into trouble. That is why intelligent people do not like groups, do not like Teachings like this because they think this is one of the weird ones. You should not be one of them. Instead, let people see your prestige, your intelligence, your beautiful life and then you will impress them. Psychics and mediums must see that there is something more beautiful than what they are doing.

Question: *Where does heaven come into this Teaching?*

ANSWER: In the Teaching, heaven is the higher mental plane and you cannot go to the higher mental plane until you pay the price. It is just like paying your taxes.

Question: *How do we as individuals have right action at any given time toward any given person?*

ANSWER: To have right action you must use your reasoning and logic. Is this good to steal? Do not steal it. The second step is to follow the laws. One law says, "Do not drive seventy miles per hour." You do not need to be a genius to know that. It is on the sign. Then you graduate from that and read, for example, rules given by Christ. I am with Christ. Then you go and read the laws given by Buddha. I am with Buddha also. Then go read *The Bhagavad Gita*. Wow. *The Bhagavad Gita* says, "If you think evil toward anyone, all your life will be met by evil." Christ said, "If you call your friend stupid, on the judgment day you will pay for it." Why did you say it? What is true Christianity? It is supreme love, tolerance, compassion, service, inclusiveness, being nonjudgmental. Christ said, "Do not judge others." How not to judge? Well, if you want to follow Christ, do not judge.

Question: *What if you have done things in this life that have affected other people, can you go back and rectify them?*

ANSWER: You will pay for them. That is the morality of it. Before it is in the computer, try very quickly to pay your debts. That is exactly what Christ said, "If you are angry with your friend, agree with him before the sun sets," which means before it goes in the computer. When it is in the computer, it is there.

Question: *Does it not go right anyway?*

ANSWER: No, there is a grace period.[3]

---

3. See *The Subconscious Mind and the Chalice* regarding the recordings in the subconscious mind.

• CHAPTER 23 •

Reincarnation

According to occult wisdom, a man's life is only a minute of time on the path of his long evolution. The life we live now is just a minute; the chain of life-minutes constitutes one endless life — the duration of our evolution.

No one knows where our evolution will ultimately end. We do know that there are those who end their evolution on a particular level and proceed to a different evolutionary process on a higher spiral.

The path of evolution is like going to school. In kindergarten, we learn a few lessons. Then we have a summer break. Then we come back to school to the first grade and pick up a few more lessons. We leave again; then come back and continue this process until we have graduated from this school — which is the Earth.

According to the Ageless Wisdom, a planet is a school. There are planetary schools, solar schools, Cosmic schools. When a person sees life from this angle, he is filled with joy because he knows that his destination is ever-expanding beauty, ever-expanding glory — that when he finishes "kindergarten," it is not the end of everything. He sees that he will be going to college, and that after graduating he will enter the great school of Life, where he will learn unimaginable wonders.

When a person completes one cycle, the next cycle opens before him with greater challenges. It is very beautiful that life always presents us with new challenges. Life is a sequence of ever-presenting challenges.

When we complete the planetary school, we will go on to attend solar schools. We do not yet know what courses we will be taking in the solar schools; hints have been given to us, but it is in the too far-distant future to concern ourselves with this information now. From solar schools we will attend Cosmic schools.

When we stand beneath the stars and watch the glories of the night sky, we see infinity opening up before us. It is like standing at the foot of the mountain and, looking to the summit, knowing that the summit is where we must go. It is infinity that we are witnessing. Infinity is the path of the human soul. Our path is very long; we know this of course. But the reward and the end of our journey is the summit. This is the greatest challenge.

When the man who first climbed Mount Everest was asked why he wanted to climb it, he replied, "Because it is there." It was a challenge. The "Everest" we are climbing is not outside of ourselves; we are climbing the Everest within, to reach the Self. In every life we approach a little more and become a little more ourselves and a little less of our physical, emotional, and mental vehicles.

On this noble path, the Ageless Wisdom says that the human soul attends school by wearing the garment of his body. This is called incarnation. The syllables "carnation" refer to that which is carnal — the body. When the soul enters a new body, we say he has incarnated; he has become objective. We can touch him, feel him, see him. And when he has finished his classes for this session, he leaves his body and disappears.

In studying comparative religions, I found that Krishna mentions that He could recall all of His past lives. Lord Buddha, in speaking to his most-beloved disciple, Ananda (which means bliss), said, "You know, I was a tortoise millions of years ago." He even remembered his animal incarnations. Christ did the same thing. He said, "Before Abraham, I was." Abraham was born thousands of years before He was, but He was there before that.

These Great Ones knew all of Their lives. Eventually we will come to know our past lives. But it will take time and great labor until we reach such a degree of development that our past lives, which are recorded in Nature, will begin to be reflected in our brain and we will be able to see them.

Our current technology has given us tape recorders with which to record our lectures. A greater genius than our current inventors will someday discover a way to pick up the speeches and events from millions of years ago because all of these events are in space.

Not only our words are recorded, but also our thoughts, even our movements and our shape and figure are "photographed" at every moment by space. A film of our lives is recorded from A to Z and exists eternally in space.

There was a time when I visited hospitals every day to visit those people who were passing away. Some who were very close to death started seeing their past lives. Like a movie passing before their eyes, they saw all that had happened in this life or other lives, and then they died.

There is a similar movie, a film that has recorded events occurring from the beginning of our evolution, continuing through to the end of our evolution. This film will eventually be made available to us as we develop our mind and intuition and purify our nature from negative thoughts, vanity, and pride and slowly become pure mirrors of these eternal recordings.

In *The Bhagavad Gita*, we are given a very beautiful teaching about reincarnation. Arjuna was on the battlefield asking, "How are we going to kill these people? How are they going to kill us?" Lord Krishna, his Master, gave him a lecture saying:

> *Arjuna, you grieve for those who should not be grieved for, and yet you speak like those who are learned. The wise man grieves for neither the dead, nor the living.*

Verily, there was never a time when I was not, nor you, nor these rulers of men; nor shall come a time when we shall all cease to be.

The Dweller in the body experiences, in this life, childhood, youth, and old age and then acquires another body. In this, a wise man finds no reason to grieve, nor to be confused.[1]

It is a beautiful thought that one always has been and always will be — even if he leaves his body. He then takes another one, leaves it and takes another, again and again — just like changing clothes. You put on a new dress, then change it when it is old and take a new one, and so on. This is similar to the process of reincarnation. Man endures by continuing his existence throughout all these changes of vehicles.

In the *Gita*, we also read:

The Indweller of the body is never born, nor does It die. It is not true that, having no existence, It comes into being; nor having been in existence, It again ceases to be. It is the unborn, the eternal, the changeless, the Self. It cannot be killed, even if the body is slain.

And Arjuna, when a man knows that this Self is imperishable, eternal, and free from birth and decay, how does he kill, or cause to be killed?

---

1. *The Bhagavad Gita* 2:11-13, tr. by the author.

As a man casts off his worn-out clothes and puts on new ones, so the Indweller casts off Its worn-out bodies and enters into new ones.[2]

The Self is the true man, the real man — and that Self is never born. Then what is born? The body. According to the Teaching, the real man is not born, nor does he die. He continues but he appears, then disappears. He appears when he takes a body, and then disappears when he leaves it.

A lot of instruction regarding reincarnation is given in *The Secret Doctrine*.[3] For example, it states that not only man but also planets, solar systems, and galaxies reincarnate. They appear; they slowly age; then they disappear and return again. This is the eternal cycle of manifestation and unmanifestation, appearance and disappearance. Every time the form appears, we say that the man, planet, universe, or galaxy has incarnated. When they disappear, we say that they have passed away.

But who or what is passing away? The form passes away, not the Real Self within us, within the planet, solar system, universe, or galaxy. The life that uses that body, planet, or solar system will one day create a new vehicle through which to express Itself at a higher level of consciousness.

Everything in Nature progresses. There is a great law in Nature which states that nothing stays at the same level forever. It changes from level one to level two, then proceeds to levels three and four, and continues eternally

---

2. *Ibid.*, 2:20-22
3. H.P. Blavasky, *The Secret Doctrine*.

forward. We develop physically, emotionally, mentally, and spiritually, working on different levels in different ways at different times. For example, someone may be developing on the physical level, but we think that because he is not developing emotionally or mentally that he is not progressing. But development on physical, emotional, and mental levels is cyclical, until the person reaches the Self, that great Spark — and then the unmanifested state. Thereafter, he rests and assimilates his experiences before returning to take a body and begin expressing, this time at a greater level of consciousness and creativity than before.

What do we mean by the term "creativity"? Creativity is the result of a person's achievement. For example, if you create a wooden toy, it is creativity at a certain level, at the level at which you are. But after 50 years, you create something more sophisticated and beautiful because your consciousness has expanded. You see greater meaning, more correlations and harmony in the Universe, and you take this harmony and apply it consciously in such a way that the expression of that harmony becomes a greater beauty. Whatever you have achieved reflects the degree of your creativity.

Each time a person "disappears," he accumulates all of his past experiences, digests them, shapes them, and then comes back to try again to manifest himself in life.

This Dweller in the body of each of us is ever invulnerable and indestructible. Therefore, you should not grieve for any creature.[4]

---

4. *The Bhagavad Gita* 2:30

The Great Teacher gave us some very beautiful instructions on reincarnation. He says that there are ten or eleven points to emphasize on the subject, beyond which it is best not to expand because our intellect stops at that point.

Every time humanity has been given a great law or truth, people slowly bring it down to the level of the common-place market and try to make a business out of it.

I remember visiting a lady who claimed to read past lives. Immediately upon seeing me, she exclaimed, "Oh, St. Paul! It is so good to see you!" Another psychic I once visited embraced me and said, "St. John! I have missed you for so long!" So I became St. John as well. Another time I was identified as being St. Joseph. It was amazing to see how they "knew" I was so-and-so but interesting that each saw me so differently. Because of this, I lost faith in all of them. There are thousands of psychics who sell their psychism, telling you for a few dollars what your past was.

Actually, in occult literature and brotherhoods, there is a law which states that **one who achieves the degree of consciousness necessary to know his past lives and the past lives of others never discusses them with anyone; he zips his mouth.** If someone discusses his past lives or your past lives with you, be assured that he has not attained that degree of consciousness. If a person is telling you about your past lives, it is a sign that he really does not know anything; he is in glamor.[5]

---

5. For more information on past lives, please refer to *Cosmos in Man* and *Other Worlds*.

Man falls into illusion and thinks that his dreams or hallucinations are his past lives.

Does it seem strange that we teach about reincarnation, but at the same time refuse and reject stories about reincarnation? This is because true esotericism is clear-seeing — taking facts as they are. Once a person loses this facility and his common sense, he can become the victim of his glamors and illusions.

Over a period of twenty years, I tried to read as much as I could find on the subject of reincarnation. In one of my notebooks I have recorded over two hundred "documented" occasions during the same time span in which Cleopatra supposedly reincarnated. Which one is the real Cleopatra? You read one book and think that it is factual. Then you read another book and see some contradictions, but also some factual information that makes you believe that it is right. After a while, you begin to see the whole picture, and you see the fallacy of their approach.

Even in certain esoteric organizations, various leading figures became trapped in astral games after doing some very nice work. They began to tell others, "You were Venus. You were this, you were that." From that moment on, the Hierarchy rejected what they were doing because they began to play in astral fields.

There are seven fields or planes: physical, astral, mental, Intuitional, Atmic, Monadic, and Divine. All that transpires is recorded in space; the Monadic Plane is the level in which these recordings are kept. This level consists of the "substance" upon which all of our life activities are recorded, referred to in occult literature as the "sea of fire," or *akasha*.[6] In some religious literature, it is referred to as the "Book of God." This substance in Nature records all our physical, emotional, mental, and spiritual activities just as if it were filming everything.

Psychics operate on the astral plane, which is full of fear, imagination, desire, jealousy, negative emotions, and so on. It is a polluted mirror in which there are millions and millions of forms. When the film of the Monadic Plane reflects upon this mirror, the psychic interprets it as reality. But that reality is merely a reflection, totally distorted and mixed with other forms present at that level. Whatever they say has a small grain of truth, but there is ninety-nine percent distortion mixed with it.

The Great Teacher says that to be able to read the Akashic Records accurately, the person first of all must totally purify his astral plane, which means he must have attained at least the second initiation. If your nature is really filled with love for all beings, if you are purified from your vanity, pride, fear, anger, and glamor, and if, in all of your activities, words, thoughts, and emotions you are totally harmless and purified, then you are a second degree initiate.

A glamor is something with which a person is objectively identified. If you are identified with something, and if that identification controls your life in any manner, then

---

6. See *Other Worlds*, Ch. 31, "Akasha."

you have a glamor; you are sleeping. If this is the case, anything that is reflected in your mirror will be distorted. At the second initiation, a person totally purifies his nature from any glamors, negative illusions, and emotions. But an important point to remember is that the astral plane can still reflect the negative emotions, distortions, and glamors of other people and the world. It is like having a clear pool into which many streams are flowing. When the pool is subjected to these different streams, you may purify it, but three minutes later, impurities are flowing into it. When *total* purification takes place at the Fourth Initiation, the astral body is totally eliminated; it is gone and the consciousness operates only from mental and higher planes.

In the mental plane there are reflections of the Akashic Records, and you can see them as they exist on higher levels. It is still a reflection, but it is much purer than the muddy, wavy sea of the astral body.

One way to avoid the trap of the astral plane, to avoid the deception that we are seeing a past life, is to reject any dream or any advice given from a psychic regarding past lives — until you are at such a degree of clarity that you can personally verify their observations. If you are not in a position to verify their information, reject it until a time comes when you are totally purified and can see the blueprint or clear photographs of your past lives.

The Great Teacher also says that those who want to read the Akashic Records must be vegetarian for at least ten years and pass through heavy disciplines so that they can work on the astral plane without being trapped.

People have the misconception that when they sense, feel, or experience emotions, they are working on the astral plane. This is not so. The astral plane is a plane, just like the physical plane. To be on the astral plane, you withdraw consciously from your physical plane consciousness and enter a dimension of consciousness which is called the astral plane. You are fully awake there.

Have you ever had the experience of dreaming and, while dreaming, know that you were dreaming? This is the first indication that you are becoming awake on the astral plane. The second indication is that you can change your dreams; this means you are awakening a little more. For example, in your dream an animal attacks you. You immediately remember that there is no fear, there is no need to be afraid because it is just a dream. Then you consciously change the animal into something good.

There are five degrees or stages of awakening on the astral plane. The astral world is the creation of your imagination, of your desire-life, your aspirations, and feelings. The moment you can change this, you are awakening into the second degree. The third degree of awakening is when you no longer dream; you know what the astral plane is and if you dream something, you see it, and then erase it in your dream — just like drawing on the blackboard and erasing it. You experience that dream-life is really a life of hallucination. You are able to control it. The fourth stage of awakening is when you enter the astral plane and experiment while you are there. For example, while on the astral plane, you sit down next to a friend and observe what it is he is doing. When you return, you record your observations and then call your friend the next day to verify if what you saw was real or unreal. Until you reach the degree that you can see things as they really are, you are not yet awake.

The fifth stage is graduation from the astral body; you never again enter the astral world. Your frequency of consciousness is such that the astral world, that sphere of vibration, never attracts you again. You surpass it, bypass it. Until this level is reached, we cannot reflect and transmit accurately what is recorded on Akashic levels.

There is a great law in effect on our planet from which we cannot escape. This law is that whether you like it or not, you are going to be born, and you are going to die; you have no control over either. I remember telling my Mother many times that I did not want to come here. She said, "Well, whether you like it or not, you are here." You can say, "I don't want to die," but you are going to die just the same. We do not have control over death and birth, so we are subject to the great, forceful imposition of this law.

A person is born and he dies because he himself does not exist as a separate unit in the Universe. For example, if you are going to be born, all the cells of your body are born with you. They cannot say, "I am not going to be born." In a similar way, humanity is a part of the body of the Planetary Being. When that Being takes incarnation as the planet, His "fingers" and "nose" are going to take incarnation with Him. Maybe you are a part of these.

In the ancient Teachings, we are told that humanity is the throat center of the planet. If that Great Life takes incarnation, He must have centers; so the centers that consist of many little lives are going to be born with Him. Whether we like it or not, we are in the process of incarnation and death, again and again.

Taking this idea a little further, the solar system is a Great Being, of which the planets are different parts. If the solar system is going to be born, the planet must be born, the lives on that planet must be born, the human beings must be born, and the cells making up the human body must be born, and so on. We are all tied together.

It is a natural law that the whole existence is in a process of birth and death. This is very beautifully explained in *The Secret Doctrine*, where Blavatsky describes it as a process of in-breathing and out-breathing. Some Great Existence exhales, and creation comes into being; when He inhales, all creation disappears. In the Ageless Wisdom, this law is called the Law of Pralaya and Manvantara.

Not only man but also planets, solar systems, galaxies, and the whole Cosmos are like great ocean waves. No one knows how many waves have come and gone in the ocean of Infinity. Nobody knows how many millions and billions of times whole galaxies have come into being and disappeared again and again.

Madame Blavatsky says that there are three principles which go together: the Law of Reincarnation, the Law of Cause and Effect, and the septenary constitution of the human being.

In regard to the septenary constitution of the human being, Great Ones have told us that we have an aura, a subtle body, and other bodies. But scientists since the sixteenth century have been laughing and joking at this idea, saying, "These people are hallucinating; there is nothing around man." Then science discovered the magnetic field; they could see the magnet, but around that magnet is an invisible field of energy. This developed to the point where we now have Kurlian photography, which depicts the electromagnetic sphere of the human body. Now they have found a sphere that extends perhaps as far as fifteen inches, but they also have found that in some advanced people, this "aura" extends as far as three miles. Science has just begun to discover that there is an aura; someday they will discover that the physical body is the shadow of that aura.

The physical body does not create the aura; the aura creates the physical body. We have proof of the first subtle body; now we are scientifically searching to find the emotional body of man. The field of psychology is beginning to accept its existence. Some psychiatrists have documented people who remember portions of their life, what their fathers and mothers were doing, while they were still in the womb. How could they remember? There must be something beyond the physical brain, and even beyond our emotions. So science is beginning to touch upon the idea of the existence of the astral and mental bodies. Some are even postulating about the existence of the intuitional body, where a person is intensely powerful, creative, and beautiful in very high moments; this leads them to question from where this glory is coming.

The idea that the physical body is the only existence is fading away. Science is trying to find the different levels at which man exists, gathers experience, and uses that experience as a vehicle for creative expression.

In regard to the Laws of Cause and Effect and Reincarnation, the rule applies that whatever you sow, you are going to reap. There are three "permanent atoms"[7] within the mind that register our physical, emotional, and mental activities. When a person dies and then returns, these three atoms will create a body that is equal to his past achievements. For example, if you were physically harmful to others in the past, that harmfulness is recorded in the permanent atoms, and when you return, your physical body will be defective because the film that you recorded in your permanent atoms is not clean, pure, and beautiful.

As another example, let us say that you achieved ninety degrees of mental development. This degree of development is recorded in the permanent atom. When you die and come back, that film will project your mental body, and your mental body will be equal to that which is recorded in your mental permanent atom.

This is in line with the Law of Cause and Effect. Whatever you do, you are going to have done to you. You pay ten dollars; ten dollars will be paid to you. You hurt someone; somebody is going to hurt you — or you pay it back in such a way that you eventually reach equilibrium and righteousness.

---

7. See *The Science of Becoming Oneself,* Ch. XII, "The Chalice and the Seeds."

These three laws cannot be separated because all are interrelated. Whatever you sow, you will reap — even on thought levels. In the Agni Yoga Teaching, the Great Sage says that we have learned to start being very careful about what we do physically; but in the New Era, we must be even more careful about what we think. A person is going to be conditioned in his life by whatever he thinks. Thought conditions not only your next incarnation, but it also conditions the friends and environment among which you will incarnate. Thought not only conditions your own existence, but it also conditions your existence in relationship to others. For example, why are you born into a family where there are constant problems with alcohol and beating each other? Why are there gangster families, families that are totally criminally oriented? A person would not like to be born into such a family, but if his thoughts were criminal, even if he did not physically commit a crime, he will be drawn into such an environment where his thoughts can find an avenue to germinate and manifest.

Through incarnation, we mature. As an example, let us take the life of a person. When he is a two-year-old baby, his teddy bear is everything to him. When he becomes seven, he is not as interested in that teddy bear. When he becomes twenty-one, his interests will be entirely different, as they are when he becomes sixty. If he is sixty years old and healthy, he has a particular outlook on life; if he is sixty, has cancer, and knows that he is going to die any day, his outlook is totally different.

In just one life you come and go, changing your attitudes and relationships according to what occurs in life. You continually mature. Eventually, after many incarnations, you reach a state of great maturity, relative perfection in which you have greater love, greater respect, and greater understanding of people.

Each person has his own life cycle. Let us say that you are born, and then you die. This cycle repeats itself until you master your physical, emotional, and mental vehicles. When this is accomplished, you enter a different cycle — the planetary life cycle. After completing this cycle, you enter a solar life cycle. For example, if you were in a cycle of being born every fifty years, when you enter the solar cycle you are born once every ten thousand years.

A Master very beautifully explains the process of birth and death in regard to human beings. He says that they are like buds, opening and then closing. This process seems very quick to highly-advanced Beings because Their life and death cycle is ten million years. During this cycle, you are born ten million times, but They are born only once.

The outer, largest wheel turns one hundred times in one cycle. By the time the largest wheel completes one cycle, the smaller wheel turns one million times, and the smallest turns ten million times. For the smaller wheels, the cycles are extremely rapid.

To recapitulate this chapter, man is subject to birth and death. Death is not the end of his life; he comes back and works out his problems again and again until all of his debts are paid. By paying his debts, he makes his creative powers more beautiful and he becomes better able to serve, eventually surpassing his physical, emotional, and mental natures to become a spiritual being. Our future births are determined by what we do in the present, so our present life is actually a preparation for the future. The future is the result of the way we live now. If we want a beautiful life in the future, we must live a beautiful life in the present and plant seeds for our future gardens.

I remember a story about a very old man who was busy planting some little trees when a child came up to him and asked, "Why are you planting these little trees? You are so old that you will die and never see them grow tall." The old man replied, "I am planting them so that you can enjoy them your whole life."

The old man was planting for others, not for himself. He was a wise old man.

Q&A

Question: *What if you refuse to pay someone back karmically? For example, if someone lends you ten dollars, and then later you have the money to repay him, but you refuse. What is the situation?*

ANSWER: Your debt will increase. You will pay "interest" on the money that you do not repay.

For example, you do ten dollars' worth of harm to someone; you caused him to pay ten dollars for which you were responsible. The next life, you will be put into such a condition that you are forced to repay him double. For example, you are driving and have an accident, and the person you owe helps you in some way. You become so grateful that you pay him double what his trouble was worth. That is a positive way to receive repayment. But there are also negative ways.

For example, you did ten dollars' worth of damage and did not repay me. In another life, I pay a visit to your home and accidentally break a very expensive object, and say, "I am so sorry, I didn't mean to break it; it was just an accident." You did not want this to happen, but it did, as payment.

Question: *What happens when you forgive someone his debt?*

ANSWER: Even if you forgive someone who owes you something, they will have to repay that karma in some way. We will pay our karma, whether we want to or not. We make payment and are compensated, whether we are conscious of it or not, according to the laws of karma. I can forgive you and you can forgive me, but the law is still in effect. If the law says that you must pay and I must receive, then so it is.

Question: *But then it is like Ping-Pong, back and forth. When does it ever stop?*

ANSWER: This is why we reincarnate, why life is in existence. Lord Buddha describes it as being trapped on the wheel of reincarnation until we are conscious of our debts and pay them all back.

The wars we fight are interesting examples. One nation is killing another nation; fifty years later, the weaker nation gains strength and tries to destroy the other.

Question: *Then what is the virtue in turning the other cheek?*

ANSWER: In turning the other cheek, you break the voltage of hatred.

Question: *Then I would benefit by forgiving?*

ANSWER: You would benefit, but you are still going to be subject to the laws of karma. One person can be the reason another person acts in a certain way; if he causes another person to act in a way that creates karma, that karma is also his karma. There is no "my karma and your karma"; there is karma for the individual, but there is also national karma. For example, you can be freed from personal karma, but then you become subject to the karma of your nation. If your nation does something wrong, you pay the national karma, whether you are purified from your individual karma or not. There is no escape. According to the Ageless Wisdom, we must pay until the very last debt is paid.

One can pay it physically, emotionally, or mentally. For example, if you hurt me ten dollars' worth, you may not necessarily have to pay me back the ten dollars physically. You may give me advice so that I make the ten dollars back; this is equal to payment. Or you could show me a life of righteousness, of beauty, or perhaps help me clean up some of my hang-ups. This is also payment.

Question: *What if you harm me and I refuse to harm you? Is this a good thing, or am I making it harder on you?*

ANSWER: Of course this is good. What happens in the example you just gave is that my karma is suspended; I must do good to erase my bad karma. It does not matter if you are making it harder on me. Let us say that I owe you ten dollars, but you refuse to accept it from me. Then I must build something for you, or give you something physically, emotionally, mentally, or spiritually so that I pay my own debt back — whether you like it or not. I do not pay you back in damages but in something good. This way I erase my debt.

The Great Sage, in speaking about karma and reincarnation, says that there are no accidents in the world. Everything that happens is due to cause and effect. At the same time, we cannot judge others because we do not yet understand the whole mechanism.

I remember a story a Master told about a massacre where the enemy gathered three hundred village children into a church and burned the building, killing all the children. The parents of the children decided that they were no longer going to believe in God or follow their religion because of this. If God existed He would not have allowed the children to be burned in His church.

They searched for reasons why this happened and came upon a wise man who told them that two thousand years before their children had put the people who had killed them in a deep hole and covered them with earth. These people returned as their enemy and repaid the debt. We do not yet have the individual power to prove or affirm these stories, but this Teaching seems very logical if we do, in fact, live in a Universe that is controlled and governed by laws which dictate that everything that happens must be according to the law.

Question: *Was the situation righteous in reference to the children?*

ANSWER: We do not know. It was not very pleasant, of course.

Question: *But was it righteous?*

ANSWER: No. Let us say that you hit me, and that I am a disciple or an Initiate who is fully capable of harming you in return. When you hit me I feel hatred, but I hold myself and start feeling good toward you. By doing this, I change my whole debt and karma in paying you with goodness. In doing good, I pay my karma.

Question: *Can we pay our karma consciously?*

ANSWER: There are millions of human beings who pay their karma consciously. For example, every time Socrates tried to discuss philosophy with his friends, his wife would become angry and say, "My goodness! Again, philosophy; again, philosophy; again, philosophy?" They lived together for forty years in these conditions. Socrates said,

"I owe something to this woman; that is why she is bugging me. But I am not going to be like her. I am going to change her as much as possible, or use her nagging in such a way that I develop and unfold myself. Her existence assists me in developing myself and in paying my former debts."

One day he was talking with one of his friends when his wife entered the room and told them they were making too much noise. So Socrates said, "Let's go outside." They were outside, talking beneath a window, when Socrates' wife emptied the wash water onto his head. Socrates said, "I knew that after thunder, rain always comes."

Look at how this wise man handled the situation. He knew that he would not have met his wife if he had not done something wrong to her in the past. The way she was was the result of what Socrates had done to her in the past. He handled the situation in such a way that he did not create more karma, and he used the situation as a means to spiritual development.

It is very interesting how disciples can handle similar situations and decrease their karma while increasing the good and, in the meantime, be learning to understand each other.

Christ emphasized that we should not judge one another, that we should forgive one another. We are not good judges because we do not know the whole picture of why certain things happen. Perhaps the whole cause is in one person and not the other; maybe one person is bugging the other because the other caused something in the past that makes that person bug him. If they can work out their differences consciously, by discussing the situation with one another and bringing the problem out into the open, then it becomes possible to find a solution.

• CHAPTER 24 •

The Immortal Spirit

Some people think that the subject of reincarnation is strictly Hindu or Buddhist. We are not talking about any doctrine, dogma, or religious belief; we are discussing a law in the Universe which can be expressed through any religion, philosophy, or psychology.

According to this law, man is sent to this or any other planet with a great responsibility and duty. We are little cells in the body of the Universe, little members of the Universe. And that Universal Intelligence, that great, great Being, sent us to refine the planet.

For example, a Spark comes, takes a body from the earth, eats food, and makes that food a refined element. We take crude oil of sorts and make it into gas or perfume and so on.

Our duty is to refine this planet, to refine the elements, such as iron, potassium, and so on, and everything that we eat. We eat and change our food into different elements. In the same way, we must refine our emotions. We must absorb emotions and refine them, making them more beautiful, making them lofty feelings of ecstasy and blessing.

We are also refining the mental realms. We either pollute space with our minds or refine it by taking mental substance and creating masterpieces with it. For example, a great creative artist takes his paints and makes something very beautiful or carves something which inspires others. What is happening in this process is that he is taking a crude substance of the earth, certain emotions and thoughts, and transforming, transfiguring, and sublimating these substances to assist in universal evolution, in universal progress toward sublimation, refinement, and perfection.

Christ advises us to seek first the Kingdom of God and that all else will be added unto us. He does not say that we should take everything. If it is given, we already have it. As part of the Universe, we have everything. This is one of the greatest tests of the human being. As a person becomes more aware of this law, all of his physical, emotional, and mental needs are met.

Life after life, a person returns to create a masterpiece body, one that will eventually reach such a degree of refinement that it will be transfigured; his light will shine to such a degree that people will be able to see that he is transfigured. Transfiguration is when an individual has reached seventy-five degrees of physical, emotional, and mental refinement. After transfiguration, he strives toward resurrection. Life after life, he comes back and transforms his body, making it more beautiful.

By refining the body, you accomplish two things. First, you create happiness and health. Second, you fulfill your responsibility to God. You came here to refine; you are changing the substance.

Imagine a planet upon which there was no life. There are only elements upon such a planet. A living soul comes and uses the elements to create a body. A stone cannot talk, but you can. What happened? The iron, calcium, carbon, and other elements entered your body; you took them in, sublimated them, and made them into activity, feelings, thoughts, imagination, and visualization.

A time comes when you must file a progress report with God, saying, "My Lord, I made my body so beautiful; I will live at least two hundred years. My body is not dying so young; look how beautiful it is!" This is what the Masters have accomplished. They worked so hard that Their bodies no longer die.

Refinement means to synchronize physical, emotional, and mental elements. Cosmic refinement is when the Spark, the seed within you, wants to expand and be like the Father in Heaven. It wants to go to the Father, but Its vehicle is not running properly. We must make our "car" perfect so that we can reach our destination.

To be perfect means to transform and no longer die. The levels at which you are born and die are equal to your failures and successes. If you are born refined only ten percent, and you give your body back to Nature having refined it eighty percent, you have succeeded. The next time you are born, you will start out life with ninety percent refinement.

However, humanity builds with one hand and destroys with the other. A person sits down before a beautiful dinner, says a blessing, and eats. Then he gets on the phone and tells his neighbor that he hates him. The next day he is ill, and his wife does not understand why because she prepared such a beautiful meal. He builds physically but then destroys mentally.

Life is like working in a workshop. The first lifetime is like your first day in the shop. You are taught what the tools are. The teacher says, "This is a hammer; this is a chisel." You try to work with the tools and you hit your finger. Then you get lazy and go to sleep for a while, which is like dying. The next day — the next lifetime — the teacher asks, "What did you do?" You say, "Oh, I learned how to hold the hammer." "Well, what about the chisel?" "When I try to use it," you say, "I cut myself." "Well," the teacher says, "then you must learn how to hold the chisel. Work on it for another seventy years."

You continue to improve in your skills until one day you are the boss in a big factory. You take responsibility; you check all the equipment to make sure the velocity, frequency, and measure are all up-to-date. You are becoming a Master. This is maybe ten million incarnations later.

As you do for the earth, you do for yourself. As you perfect life, you perfect yourself. Whatever you do for other people, it is done for you. People often think differently, but when you do only for yourself and not others, you have no equilibrium or balance. And that is how people live — big house, three cars, certain traditions, and so on. Even when they have it, they do not enjoy it. We must make other people prosperous, happy, and healthy if we want to be healthy ourselves.

Thus, we came here to refine. Eventually we dedicate a refined body and elements to Nature. For example, say that I own a Rolls Royce which I keep in the best condition. When I depart, I leave it to one of my friends. If he knows how to drive and maintain that car, he will be able to use it just as I did. It is the same with our astral and mental bodies. We will dedicate astral and mental bodies that are really rare.

This is hinted at in the Biblical story of Elijah. When Elijah departed, a carriage arrived into which he jumped and flew into the sky. His disciples were waiting and he took his mantle and threw it to them. When they dressed in his mantle, they obtained the same spiritual powers that Elijah had. People think this story is an hallucination, but it is not. This "mantle" was one of his bodies, perhaps his intuitional or mental body. That is why the Great Teacher says that the intuitional body of Buddha must be used by Christ, or by any Master, because it is such a complicated and intricate mechanism that every kind of feature has been constructed into it throughout the ages: clairvoyance, clairaudience, sensitivity, impression, and so on. Blessed are those who can own and operate such bodies.

We must proceed toward perfection, toward improvement and completion, life after life, because we cannot yet resurrect ourselves. We are instructed to "be perfect as our Father in heaven is perfect." But show me one person who is perfect. This means that we cannot accomplish this goal in one life. We can, however, improve in each life, getting closer and closer, so that one day we will be successful.

So our first duty is to make our bodies beautiful, to be harmless to our bodies. It is not only a matter of eating the right foods and drinking the right water, but it is also a matter of right feeling. For example, if you hurt someone even in a subtle way, you also hurt your own emotional and mental bodies. When you hurt yourself and others, you are not working for perfection; you are working for degeneration. You must improve physically but also control and sublimate your emotions so that they do not create friction in the body. If your emotions and physical body are good but your mind is crooked, it will not work. You will always have mental friction and be unhealthy.

This is why we die. We have not yet learned the secrets of immortality. We are in a labyrinth; we go in a certain direction thinking that it is correct and then find out that the road is closed. Then we make turns to the right and left and find ourselves in the same place we started. Soon we do not know where we started from or where we have already been. We feel anxiety; we feel lost. Only through Intuition, true "smelling," can we find our way out. We have not yet learned the labyrinth of life. When we do, life will no longer be stealing and killing; it will be a continual process of giving, harmony, and joy.

Reincarnation has one aim — to perfect. Incarnation is not satanic or being lost in the labyrinth; it is a law. Everybody incarnates. Look at the trees. They "die" in winter and are "re-born" in the spring. Planets and solar systems disappear and then come into being again.

We all want to learn how to prepare to die. When a person feels the approach of his death, it is important that he settle his personal property matters. People often leave everything in a mess behind them. Actually, after the age of seventy, if a person is healthy it is better for him to have less property; he should distribute his accumulations to his friends and family members, with his blessings. It is better to give them away before dying because after death it will be taken anyway, and the person will not benefit from the process of giving. If the person gives, the blessings and joy that he receives are like fuel which propels him to Higher Worlds.

It is more profitable to give things than to have them taken from you. Helena and Nicholas Roerich were examples of this. When they felt it was time for them to go, they went to their house, which was like a museum filled with precious pieces of art, ivory carvings, jewelry, chalices, statues, carpets, and so on, and distributed the majority of their most loved possessions, saying, "Thank you all very much. You helped us so much, and you are so beautiful." Alice Bailey did the same thing; she even distributed the pencils she used to write with, her ring, and other jewelry. This is a great blessing.

It is important to settle all debts. Pay back those to whom you feel endebted. At least call them and say, "I cannot repay what I borrowed, but please take this instead or whatever else you want. I am so sorry, but next life I will repay you totally."

When Mohammed was dying, he remembered borrowing a chicken from one of his neighbors. He called one of his followers and asked him to take a chicken from his yard and repay the neighbor so that he did not die with an unpaid debt.

Debts are not only material; they are also moral, spiritual, and mental. How can we repay them? Say that you did something wrong to someone, and you feel that you hurt him, that you damaged him. You need to settle this debt before you die because you do not want the same animosity, tension, and irritation to continue in the next world. Forgiving and asking for forgiveness are the same thing. Visit or call him and say, "I am so sorry; I should not have done those things. I really feel miserable. What can I do? Will you forgive me?" You must really mean it with all sincerity; this must not be a technique of escape.

One must also express gratitude to those who have helped him in any way because when gratitude increases in his soul before he dies it becomes a tremendous source of energy in the next world. Gratitude must be expressed with the mind, with the heart, with singing and speaking.

If someone awakened you to something beautiful, you must express your gratitude to him. Maybe someone saved you from an emotional dungeon; someone opened the spiritual path; someone taught you to be more beautiful. Do not die without feeling gratitude to these people — and total gratitude to everyone.

As you grow older, begin making a list of those to whom you are grateful, and send them your blessings and love. If you are wealthy, you can send money to them also, with your thanks — for example, "I am so grateful for the time I had an accident on the freeway and you helped me and visited me in the hospital, encouraging and loving me. I never forgot that day. Here is a check for five thousand dollars."

But humanity is not living like this. Humanity is living in a jungle psychology — I eat you; you eat me. If your mouth is bigger, you are more successful. Humanity lives this way because they do not know about the Other Worlds. When they go there, they will be terrified at what they find.

We must prepare ourselves to confront the unknown. Fortunately or unfortunately, we do not remember that we were once there, but we still need to prepare. We can do this by deciding before we die that no matter what obstacles, difficulties, and problems arise on the path of our soul, we will work for beauty, goodness, and truth and hold to the path of perfection. The Great Sage says that those who die with such thoughts are totally different from those who die in a miserable state of consciousness; they are energetic and progressive.

People who do not believe in immortality are like blind corpses when they reach the subtle planes. They stay there for two or three thousand years and then come back. Many religions do not believe in immortality. To these religions, nothing exists beyond because to them the soul is the same as the emotions, mind, and physical body. When these three die, you are like a balloon which bursts.

After death, when scientists who do not believe in immortaility reach the subtle planes they are totally blinded and paralyzed. They wait for many centuries and return with defective bodies and brains because in passing from darkness into light, and from light into darkness, their mechanisms received tremendous shocks. Sometimes you see signs of this in children who are very smart, but at the same time very stupid — both extremes. This is because they were smart but not in line with Truth, so they were shocked. The effect of this continues for two or three lives.

We must not carry any feelings of guilt or sin with us when we pass to the other side. We must go guiltless, sinless. It is important to say, "Lord, I know I did wrong, but now I want Your grace, Your forgiveness, Your light. Please lead me." This is important because the light of the Almighty Presence can heal and purify. We must surrender with the thought that we are going to continue with beauty, goodness, and truth wherever we are, at whatever level we are, and never lose our striving toward perfection. Going forward with these thoughts elevates the soul into higher planes.

In Chinese and Tibetan traditions, it is believed that the last thoughts of a dying person are his most important ones because they determine his future destination. When you are dying, think of the Hierarchy of Light; think of your Master, whether He is Mohammed, Moses, Christ, Krishna — Whomever you like — so that a mental link is established. Thought is electrical. It immediately finds the one about whom you are thinking, and a ray of energy will come to you and direct, protect, and lead you. Put your hope in the Master. Invoke your Solar Angel to guide you.

Try to establish and maintain continuity of consciousness. I have administered Holy Communion to people who were dying in hospitals and stayed with them in their last moments. Some people identify with their bodies, and when the body is failing they think that it is over and that it is really finished for them. They die, hypnotizing themselves, blocking their soul. Some people panic and think that they are going to go to hell forever and burn; they do not want to die, and they struggle. Sometimes it takes several days for them to pass away, and at the last moment they hate it because they are afraid.

By observing such cases, one can learn a lot. Those who believe in immortality say, "Lord, please take care of me. I am with You." When my Teacher was dying, he saw me enter the room and said, "Do not cry now; come on. I want a smile." So I sat beside him. He put his hand on my shoulder and then suddenly his eyes opened wide. He reached out to take a hand I could not see, and he said, "Thank You, O Lord, I am holding Your hand." He never lost continuity of consciousness.

When the day comes, no matter what you are, where you are — even if you have a bad accident and your body is crushed — do not think that you are dying. There is no death for you. By putting this thought in your mind, you will be able to see what is happening to your body, but you will not be in the body. You will already be five or six miles away; you will see the body because your soul will jump away from the body.

When you identify with dying, you cannot escape the body. Keep in mind that you are the Immortal Spirit, that God is within you, that you were not created to die, that you are a Spark, a part of God. The "picture" of you may be broken — but not you.

When I was living in the Middle East, I used to read about the art of dying. I practiced continuity of consciousness exercises, trying not to lose consciousness during sleep. One night a great, tall man came to me in my dream and said, "Well, we are going to test you to see if you can pass." I said, "Okay, I will do it." He took me to a busy street; it was as if I were awake and not asleep.

A car passed by, going ninety miles per hour. "Did you see that car?" he asked. "Yes," I replied. "Another one is coming, and you must throw yourself in front of its wheels." When the next car came by, I threw myself in front of it; it was quite a mess. "Do you see your body?" he asked. "You are not dead. You must do this three more times." I repeated this exercise at least thirty times more. I loved it so much. I was taught in my dreams.

This is not to say that one should commit suicide. Eventually we are going to develop the consciousness that death is not for us.

• CHAPTER 25 •

Birth, Death, and Reincarnation

Q & A

Question: *Are you saying that we do not necessarily have to build our own astral, mental, and intuitional bodies, that we can use ones built by others when we are ready?*

ANSWER: No. Unless you learn how to operate your own body totally, you cannot operate another body. You must first have experience, clarity of mind, dedication, and pure motive. Then you are prepared. If you give a Rolls Royce or another piece of complicated machinery to a little child and tell him to operate it, what would happen? He will be hurt, or he will damage the equipment.

Question: *Is it important to have Holy Communion before dying?*

ANSWER: Holy Communion is an event that creates a certain attitude, a state of thought and consciousness. It is not the mechanics of Holy Communion that help but the symbolic meaning and reception of that mystery that helps.

I once visited a young teenager who had been crushed in a terrible accident. She was terrified because she thought she was a sinner and that she was going to burn in hell. "Well," I told her, "don't worry. I will talk to God and everything will be okay." Then I prayed, "Lord, this young girl has done nothing. If she has done wrong, put it on my bill." I told her that Holy Communion is connection with Christ, so that she would be under His protection and not to worry. Then she took Holy Communion, slept a few hours, and then passed away in peace.

Question: *Who are the Immortals?*

ANSWER: They are people, just like us.

Question: *They no longer incarnate?*

ANSWER: No, They are finished. For example, if you already know about everything that is being lectured on in school, you no longer attend the lectures. Why waste your time? There are other things to do.

Question: *Why did your instructors in the dream about dying in front of the car have you repeat the exercise so many times?*

ANSWER: To impress my mind that I am immortal. Because of this I have become so fearless in dangerous moments that it surprises people. Once during the war the enemy opened fire upon us with machine guns and I jumped out in front of them and yelled, "Stop it!" and they stopped. My friends in the trenches said, "You are stupid and crazy! What are you doing?" "Well," I said, "it stopped them!" Another time there were twenty of us walking when the enemy opened fire. Ten people on one side of me fell, nine on the other. I stood there checking myself to see if I was wounded, but I was left untouched.

A fearless attitude protects you. Most of the time we bring calamities upon ourselves by having fear and worrying that things will happen to us. I can recall many instances of error and failure because of this. I think something is going to happen, and it happens because fear attracts it.

Question: *How does fearlessness prevent it?*

ANSWER: Fearlessness prevents it because you do not need the lesson. Immortality is nothing more than total fearlessness. Fear is death; the more fear you have, the more you are dead. The more you are fearless, the more life you have. If you observe those times in your life when you were fearful, in any way, to any degree, you will see that you were weaker, losing the point and failing in those moments. A leader once said that we have nothing to fear but fear itself. We can add to this statement that we must not even be afraid of fear. If you are in fear, you attract fear to you. If you are not identified with your bodies and more identified with your spiritual part, you will have less fear.

For example, if I am identified with the carpet, I become the carpet. Anything that happens to the carpet happens to me. This is how we kill ourselves by identifying with our possessions. We become afraid when we think that we will lose our body. If a person knows that he is not his body, he does not have fear.

There is always a battle. If you are fearless and find yourself in a dangerous circumstance, you can fight off the fear to which the vehicles may be automatically reacting. If you are not identified, you can fight this pollution; you can reject it, refuse it, balance it, and eventually conquer it. But there is always the battle.

You can go to a room and feel differently because someone quarreled, or a crime was committed there and it affects you. You find a new boyfriend or girlfriend, and after visiting with him or her, you come back feeling irritated — because you take the other person's aura into your own.

Our intention is to refine our body, emotions, mind, and our relationships with other people. We must ask what it is we can do that will make ourselves and others more refined. This is the greatest test given to us by the Creator.

Perhaps it may be difficult or painful, but this does not matter; create refinement. This is what karma does for us. We become sick and suffer; we do not realize that our sickness is an accumulation of all of our hatred. Five hundred lives lived in hatred create a tumor for which no doctor can find a cause. But when awakening starts in the Subtle Worlds, in the astral plane, we can see what is happening.

For example, fear creates problems with the pancreas. One big fear two thousand years ago, another big fear a thousand years later, another fear after that, and before you know it, the pancreas no longer works. Our health depends upon our morality. The Great Ones tell us that biology and morality are the same; whatever is going through your mind affects your aura, and your aura immediately affects your body. Whatever you think conditions your next incarnation.

To be very truthful, your body, emotions, and mind are the result of the accumulation of your actions, speech, and thought. If we analyze only the mental body of a person, we will see that all he has ever spoken is stored in his mental body. All of his past feelings and emotions are built into his emotional body. All that he has done physically is incorporated in his physical body. This is why it is a logical conclusion that man creates and destroys himself with his own hands.

Morality and biology go hand-in-hand. Because a person defeats and misleads people, because he is a sneaky liar who takes advantage of others and misuses them, he creates a totally corrupted brain. His thinking eventually disturbs and distorts the mechanism of his brain, and the brain no longer knows what to do. The brain is created to function naturally, beautifully, to answer questions. When a person corrupts it, it creates turmoil and the brain cannot function properly.

I saw an experiment performed in a monastery. Three boys were connected to a very sensitive electrical instrument which recorded their electrical responses on a monitor. They were placed in a room where a gold watch had been left and instructed that for the next three hours they could do anything in the room that they wanted. We observed them from another room only by the responses recorded on the monitor. Suddenly, the recordings of one of the boys became erratic and extreme, and then it eventually stabilized. When we entered the room the watch was missing, and the boy whose recordings had been so extreme confessed to taking it. His actions, thoughts, and feelings while stealing the watch affected him electrically, and those responses where recorded on the instrument.

Whatever you sow, you are going to reap. In a dream I saw a war in which five thousand people were mercilessly massacred; in this dream, they were reborn as babies in the nation that had massacred them. They proceeded to create revolution in that country, which resulted in the death of millions of people. The same thing is happening in the world today, but we cannot see it.

In Taoist, Buddhist, Hindu, Christian, Jewish, and Moslem religions we are taught that whatever we sow, we reap; whatever we plant, we are going to reap. It is better for us to plant good crops than weeds, if we want good produce. From another viewpoint, to be born into the world means to plant yourself as a seed. Whatever you plant here, you are going to reap. If you are an onion here, you are not going to be garlic there; you are also going to be an onion there.

In order for people to understand this, they need ten thousand lives of suffering. We cannot really understand this just by talking about it or reading about it. It is not for us to become religious fanatics who preach these subjects; people are not ready, for the most part. But we can begin to help people understand that they are Spirit and not matter. But care must be exercised because if people do not understand or agree, they may react in harmful ways.

I was once visiting a man who was dying, and in trying to help him, I began to discuss immortality. He pushed the buzzer to call the nurse and had me thrown out of the hospital. If people understand, discuss the subjects with them; if they do not, let life teach them. But help them any way that you can. Maybe they do not need a lecture; maybe they just need a massage or your friendship. Maybe they just need to know that you love them.

It is important to write down your various observations and experiences in a piritual diary; in fifty years, you will have valuable, documented evidence of what is happening. In this way, you teach yourself.

Question: *What if someone is dying over a long period of time? How does that usually affect transition?*

ANSWER: The person is "paying his bills," that is all. If he understands that he is paying his bills, he will see that what is happening is good, and when he leaves his body, his bills will be paid.

Sometimes we think that people who go through slow and painful deaths are wiser because they seem to see and understand everything. This is because their subconscious opens up and shows them why these things have happened to them. Nature is so professional.

The law of incarnation is sometimes viewed as a kind of curse where you are forced to be born, suffer, and die. This is not so. Every time you leave your body there is tremendous joy and festivity. This memory is blocked when you come into physical incarnation, but when you pass over, both sides are open to you. You see that the seventy years of life you had are nothing compared to the ecstasy you now have. Reincarnation must not be related to suffering and dying alone.

It is good to discuss dying, just to know that such things exist and that we can pass away in a better way than we are at present. We tend to emphasize the pain and suffering of death, but sometimes it is the most beautiful experience to die. There are ecstatic feelings, great beauty and blessing. When you love and unite with a person, you experience lots of different feelings. But the blessing and ecstasy of the moment of death are beyond any other ecstasy because you are totally free, uncaged. Yet people make it so miserable; a visit to a funeral home will convince you of this.

There are examples of the ecstasy of death in the Teachings of Christ. One example is the life of the first

Christian martyr, St. Stephanos. He was teaching about Christ, and people attacked him by throwing huge rocks at him to kill him. Witnesses noted that when a stone would hit him, crushing his bones, he would glorify God, saying, "Thank You, Lord; even my suffering is beautiful." There are other historical examples, such as the martyrs who died in the arenas in Rome. The Romans would place several hundred Christians in the arena and release wild animals to devour them, while millions of people watched. But all the while, the martyrs would sing praises to God and glorify Him because intuitively, or in their state of consciousness, they knew that they were not the bodies that were being eaten. If one reaches this stage of psychic development, the minute any danger comes to the physical body he leaves the body and watches; he does not feel anything.

There are also examples of martyrdom in Hinduism, Zoroastrianism, in other religious and even scientific fields. It would be an interesting project to go to the library and compose a compilation of how many scientists, philosophers, great artists, and so on were put to death by inquisitors and their kind.

Verily, there was never a time when I was not, nor you, nor these rulers of men; nor shall come a time when we shall all cease to be.[1]

---

1. *Bhagavad Gita* 2:12

There are some steps we can follow which will help ease a dying person's journey toward Higher Worlds and also ease their reincarnation.

It does not matter whether a person is conscious or unconscious when he is dying — because in reality he is always conscious.[2] Sometimes he is out of his body and cannot control the mechanism of his brain to contact you. Sometimes certain nerve centers are paralyzed so he cannot talk or move. But his soul listens; he senses what is going on around him. Sometimes his senses are more sensitive than you can imagine; sometimes dying people can hear things that are being said two or three rooms beyond. So if you speak to a dying person, do not think that he is not listening and use care in what you say.

1. **Inspire the dying person with fearlessness.** Talk with him about how God is love and tell him not to be afraid. Explain that all he did wrong is nothing compared to all of the good he has done throughout the ages, that the balance of good will increase and that the love of God will embrace him. Cast out all fear.

The Teaching tells us that those who enter the Subtle Worlds with fear are paralyzed for as long as forty years. Like a bug which pretends it is dead when you hit it, a person who is hit with fear is stunned when he enters the Subtle Worlds.

I once asked a surgeon, who was also a psychiatrist, why one of his patients was having difficulty awakening after surgery. Every possible means was used to bring the

---

2. For more information see *Other Worlds* and *Cosmos in Man*.

patient to consciousness, but he was just gone. The doctor told me that the man had gone under the anesthetic in a state of fear. Those who are not afraid of the anesthesia awaken much better; those who are fearful have a more difficult awakening.

The same is true in the Subtle Worlds. Fear paralyzes a person's senses, his striving, and prevents him from seeing his vision for the future. A dying person often has a tendency or inclination to identify with the state of his body, emotions, mind, and failures. This leads him into a state of fear. Because of this, it is important to help the person overcome fear by strongly impressing him with fearlessness.

2. **Never mention any failure or wrong-doing the dying person may have committed in the past; this will cause him to identify with his failures.** Any human being who is identified with his failures is not successful; he is a failure and cannot go forward. For example, if he opens a new business, it will fail because the image of failure controls his mind.

Talk with him about how beautiful he is, how many friends he has, how many people love him. Make him feel that he did good things.

3. **If he has transgressed in any way against you, tell him that you forgive him and ask him to forgive you.** Make him lighter so that he does not attach to any thing he may have done incorrectly. This is because we carry each failure image with us.

The Great Sage advises us to leave as much of this trash behind as possible; you can supply a dying person with better luggage than failure images.

4. **After the person dies, it is good to give a dinner party in his honor, inviting his friends and family.** Everyone must speak very beautifully about him and not mention his negative qualities. The discussion should center around his good qualities and the good deeds he performed.

Often a person does not know he is dead for a period of one week to forty days after he has passed away. He thinks that he is still with you, and he is sometimes surprised that you do not answer his questions. Sometimes you answer his questions mentally, and he thinks that it is verbal communication. But if you speak evil of him or mention his short-comings, you make him identify with his failures, which makes him earthbound, and he will have the same emotional and mental disturbances that he had while he was in the body.

There is a tradition in many Moslem, Sufi, and Christian monasteries that for forty days after a person dies, a place is set for him at the table. I once asked a monk why this was observed, and he said that the person does not know he is dead yet, so he comes to eat. He does not actually eat, but he thinks that he is eating.

A person who has died is still in the same etheric and emotional bodies, which appear like the physical body. However he imagines he is dressed, he is immediately dressed. He listens to everything. He sits down to eat and supposes that he is eating. He sees that he is eating, but the food is still there. But if a chair is not left for him, he receives a great shock and wonders why he has been omitted. This causes him to grieve.

When a family member dies, it is a contemporary custom to take everything he owned and either give it away or throw it away. The person is so surprised to see this happening because he is still "alive." How would you feel if your father and mother took all your possessions and threw them in the rubbish? It is important to make the person feel that everything is the same until he awakens naturally. Give him the impression that everything is all right until he slowly feels that he is departed, that there are no hard feelings, pain or suffering, and that it is okay because there is no separation.

There are also invisible helpers which assist in his awakening. Sometimes his own Solar Angel awakens him; sometimes it is a friend who is still living.

If a person has continuity of consciousness, these problems are solved. Astral consciousness is different from physical consciousness; physical consciousness is related to physical life. There is also mental consciousness. If these three are awakened, there is continuity of consciousness on three levels. If only one level of consciousness is opened, no matter where you are you think you are on earth because only the earthly "radio" is in operation.

5. **Every Saturday or Sunday night, light a candle and some nice incense and say, "We remember**

you; you were so beautiful." Say a few nice things to the person, and then say a prayer for him. This is a tradition which is very helpful to those who have passed away.

6. **If someone passes away, it is helpful to pay any of his remaining debts.** For example, if your father passes away without paying his debts, it is marvelous to pay them for him because you release him from any anxiety he may feel in the astral or mental plane as to why he did not pay them. Paying them is a great release for him; you really advance his evolution and help him prepare for a better incarnation.

If the person who is dying has done something harmful to you, it is important to find him before he dies and tell him that you forgive him, that he should not worry. This also cleans your account with him. As you clean your account, you prepare yourself for a more successful experience at the time of death and a better incarnation when you return.

If the person used malice and slander against you, tell him that you have no hard feelings and always bless him, especially at the time of his death.

There was a warrior king who had an enemy, and as they fought, the enemy was wounded and fell to the ground. The warrior king carried him to a lake where he washed his enemy's wounds and waited with him until he died. The enemy asked, "Why don't you just kill me?" to which the king replied, "I did not want to harm you; I wanted to kill your animosity. In truth, I love you. The next time you come, be a commander in my army. You are free to die in peace because I will prepare a place for you in my army." The story says that after the man died, he was born again as the warrior king's son. Because the king had mortally wounded him and created tremendous pain and suffering for him, the king owed his enemy everything he owned — even his entire kingdom.

When people die, they need energy. We not only need energy to maintain our physical bodies, but also our emotional and mental bodies. Energy is needed to feel, to sense, to express emotion, to move in space. There are three things that create energy: beauty, goodness, and joy. Events in our life that are beautiful and joyful are charged with the good that is buried in our subconscious.

For example, I do something very good for you, something beautiful and joyful for you, but I forget about it. I hardly notice that I have done this, but it is still buried in my subconscious mind and inactive in my being. When I am dying, you mention the incident, and by doing so, you release this buried source of energy that has been stored, and you equip me with more energy to use in the Subtle Worlds.

If someone is passing away, even if you had trouble with him, do not allow the trouble to continue into the next world. Just mentioning any act of beauty, goodness, or joy that he may have done will create a subconscious release of energy which will assist him in his journey.

Question: *Does the Solar Angel stay with us while we are discarnate?*

ANSWER: First of all, the Solar Angel does not impose; secondly, not every person is in contact with his Angel. Eighty to ninety percent of humanity are unaware of Its influence, impressions, and suggestions. But They do Their utmost to awaken us through various sensations.

For example, you do something that is not good for you, and you feel very bad; that is the Solar Angel impressing you, reminding you. You make a decision and want to change; your Angel helps you change your direction, thinking, feeling, and actions. When you are well-developed in your physical, emotional, and mental consciousness, you will be in direct contact with your Angel.

There is another important stage in this relationship. When you develop your physical, emotional, and mental consciousness, your Angel will leave you for fifty or sixty years and no longer communicate with you so that you exercise being independent and do your own job. It is important not to depend on the Solar Angel. If you have not established lines of communication with your Angel, your faith and expectation create a kind of magnetism between you and your Angel so that you can communicate better.

When we say that the Solar Angel stays with us, it is a misleading statement because the Solar Angel is never limited to us alone. It watches us with one eye, but at the same time It is engaged in universal, Cosmic duties. It is not our prisoner. Many times our own attitudes create limitations to our contact.

The Ageless Wisdom teaches us that long ago there were human beings who entered Nirvanic consciousness.

In Lemurian times, which was two hundred to three hundred million years ago, these Great Beings were called upon to come and help humanity because humanity was not doing very well. They made three visits, finally entered into our aura, and upon Their doing so man became creative. These are the Solar Angels. Other beings do not have Solar Angels.[3]

There are more Solar Angels in existence than there are mortals on earth. There are individual Solar Angels, group Solar Angels, family Solar Angels, and so on. It is not a well-known fact, but every family has a Solar Angel. If the family is involved in wrong-doing or wrong human relations, the Solar Angel will leave and the family disintegrates. Every group has a Solar Angel, as does every nation.

Question: *What if family members are scattered three thousand miles apart?*

ANSWER: Distance does not matter. There is a magnetic link which draws them instantaneously. Some mothers feel this immediately.

For example, a mother of a young man who was fighting in Vietnam was sitting in church. She suddenly screamed and cried that her son had just died. "I saw him," she said. "He came and said, Good-bye." She wrote to the State Department, and they confirmed his death.

I read about an experiment where they took a mother rabbit and hooked her to a piece of equipment that registered

---

3. This topic is dealt with in detail in *Other Worlds*, Ch. 59, "The Guardian Angel."

her heartbeat and other electrical responses. They took one of her babies onto a submarine and after traveling ten thousand miles away began running a medical experiment upon it, eventually killing it. At the exact moment of its death, the mother rabbit registered violent responses, very unusual vibrations, ten thousand miles away.

Time and space are not obstacles to communication; communication is instantaneous. Time and space are related to the brain. But when we are working in different dimensions, time and space evaporate.

Question: *Can you relate to other people who are in the astral plane?*

ANSWER: Yes. They are exactly like us, but they do not have a physical body; they have an astral body. They can go anywhere in the world they want in one instant.

If someone who was planning a trip to Rome dies ten days before the time of his intended vacation, while he is on the astral plane he may suddenly recall that he was supposed to go to Rome. So he will "buy" a ticket and sit in the airplane and travel to Rome. Or when night comes he will prepare for bed and go to sleep. He does not need a bed or sleep, but he does not know this. Some people even construct houses and go to work in astral levels after they die.

If they are close to a place where war is being waged, where bombs are flying and machine guns are being fired, they may start hiding themselves, fearful that a bullet will hit them. They may notice the bullets passing through them and think, "This is crazy; what is happening?"

All of these experiences suddenly awaken them to the awareness that they are no longer in their physical bodies. It sometimes takes a person hundreds of years to realize that he is living in a different dimension, subject to different laws. At that level, every time you think that you are in a physical condition, you are in a physical condition. But the moment you change your mind and say, "Now I am Spirit," you are released.

Question: *When you awaken on the astral plane, is this your opportunity to go to the mental plane, or do you decide on other things to do?*[4]

ANSWER: A long time is spent in the astral plane. There are several levels to which one who passes away may go. Those who are very low-level go to the bottom level of the astral plane, which is sometimes called "Hades" or "hell." It is a very bad place. There are animals, such as vipers and scorpions, even dogs which have died, and low-level people. It is the hell about which we hear so much. Sometimes the inhabitants spend several thousand years on this level.

The second option is to travel to higher astral levels and then to the mental plane. Those who are mentally advanced and really advanced in their consciousness enter the Intuitional Plane, and do not have to come back. As long as you are in the astral and mental planes you return.

---

4. For more information on the inhabitants of the Subtle Worlds see *Other Worlds*.

There is another condition after leaving the mental plane called Devachan, a place of rest where people may linger for three to five thousand years, because it is paradise. There is amusement and great beauty there. But really advanced souls do not visit Devachan because it is leisure; it is considered a violation of the time God has given. Instead, advanced souls go immediately to the mental plane, then enter the Intuitional Plane, and then return to serve.

> **Question:** *When a person dies and goes to the astral plane, does he ever go to sleep on that level, or the more subtle levels?*

ANSWER: Yes. You are in the same world, but you are stuck there because that is your frequency. You cannot enter the mental plane because the mental plane is very advanced. It is called the "Fiery World."

Suppose you have an impurity in your mind when you approach the mental plane. The closer you get to the mental sphere, the impurity ignites and burns you to such a degree that you escape and return to the astral plane. You can only enter the mental plane if you have no inflammable substances — impurities — in your mind.

> **Question:** *Let us say that a parent dies. When he passes over, does he really know your thoughts?*

ANSWER: Immediately.

Question: *Some children do not like their parents; they cannot fake it, can they?*

ANSWER: That is why I suggest to change the situation before they go.

Question: *What if other family members are the ones who dislike the parent? How do you change the situation?*

ANSWER: Teach them. Before the elderly person passes away, go to him and say, "You know, I hated you so much, but now I love you. It was really stupid of me to be so hateful because you really did not do bad things to me." By doing this a person really creates renewal within himself, which cleans the system. It is the most beautiful healing quality in you.

Question: *Is there anything a person can do to make up for others who do not do this?*

ANSWER: Tell them, "What are you gaining by keeping that anger in your mind? You are polluting your own atmosphere." Say that the person replies, "I cannot forgive this man; he is so bad. He harmed my mother and sister." You can tell him, "Still, what are you gaining? He is poisoning and killing himself with these actions. Do not poison and kill yourself by your actions."

When a person forgives, his consciousness begins to work more efficiently. His glands and nervous system come into harmony; his business will improve. Some religions and traditions suggest revenge, but in spite of these teachings, the Bible contains a very beautiful phrase: "Revenge is Mine," saith the Lord. We do not need to take revenge on others; leave it to God. He does a very good job through the laws of karma, so you do not need to involve yourself in it. Revenge must be eliminated from our lives.

Of course, because of the state of worldly conditions, people think that it is right to take revenge. Do not blame them. But it is not the way for peace and harmony, for everlasting right human relations. Revenge is a vicious circle which perpetuates itself. Humanity to this point does not have the wisdom to stop the devil we call war; with all its collective intelligence, humanity still fights wars.

Question: *Do we take our subconscious with us to the various levels when we die?*

ANSWER: Of course. The subconscious is a recording within you. Your permanent atoms contain recordings; everything that has happened, in the minutest detail, can be remembered in the subtle consciousness.[5]

Question: *Can you work out problems that you can see on the "other side," that you could not see when you were in body?*

ANSWER: You cannot. What you begin here continues. Subjective life is totally the result of what you do here. That is why you must work and prepare here. Once you

---

5. See also the *Subconscious Mind and the Chalice.*

push the vehicle and it begins to roll, once you are conscious and on the ball, it continues. But it must start here. This is a hard lesson to learn.

> **Question:** *How is it that people who may not be doing obvious things on the physical plane to bring them fame and reputation are sometimes said to have great fame and reputation for their works in the Subtle Worlds?*

ANSWER: Because they are conscious in the Subtle Worlds. Let us say that you are an average philosopher, esotericist, and initiate. You pass away and perform marvelous works in the Subtle Worlds. That ability is within you, but you did something karmically wrong which prevented you from becoming famous in the previous incarnation. You still have the ability. It is possible that some of you have done great things in the Subtle Worlds, but you do not know about them.

> **Question:** *The etheric body is the prototype of the physical body. If something is wrong in the etheric body, it reflects in the physical body. Does this mean that the cause is in the etheric body?*

ANSWER: No. The etheric body dies three days after the physical body. The etheric body is not the subtle body; it is physical. The Tibetan Master constantly repeats that when He says "physical," He means "etheric" because the etheric body has no survival. The etheric body dies, disintegrates with the physical body. If the etheric body does not disintegrate, it becomes a ghost.

Question: *Is the mind physical?*

ANSWER: The mind is physical because it is "brain vibration."

Question: *In other words, is everything we think, while in physical consciousness, physical?*

ANSWER: It is in the physical world, but it affects the other worlds.

Question: *Blavatsky says that entities fear a sharp blade, even though it cannot kill them, because it can give them pain. But you said something about walking through bullets and not feeling things on the astral level.*

ANSWER: If you are on the astral level and you receive an astral bullet, it really hurts you. If you receive a physical bullet at this level, it does not affect you at all because for you it does not exist.

An astral entity can enter through a wall; he has no limitations in physical elements because they do not exist for him. If you are going to hit an astral entity, you create an astral arrow or bullet. This wounds or kills them; they sleep for months, thinking that they are dead on the astral plane. When they awaken, they are again revived, and they fight against you again. This happens only on the seventh through fifth levels of the astral plane. From levels four to one, it does not happen because you are going toward beauty, goodness, righteousness, truth and harmony.

Question: *I thought that the physical plane was just a shadow of the subjective plane.*

ANSWER: This is not correct. The physical body is a shadow of the etheric body, but this does not mean that emotions and the mind do not affect the etheric body. Whatever affects the etheric body is then filtered down to and is reflected by the physical body.

Question: *Regarding the example that you gave about the philosopher and esotericist who was not famous on the physical plane, is it always karma that blocks us from being here what we are there?*

ANSWER: Exactly. Everything starts and ends here. For example, you must take your initiations here. You must, for example, achieve resurrection during physical incarnation. Christ is going to reappear on the physical plane in order to take the Seventh Initiation.

Question: *I thought that after the Fifth Initiation, a person no longer needed to incarnate. Don't you have a choice to leave after the Fifth Initiation? Where is the decision?*

ANSWER: Christ took His Sixth Initiation here. If you want to continue on this globe, you are going to obey the laws and regulations of this government.[6]

Question: *I have heard that sometimes people must work on subjective levels because they have done it on the physical plane before.*

ANSWER: It can be something like that, or perhaps their Solar Angel is blocking them. For example, a man may be a very famous judge who is a masterpiece in the courtroom, but he can be a total idiot at home. He may not be able to repair a simple light switch, cook an egg, or even love his wife. You have known or heard of such people, haven't you?

Question: *How does the Solar Angel block one?*

ANSWER: The Solar Angel is like your teacher, if you really give yourself to the Solar Angel. Let us say that I am your Solar Angel and I see that you are doing certain things that will limit you. I say, "Don't do that; do this instead; follow this line of work." You say, "I want to be a dancer. I want to be a doctor. I want to be a painter. I want to be President of the United Nations." So I say, "Take only one thing." You may hate me for it, but it is good for you. The Solar Angel looks at the situation and sees that as a dancer you would die in a car accident on the way to a dance. He says, "Honey, I would like for you to be a dancer,

---

6. For further information on Initiations, see *Christ, The Avatar of Sacrificial Love*.

but I do not want it." He does not explain why, but you must be a doctor because He sees that in that line of work you will develop. If you listen to the impressions coming from the Solar Angel, it prevents future dangers on the Path. In the meantime, you feel as if you are being limited. He saves your life, and you think He is limiting you. This is why it is very important to develop communication with the Transpersonal Self, the Solar Angel.

Question: *How many times do we come as a woman and as a man?*

ANSWER: In various esoteric and advanced Teachings we are told that a person incarnates as the same sex for not less than three and not more than seven consecutive times. After seven incarnations as one sex, you incarnate as the other sex.

Question: *Is there any way to know what sex we will be next?*

ANSWER: There is a way, if you awaken. There is one exception; after the Fourth Initiation, a person can choose his sex. He has power over this. Most Masters choose to be men, but over the last one hundred years this is changing. A lot of Masters are incarnating as women, and Their numbers will increase. A female Initiate is more than a male Initiate.

Question: *Then why do most Masters prefer to be men?*

ANSWER: In our current world situation and environment, men can more readily become a president or talk effectively with leaders of nations and armies. This is the trend, the consciousness of humanity. If They appeared as men, They were better accepted. For example, fifty years ago if a woman ran for president, she would have been rejected. But now the mentality of people is changing, and when the mentality changes, Those who are able to choose Their sex will appear more as women than men.

Question: *Is it the change in sex that causes homosexuality?*

ANSWER: Homosexuality has a very deep, complex mechanism. It is not a matter of blaming anyone. It adjusts itself, by the way.

Question: *Regarding miscarriage and abortion, at what point does life begin?*

ANSWER: The moment conception takes place, the soul is there. When a man and woman have intercourse, their united aura creates a funnel at the head through which the baby's soul travels to the mother's womb and the seed begins to germinate.[7]

In esoteric books, abortion is condemned unless the mother's life is endangered because it violates a person who has worked very hard to leave the subtle planes to enter the womb. You are breaking the house that he is building for his survival.

---

7. See also *Woman, Torch of the Future* and *Sex, Family, and the Woman in Society* for detailed discussion on marriage, sex, conception and family relations.

Question: *What about miscarriage?*

ANSWER: Miscarriage can be karmic, or it can be a dark attack. For example, let us say that a masterpiece child is coming; the dark forces will attack and try to kill it. There are hundreds of cases in medical history where the mothers of very advanced human beings tried abortion but were unsuccessful. The dark forces attack the child through the mother because a soldier in the Army of Light is a danger to them, and they try to prevent his birth. There are powerful politics waging in astral and mental planes.

Remember that nothing happens by accident. One does not really know what is happening — whether miscarriage is karmic, self-created, or a dark attack.

The first three months in the womb the child is still in astral consciousness, developing the physical counterpart of the astral consciousness. During the third to fourth month, a time comes when the soul makes contact with the developing body. This is the moment of "quickening" in which a woman feels the movement of the child. Then in the remaining seven to nine months, the soul makes a connection with the mental and astral bodies, and then takes birth. He makes a connection with everything and then "lands" his instrument.

The process reverses in death.

Question: *When an egg is fertilized by the sperm in vitro, when does the soul unite?*

ANSWER: The moment they fuse. When the fertilized egg is transplanted into the woman, it grows there.

Question: *The soul is present in the test tube?*

ANSWER: You must know what kind of soul is present at this sort of procedure. If science continues, we will see many zombies walking the streets — without feeling. Why is marriage sacred? The marriage ceremony creates an etheric and auric atmosphere for coming children, with prayers, chanting, and blessings. When the prayers and the intention of the marriage partners are very high, a high-level frequency is created which attracts only high-level souls.

When a man and woman decide to have a child, they should spend several hours in meditation and prayer prior to intercourse, so that they attract a genius, a talent, a beautiful leader. This is why many religions forbid kidnapping a bride, or making a woman pregnant in a nightclub or motel. What happens in these instances is that the parents attract entities living on the etheric plane, who are mostly criminals or people trapped in vices. Sometimes they are victims of war who are full of tremendous anger, revenge, and hatred, the results of which fill our prisons.

I heard a man interviewed on television who had molested ten young girls. He had spent five years in prison for the crime. When he was asked what he would do when he was released, he said that he would do the same thing again. What kind of consciousness is this? This person had some kind of hang-up, revenge against women. Maybe a woman killed him and he was stuck in the etheric plane for five thousand years, so now he wants revenge on women. By chance, perhaps one that he molested is the woman who organized the crime against him. No one knows exactly.

Incarnation is a science. When a person understands reincarnation, he becomes tolerant. His national and racial hang-ups disappear because he may be Armenian now, then German, Arab, Jewish, and so on. One does not know what he will be in his next incarnation. A person who understands reincarnation does not give much value to separatism; he becomes human. He understands people.

The Tibetan Master wrote in *The Reappearance of the Christ* that when Christ comes, He will give us a more advanced Teaching regarding reincarnation and karma. Our current understanding is not what He wants.

Question: *How do the dark forces know whether the incarnating soul is advanced or not?*

ANSWER: The dark forces are more thorough than the FBI or the CIA. They have a "computing system" in the astral and mental planes. They can detect every movement. This is why in one of the schools in higher planes we are trained to keep our thoughts and emotions secret.

Any time a soul incarnates, their automatic registration shows them where. What is our protection? The White Lodge can disturb their instrumentation, if the incarnating one is really pure and under Its guidance. That is why we pray, "God protect us."

People often take blessings, such as "God bless you" or "Have a safe journey," very lightly, but these are a form of blessing, of protection. A person can protect with his wishes, desires, and thoughts.

Question: *Yet you say that nothing happens by accident, that it is karma.*

ANSWER: Let us say that a very beautiful worker, a savior of men, is coming. The dark forces do not like this, especially if he is incarnating into a family and environment where all of his qualities will unfold and bloom. They will create everything possible to prevent his birth. If his karma is bad in certain aspects, they can harm him according to his karma. But if he is without karma and they attack, the White Lodge destroys them.

In *The Externalisation of the Hierarchy*, we read that in 1939 and 1940, during World War II, the dark forces were attacking humanity from subjective levels. In 1940 and 1941, the dark lodge began to incarnate, entering and possessing commanders and other officers in the armies of the Germans, Japanese, and Italians. Upon this, the Hierarchy immediately took action and began to inspire and impress the Americans, Russians, English, French to win the war.

If we had not had karma, they could not even touch us. With all their power, they cannot touch one who is karmically clean because his purity protects him.

I once lived in a monastery which was situated next to a graveyard. I shared a small room with another person, a very nice boy who is now a minister. At the time, however, he was very mischievous; he would steal bread and cheese and hide them in our room. Still, we were good friends.

One night, during the full moon, I was sleeping but was awakened by choking sounds. At first I thought the boy was throwing up what he had over-eaten, so I did not bother to open my eyes. I wanted every moment of sleep because at four o'clock every morning we had to get up and jump into a very cold river. But because the choking noises continued, I decided to get up and rub his back. When I opened my eyes, I saw someone else in the room over my friend's bed who immediately disappeared.

My friend said, "A tall figure came, a spirit with fiery eyes. He approached you as you were sleeping, but when he was about two feet away from you, he received a shock, like lightning. I was freaking out, watching it happen. He tried again, and again he was shocked. So he came toward me and grabbed me by the throat."

For three months after this incident the boy had bleeding from his throat. What kind of energy was that?

In another incident a neighbor girl, who lived a few miles away, fell in love with me. She wanted to sleep with me, but though she was very beautiful, for some reason I did not like her. I tried every method to repel her, but she was so "sticky" that she insisted on trying to come to my house. Whenever I saw her face at meetings, I avoided her, and for several nights I slept with a gun.

One night, I heard someone walking on the dry leaves in the yard, and I saw that she was approaching my house. I opened the window and thought, "Let her get a little closer, and I will shout at her and scare her away." She came about twenty-five feet closer, and then suddenly backed away and began running.

An hour later, the telephone rang. "You are a magician," she said to me. "I can't come over; something is preventing it." "You know," I told her, "I have five spirits who are waiting to beat you." She tried three or four more times, and then she disappeared.

A person's magnetism can create this protection. I am not implying that I am special; a person has at his level a way to protect himself from danger and attack that are beyond his imagination.

Question: When a child dies, is it karma or attack?

ANSWER: It is most often karma, but sometimes it is an attack. There is a very important verse in the Psalms which says, "Let not the watchman sleep, so that I do not fall into danger." Sometimes the "watchman" sleeps. As the mother sleeps for just a second, her child falls into a well. Keeping awake is very important.

Three-fifths of advanced human beings do not reincarnate. Two-fifths, who are neither hot nor cold, continuously incarnate because they are "downed" by two electromagnetic energies. Electricity repels them; their magnetism brings them back. They perpetuate their existence in the world by being dark and light together. There is no release for them. If they are totally dark, they remain in the lower astral plane. If they are really pure, they remain in higher levels. It is the "middle class" that is incarnating, dark and light. They have twenty righteous qualities and twenty dark qualities.

Those who have a really pure light are radioactive, not magnetic. Those who are material are attractive, which means that they accumulate matter and bury themselves beneath it. I am defining electromagnetic energy in a different way. When you are radiant, you just radiate; you no longer receive anything, just like the sun. The earth, on the other hand, pulls.

If you are going to be bad, be bad. If you are going to be good, be good. We call the middle class "mules" in esoteric language because they are neither horses nor donkeys.

Question: *What is considered advanced humanity?*

ANSWER: Third, Fourth, and Fifth Degree Initiates. They incarnate not because of attraction but because They are given duties and responsibilities to come and work. When you enter the Hierarchy, you no longer have a little will. The Hierarchy says, "You are going to go to this place and work," and you say, "Yes, Sir." You incarnate not because of punishment, guilt, or hatred, or because you massacred people, but out of duty. Whatever happens to you in such an incarnation goes into your savings account.

Question: *Can a person overcome his karma?*

ANSWER: Yes, if he works very hard. Overcoming karma is like building a successful business. If you owe two hundred dollars, you must pay it. Overcoming karma is not escaping karma but paying it. You can do this without suffering.

For example, a friend gives you ten million dollars, but you only owe five hundred dollars. Five hundred dollars is nothing to pay, so you overcome your karma. There is no escape; you must pay. There is a kind of payment where you do not have the money to pay, so you are "needled" until you can pay.

Paying karma is becoming more light, less darkness. It is not suffering to become more light. It is a joy to be sacrificial, to help other people.

In parts of Asia when people reach fifty years of age, they assume a different life-style. They finish their business affiliations and prepare to die. They give their money and belongings to the people, their land to their children. They make everything good. When this is finished, they look for anyone they harmed and make restitution, somehow easing the burdens of those they hurt. Then they go on a pilgrimage. If they are Moslem, they travel to Mecca. If they are Christian, they go to Jerusalem. If they are Buddhist, they visit different shrines and centers. If they do not believe in pilgrimage, they begin a life of retreat, going to the mountains for several months, returning to their homes for a short time, and then leaving again to meditate and study their holy books, their philosophical books, and so on. In Afghanistan, Persia, and Tibet, thousands of professionals, such as doctors, lawyers, other leaders, and so on leave on retreat.

In one Sufi ashram I met a British colonel and a millionaire from France; another man was a masterpiece surgeon who studied with Gurdjieff; they were dressed very simply, like dervishes. These men were cleaning bathrooms in the monastery, doing meditation at eighty years old.

This is the custom in the Middle and Far East, but in America we still have houses and land at age ninety. We work to develop them and die of a heart attack in the process. Instead of going to heaven without property, we end up going to hell with everything.

The influence of television and our fast life-style has us so involved with life that we have no time to think about the everlasting effects. This is the success of Satan. With television, radio, movies, businesses, taxes, accountants, problems, and court dates keeping us busy and stimulated, we do not have time to read, meditate, and reflect on our lives. Sometimes it is impossible not to be involved. But when the time comes, retreat. Say "Good-bye" to everybody and retreat. If you do this, you can prepare.

That is why it is good to make a little money at honest work, settle everything, and start creating — painting, music, sculpting, writing, and so on — in total retreat. Before leaving you can teach a few selected people and then fade away.

By doing this, you prepare a beautiful future incarnation for yourself. Read and search out these ideas before you pass away. If you are going to visit London, you at least take out a map and look at where you are going, and you try to find out about the weather, the laws, and so on. But for some reason we give little planning to the future life we are going to have for three or four thousand years in the Subtle Worlds. Is there hell? Is there heaven? Find out.

If a person has plans and is unable to finish them, and it is a really good plan for humanity, the greatest service you can render is to continue his plan so that his soul can rest. If you continue and finish it, it is more profitable for you; in the future he will return and do the same for you. In higher levels of consciousness the only valuable thing is to finish a creative project, not one that is personality-oriented.

For example, if a person wants to build a holistic hospital and he makes plans but then passes away, and if it is within your capability, collect the doctors to staff it, build it, and dedicate it to him. In this way, he can inspire people from the Higher Worlds. In his next incarnation, he will help you in a similar way; he has debts and he pays them.

Publish his works. For example, Helena Roerich wrote thirty-two books, many of which are published. The rest are masterpieces rotting in garages. Because she is very advanced, she probably does not mind, but there is some failure in this. The Teaching that she gave should be published because it is a project, a plan, for humanity.

It is very special to help orphans. If someone who is dying has children, they must be told, "Do not worry about your children; I will take care of them." This is a great release for mothers, especially if the children are young. There is a chapter in the Koran dedicated to the care of orphans. Orphans are very sacred. They must be schooled until they are self-dependent.

It is very important that after people die, you do not tell their children bad things about them. You should never speak evil about one who has passed away because he may take revenge on you. If he is in the lower astral plane, he will obsess or possess you; this is one danger. Secondly, you prevent him from advancing because you remind him of his faults and errors and perpetuate them in his consciousness.

Question: *How does grieving affect the departed one?*

ANSWER: Any time you are grieved, really sad and depressed, they try to appear around you, to be around you. They feel very bad because they know they are immortal and see how stupid you are. But, because they love you, they miss their "plane" to the Higher Worlds because they are tied and limited by your grief.

When my Uncle, who was a very joyful and beautiful surgeon, passed away, my Father smiled and said, "He is released." I said, "Why are you laughing? He died!" My Father said, "It is good; he is released." Twenty-five people, with drums, flutes, and different instruments, went to his grave and danced for hours because he loved dancing. They dressed a man exactly like him and celebrated. When I asked my Father what was going on, he said, "He will be so happy! If you sent a man to the palace of the king, would you get depressed? So we are seeing him off."

We are brainwashed to such a degree that it is hard for us to think in these terms.

> **Question:** *You said that animals incarnate again after only a few days. Is there anything special we can do for them?*

ANSWER: Just send them your love. They will follow you astrally for three or four days; you can say, "Poochy, I love you. You are here; I feel you," and put out some dinner for him. Many advanced animals come back in different forms.

> **Question:** *Do they suffer when they die?*

ANSWER: They go directly into their astral body and do not hurt like humans do. Humans have imagination, which makes them hurt more. Animals do not have this kind of imagination; they withdraw immediately to the astral plane. That is why if an animal breaks its leg it can sit for three or four days without making a sound. It is in the astral plane watching its body.

> **Question:** *Do animals take longer to incarnate if you killed the animal and it is mad at you? Can it bug you?*[8]

---

8. See *Other Worlds*, Ch. 13, "Vivisection and the Astral Plane," and Ch. 14, "Organ Transplants."

ANSWER: I think that killing animals is very bad because when you die they find you and really harass you. Can you imagine what will happen to butchers and the people who eat meat? They do not know what they are creating.

A scientist who kills three or four hundred monkeys has his astral body eaten day and night by the astral bodies of the monkeys. The Ten Commandments say, "Thou shalt not kill." But we kill: guns, bombs, war.

All great philosophies and Teachings are not created from earthly points of view. They are created from a higher viewpoint. When Moses received great laws and inspiration on the mountain, this symbolized the spiritual mountain — the heart, the elevated consciousness.

For thirty dollars, Judas went to the high priests and said, "I know where Jesus is; follow me." The soldiers followed him and found Jesus in the Garden of Gethsemane. Judas kissed Him, which was a signal to the soldiers. The Master looked at him and said, "You betray your Master with a kiss?" When the soldiers were binding His hands, St. Peter rushed forward with a sword and cut off the ear of a soldier. He was trying to cut his head off, but the man turned his head at the last minute. Jesus took the ear and healed it, yet this miracle did not even affect the consciousness of the soldiers. Then He turned to Peter and said, "Put your sword away. Whoever kills by the sword will die by the sword." That was one of His last lectures.

But we say, "Your nation bombed my nation; well just wait and see what we do!" Yet, all religions advise us not to kill. One can kill with his thoughts, emotions, and actions.

• CHAPTER 26 •

Self-Renunciation

The progress, the advancement, of a human being's spirituality depends upon self-renunciation. As much as one renounces himself by giving up his vanity and pride and humbling himself, the more he advances on the spiritual path. Vanity and pride, the "self-confidence" a person feels when he thinks that he is somebody or something special, separate him from the reality of God. That is why the start of new growth, the beginning of each expansion, stems from the seeds of humility, renunciation, and the disbursement of the little self.

In discipleship, there is a very ancient method or exercise for renunciation based on universal laws and rules. Whenever a person begins a new creative endeavor, starts a new business, makes new arrangements or engagements, or begins a great plan and labor, he must first renounce the self. This is very hard for most Western people because they are pumped from beginning to end with me, me, me, I, I, I, and with being the most beautiful, rich, and powerful people in the world. But we must renounce this. Unless a person humbles himself, he cannot grow in the soil of God. That is the rule.

We must renounce daily. Renunciation is like taking a shower first thing in the morning. Every day a person accumulates a lot of pollution and dirt, even though he is not aware of this. If he examines himself, he will find lots of chemicals in his pores, on his skin, in his nose, lungs, and brain. His body is loaded. When the outside of the body is really polluted, he takes a shower. But a person becomes polluted not only on the outside, but also he discharges a lot of polluting emanations from the inside. He must also take an inner shower by renouncing.[1]

Everyone from the highest saint to the lowest peasant pollutes himself daily through wrong thinking, wrong speech, and wrong action. When this pollution accumulates within the person, he is cut off from the life-giving energies in the Universe. When pollution accumulates in his aura because of wrong thinking, wrong speech, wrong feelings and actions, it builds out of finer elements an electromagnetic shell around him which prevents the Spark from communicating with the Invisible Presence in the Universe. The more pollution that accumulates, the more a person is deprived of life, light,

---

1. See the booklet *Mental Exercises* for purification visualizations.

love, and wisdom. Something goes wrong with him because he has polluted himself and has cut himself off with a self-created shell.

Just as one takes a daily shower, he should take a psychic shower by renouncing. In the Far East, I visited many temples and monasteries in the mountains where they renounce in a ceremonial way.

Exercise

Ceremony of Renouncing

1. Kneel down. Close your eyes and take a deep breath. Feel that you are a light in the presence of God. Repeat:

My Lord, I forgive everyone who has hurt me.

May my love be a blessing for them.

My Lord, forgive the wrongs I have done

with my thoughts, words, and actions.

2. Visualize a white light, cleansing all your body, emotions, and mind. Feel peaceful, joyful, and let your heart fill with hope.

This is a wonderful exercise which you can do daily to regenerate yourself. Without regeneration and purification of our lives, we cannot understand and assimilate the Teaching. I am not saying that we are now holy and perfect. It is written in the Bible that even the best human being is like a dirty cloth before God. Every time we clean ourselves, we start to regenerate ourselves, increasing our creative powers and tuning in with the Cosmic direction.

One must give up something to receive something; this is a great law in the Universe. People who do nothing but take become empty. In order to receive greater wisdom, greater life, the greater Self, one must give up.

There is another very interesting Cosmic law functioning throughout the Universe which is seldom mentioned in books. It has no name, but reincarnation is based upon this law which has not yet been discovered by man. This law states that all that is projected from a core or center departs from that center and then returns to that center. For example, I am a center; I radiate out my thoughts, emotions, words, energy into action. All that I radiate is out in space. It goes with a certain velocity to a certain distance and then restricts the core to some degree. What a person projects is like his child, magnetically connected to him, sometimes for thousands of years.

A person has two energies: electrical energy, which radiates out, and magnetic energy, which pulls back that which has been radiated — just like breathing. The self attracts everything that it creates. If it creates beautiful things, it will attract beautiful things; if it creates pollution, it attracts pollution. This continues level after level.

Let us say that the self changes its focus of consciousness from the physical plane to the emotional plane, then to the mental plane and Intuitional Plane. Whatever is projected will return to the level from which it was created and create the person at that level. He is first a physical entity, then an emotional entity, later a mental entity, until the self is so "empty" that it can no longer give anything. At this point, it unites with the Self.

Solar systems, galaxies, chains, and rounds all radiate energy, thought, emotion, sound, and color. All these radiations are projected into space, returning to take their previous forms around the nucleus again. In esoteric literature, this process is called *Manvantara* and *Pralaya*. In Pralaya, everything disappears; in Manvantara, magnetic energies are again activated and the cycle of action begins.

The secret to breaking this cycle is that we reach a stage in which we no longer radiate physical, emotional, and mental energies but radiate only spiritual energies. Hence there is no reaction. This is a great liberation sometimes referred to as *Nirvana*. If a person radiates pure Spirit, without emotion, body, or mind, there is no reaction. This is how one is freed from karma. The result of this is bliss, a stage in which the process of coming back and going out ceases. The person becomes new, existing without cause and effect. Cause and effect exist only in the physical, emotional, and mental universe. Beyond this, there is no cause. This is the basic law of reincarnation.

To be empty means to be free of physical, emotional, and mental elements. God is a vacuum because no impurities exist in Him. You cannot see, feel, or touch God; He is like a vacuum because He contains no element through which a person can contact Him — unless he "vacuums" himself.

The "old man" must die so that a "new man" comes into being. One must resign himself to find himself. One must "vacuum" himself from his ego. We do not know what a painful thing the ego is; all physical, emotional, mental, social, and universal problems originate from the ego.

Ego is the Divine Self misidentified with and blinded by the physical, emotional, and mental natures. When It is blinded, It does not know what It is doing. Like a blind bull, It eats, kills, and destroys. One can empty himself of ego by using the renunciation exercise, saying, "I am just nothing; I know nothing; I can do nothing. God is all." When a person resigns himself in God, he becomes one with God.

Take time to observe how much pain, suffering, anxiety, noise, and fear you have because of your ego. If you do not have physical ego, such problems cannot hang on you. Any time you find yourself in ego — having a mental debate, being mentally critical, being angry and fearful, just remove the ego and you will be surprised how peaceful you will become. Ego is separation from God; renunciation of the ego is a process of entering into God again.

Terms like "disciple," "Initiate," or "Master" are hallucinations of sorts. Only one thing exists. These terms describe the stages in which a beam of light increases in light. What these stages are called does not matter; the terms are human fabrications.

By increasing in light, you will be freed from pain and suffering. Second, your knowledge will expand to solar and galactic space. Third, you will become a co-worker with Cosmic creative forces. Beyond that, we do not know what will happen. The first step is to liberate yourself from your physical, emotional, and mental pain and suffering.

Lord Buddha called His five hundred disciples together and said, "Do you want to be Arhats, never returning to this earth again?" Being an Arhat means to be immortal, never returning to physical incarnation unless you want a test or for a certain responsibility. The disciples all wanted to do this, so Lord Buddha said, "The first lesson I am going to give you is renunciation of the ego." The disciples renounced everything that was ego, and all five hundred of them entered into Masterhood, conquering space, time, and death.

Christ produced five thousand Arhats. Until the year 2000, there will be five thousand Arhats around Christ. We must work harder to become one of them by the year 2000; this is the goal. We cannot do this by drinking, watching television, gossiping, hating, criticizing, condemning, and judging; it does not work.

If we knew how beautiful the Other Worlds are, we would never want to stay here. But we say, "No, no, no! I want to return to this. I enjoy my property, land, money," and so on. This is the madness we are in. We cannot liberate ourselves because we are not ready for it. Until a person's natural cycle is totally transformed and his karma cannot catch him anymore, he reincarnates. Why are we here? Because of karma.

Centuries later, when we become Masters to a high degree of enlightenment, we may see that something went wrong in Cosmic space which caused us to fall into the trap of incarnation. We know something happened, but we do not know what it was. We went through a tremendous shock and lost the memory. If one receives a shock to the brain, he even forgets his own name; he does not know what he was. We were Sons of the King, but we think we are nothing. The mechanism was disturbed, distorted, and no longer functions properly.

We have gone through many shocks on earth. We received a tremendous shock in Lemurian times when all Lemuria was destroyed. Again, in Atlantean times when everything was sinking to the bottom of the ocean, we went through another shock. If we have a global atomic war, it will be another severe shock, and it will take humanity millions of years to recover. Why not work on liberating ourselves? Then if certain shocking events happen, we will be able to handle them.

One can think on the physical level; that is physical thinking. One can think emotionally, which will cause a reaction. One can think mentally, which means separative thinking. These three kinds of thinking cause us to return because they are separative. But there is a thinking that is intuitive, which is for the Self in all. Because we are in wholeness at that stage, we do not return. Most human thought is related and limited to the physical, emotional, and mental planes. This is what creates cause and effect, magnetism and radiation.

We can rid ourselves of this by changing our state of consciousness. For example, if you think about your body ninety-nine percent of the time and Spirit only one percent of the time, you will not be liberated. If you can change your thinking to ninety-nine percent spiritual, which is thinking about the seven principles of Beauty, Goodness, Righteousness, Freedom, Joy, Striving, and Sacrificial Service, then you will free yourself. Only that energy which stimulates the lower atoms and molecules causes them to return because it magnetizes them. For example, I magnetize this physical atom and radiate it; because of the magnetism in the atom, it returns and finds me.

We magnetize our emotional substance with hatred, jealousy, revenge, and greed and then project it. Because we vibrate at the same frequency as our emotional substance, it finds and returns to the source of its frequency. This is karma and reincarnation. I magnetize my thoughts; they fly away, and then say, "Where is our nest?" Eventually they return to the nest, the originator of the thought.

Q&A

Question: *Can we change those thoughts?*

ANSWER: In a sense, we can. Everything is possible in the Universe. Let us say that you owe me ten dollars and it is very difficult for you to pay it. You gain two hundred dollars, so it becomes easy for you to pay me the ten dollars. If you "tune your car," making it more light, more love, more wise, more joyful and free, you do not accumulate debt, and past debtors never reach you because before they even enter your house, your servants pay them. It is magnificent.

Question: *Where does the ego come from?*

ANSWER: Ego is misidentification. Say that you go to a party and there is a bottle of wine on the table, which you start drinking. After drinking for a while, you will notice that you become one with the cup and with the bottle; you are gone.

Both Christ and Lord Buddha have said that, in a sense, we are intoxicated. We are intoxicated with Nature, with beauty, with flesh, with sex, with our bodies, money, food, property, and so on. Is there anyone sober from these things?

When you perform good actions, you gain more capital with which to pay past debts. If you insist upon accumulating debts that you do not want to pay, then you increase your taxation tenfold.

In Cosmic existence, we must try to increase our light so that darkness decreases. If you go outside at night and look up at the sky, you will see billions of stars. They tell us that behind all planetary and stellar motion, behind all creation, there is a law. This Universe is not in chaos; it is a mathematically-created Universe.

A person creates his own period of incarnation according to the velocity and charge he puts into his manifestation. For example, if he has five hundred thoughts which travel for five million years, he will incarnate for five million years. But if his thoughts are totally spiritual he does not come back, because those thoughts are not magnetized. They do not return to create a physical, emotional, or mental body because the person has become the Cosmic Self, Life itself.

Physical existence is terribly limiting. Once a person becomes conscious on the astral plane, and then on the mental and higher planes, he never desires physical incarnation again because the higher levels are so fantastic. For example, let us say that you are in your emotional body. You can be in China in a matter of minutes without an airplane. You can penetrate into any library, read, and learn. When a disciple sleeps, he can visit the Vatican library and search out a secret book about Christ written in Latin. Perhaps he does not know Latin in his physical existence, but suddenly his mind opens and he understands Latin. He reads the book and then comes back. Why would he want to be limited to the physical plane? It is so limiting that we are crazy to remain here, but we have no choice.

Many of us think that we have come to this planet to develop powers and energies to become gods. We must remember that we are nuts and bolts in a large machine; we are like leaves on a big tree. We are important, but the tree is more important. We have come to this planet to serve. Spirit comes to this planet and uses the chemicals It finds, refining them to make a body.

The human being is a refinery. On the physical level, he takes a raw element from the planet, eats, and digests it, changing the vibration, velocity, and intensity of that element to refine it one hundred percent. He also takes elements from the astral sphere out of which he makes his emotions, either polluting or refining space with his creation. He takes elements from the mental sphere, creating either tremendous beauty with his thoughts or polluting space with them.

We have come here with a great task, a great responsibility. If a person incarnates and creates a body that is inferior to what he created before, he generates a lot of taxation because he has not done what Nature has given him to do. When he leaves, Nature wants a body that has been chemically refined and sublimated so that it can use the elements of that body to build another animal form in which Spirit can better develop.

If in your last incarnation you refined your body fifty percent, then you left Nature a fifty-percent refined body. You took crude oil from the earth and made it into gasoline, which you give to Nature in place of crude oil. In the same way, you take elements from Nature and refine them to make your body, and then when you leave your body, Nature has more highly-refined elements with which to construct more refined bodies in the future.

After a person leaves his body, the body dissolves, but the atoms in that body do not. Even after burning the body, the atoms that made up the body stay the same as they were. They go to space and accumulate, forming another body, or they return to the person. It is said that on Judgment Day your mouth, your eyes, and ears will bear witness against you. You will stand before the Judge and say, "I did not lie," but your mouth will testify that you did lie.

The physical body is not a principle; a principle is something that causes other things to happen. The body does not cause things to happen; it is a shadow which follows. The body does not cut the body; there is an active, dominating side which is the causality that cuts the body. This is the principle. Effect is not the principle; it is the material, physical aspect of a principle.

We inherit atoms from other people, and it is our job to keep improving those atoms. When a person thinks, there are thought atoms, mental atoms, all around his head. When he thinks very creative, supreme, beautiful, high-voltage and pure thoughts, these atoms take initiation. When they are ninety percent pure, one can see a halo around the man; this is the mental aura which becomes illuminated.

When a person passes into the Intuitional Plane, he leaves behind his mental aura, which then can be used as material to make a dress for someone else. In the biblical story, Elijah threw his mantle to his disciples before ascending into heaven. What he left them was his mental body so that this organized machine could be used by them for Cosmic communication. But people think that he was just throwing them his coat.

When a woman becomes pregnant, she gives her child physical atoms, emotional, and mental atoms which condition his existence. When a person dies physically, he gives his physical atoms; when he dies on the astral plane, he gives his astral atoms; when he dies on the mental plane, he gives his mental atoms.

We are here for two reasons: to help the whole Cosmic Nature and to be a refinery. In the meantime, as we improve our bodies, they become communication links with progressively higher spheres. For example, the body of an aborigine is less sensitive to higher impression than a twentieth-century artist. Eventually, our bodies will be able to register impressions from the stars, from the Hierarchy, from Shamballa, and even higher forces.

This process of refinement takes place incarnation after incarnation. If you are really following the progressive path, which a Great Sage refers to as the "path of striving," then you will build a better body each time you come, eventually enveloping all of your bodies into the "body of glory," the Divine Body, the Intuitional Plane.

This body will be so sensitive that you will no longer need a radio or television.

In the *Bhagavad Gita*, there was a wise man named Sanjaya who kept the king informed of what was happening on the field of battle. They were ten thousand miles away, but Sanjaya would look to the mountains and say, "Now Arjuna is talking this way; the battle has begun and people are fighting. Ten people have died and Krishna is driving His chariot." Sanjaya could do this because he had refined himself. Because of her degree of refinement, the Great Sage says that Helena Roerich could communicate with extra-planetary beings during her waking consciousness.

Year after year, life after life, a person becomes more beautiful, more refined, more fantastic. It is interesting how we are passing through a period in which a large number of people are interested in diet and health food. This is because they are feeling that unless they refine themselves, they are not going to make it.

A ballet dancer takes care of her body so that it can respond properly to the music of the dance. The music is transformed into dance through her body. The body becomes so adapted and synchronized that every note becomes a movement in the body. If the dancer can create this kind of adaptation and synchronization to develop an astral dance and then a mental dance, what great beauty she will be able to express to us!

A singer pays a tremendous amount of attention to his throat, voice, vibration, and so on. He tries to explain and manifest all expressions of pain and suffering, emotional desire and anxiety, mental vision and revelation through his voice.

When a cat wants to play, he meows a certain way. When he is hurt, his meow is different. Even animals try to put concepts into higher expression.

Question: *Can anyone use the subtle body of an Initiate?*

ANSWER: No. The body is such a high voltage that if an unprepared person tries to use it, the person would shatter. It would be like touching high-voltage electricity.

Those who are prepared can use it. When I was a child, my Father had a five-foot sword which I could not lift. But when I became eighteen years old, I could lift it because I had developed to the degree necessary to use it.

For example, I have a car which I really know how to drive. A friend of mine, who is going to take a trip to Europe, gives his car to me. It has a radio, television, telephone, and everything in it, so I use it. But if he gives the car to someone who cannot drive, it would be a catastrophe.

In one of His books, the Great Teacher says that Christ will use the intuitional vehicle of Lord Buddha. Christ will use this body because He will not want to start from scratch, as a matter of Divine economy. Instead of waiting thirty years to develop the "car," he uses one that is already made.

A great Initiate can use or adapt his vehicles, or he can leave his vehicles and use those created by others. When he leaves his vehicles behind, someone else who is capable of using them can use them. It is like going to a garage sale and using the clothing and shoes that are available.

Question: *How do you explain the population explosion?*

ANSWER: There is no population explosion. There are sixty thousand million Monads in and around our globe. Some are incarnated; the majority are not. As the planet becomes more capable of nourishing the body, they take incarnation, in turn.

Natural calamities[2] restore balance to the planet. They clean part here, part there, putting the planet in equilibrium. They have happened in the past, and they will happen again. Those who are advancing will be untouched because the five-pointed star of Christ is on their forehead.

Question: *Are we our consciousness?*

ANSWER: We are not our consciousness. We use the consciousness. Consciousness is our mirror, made of a very high substance in which things are reflected for us to look at until we surpass our consciousness. A day will come when we do not use our consciousness. We

---

2. See also *Earthquakes and Disasters — What the Ageless Wisdom Tells Us.*

will be aware, and then the day will come when we will no longer need our awareness; we will simply be.

For example, I think about you and use my consciousness, defining you in certain ways. Later, I will surpass that and become aware of what you are, without reason or logic. In the third stage, I will no longer need awareness because I am you! This is progressive beingness.

We use our consciousness; our awareness determines the consciousness which we use. The level of consciousness which we use continuously affects the atoms in our mechanism. Consciousness sets the pace, the rhythm, and the measure. According to that measure or vibration, the physical, emotional, and mental atoms absorb and synchronize. Whatever the consciousness is, that is what the bodies are.

Consciousness determines the level of matter, the elements which you absorb from space and use to build the bodies. The mechanisms you use constantly ascend and change; they change as you change. Until your body is one hundred percent pure, you cannot be free of it; you are stuck to it. Until your emotional body is totally pure, you cannot rid yourself of it. Any impurity in the body attaches it to you. Only by refining and purifying the bodies can you break your link with them. The mental body must be illuminated ninety percent to be free of it.

But the human being builds a house and then destroys it the next day. He builds a chateau or a palace and then destroys it. He builds a road and then bulldozes it. He builds a nice body, then goes out drinking and does wrong things, destroying his body. He makes his emotions happy and beautiful, then hates, feels angry and greedy, and takes revenge. Mentally he thinks about great, beautiful plans, and then he gets on the telephone and gossips. He builds with one hand and destroys with the other. He builds himself and then destroys what he has built. We must pay attention, building continually toward perfection, being careful that we do not do something which will bring the whole building down.

It is very important to build a strong foundation. Without a foundation a person may build for fifty years, but all that he builds will eventually collapse on his head. He will say, "God did not will it," but the truth is that he did not construct it right.

When I was in the monastery, my Teacher selected a few boys to start giving lectures and organizing groups. I said, "What about me?" He looked askance at me, and did not answer. One year later I asked again, "What about me?" Two years later, I asked again; I was burning up. I listened to their lectures and thought, "I can do better than that." Six years later my Teacher told me it would be at least another two years. "That's all right," I said to him, "because I realize that I am not ready for it." He looked at me and a big tear came to his eye. He said, "Tomorrow you start, my son." "But I am not ready!" I said. "When you think you are ready, you are not. If you are ready, you will not talk about it," he told me.

We need to get ready. In our current system, a minister begins talking at a young age and continues until he is in his eighties. There is something wrong with this. Christ worked for thirty years and talked for only three. He worked until the Father told Him to start talking. We build very beautifully but forget that just one stick of dynamite can destroy everything.

Until the physical, emotional, and mental bodies reach a certain stage of perfection, one cannot be free from them. For example, if you do not have a toothache, you do not even notice your teeth because they are pain-free. But the moment the pain starts, you know that your teeth are there. Any imperfection in the body "sticks" you to that body. The best way to rid yourself of the body is to perfect it because in making that body perfect, you fulfill the task that God has given to you.

As a person evolves, purifying and sublimating those elements and chemicals within himself, he acts like a laborer who is shaping and polishing a very nice stone. An engineer takes that stone and uses it to make part of a room in the Cosmos; another engineer takes the room and makes it part of a palace. It is not really our concern what these great engineers are doing; our part is to shape the stone, to refine the body.

Question: *How does our speech, thinking, feeling, and action affect the atmosphere, the structure, the atoms, and everything that makes up this planet and the life on it?*

ANSWER: Whatever you are is what the planet is. In whatever condition humanity finds itself, those conditions exist within you. When a person radiates love, light, power, beauty, goodness, righteousness, joy, and freedom, he is already consciously or unconsciously sublimating elements that make up the planet. That is what we have been created to do.

If we pollute space with wrong thinking, wrong action, and wrong speech, that pollution will return to build a prison around us. To destroy that prison, that pollution, will take another five thousand lives of suffering to pay back what we did.

We come back to the idea of the foundation. As much as possible, we must not violate the law of love. God is love. Everything we do, we must do with love: improving our physical body by eating right, sleeping right, and taking care of it; taking care of our emotional body; and mentally taking care of ourselves.

Science, politics, business, and so on are not as important. They are all exercises to make us want to purify our bodies. Who cares how much land a person has? People are killing each other, saying, "This land is mine, not yours." Robbing, killing, and destroying does not work because in time it will all come back to us.

A person who increases his pollution is a criminal. To be a criminal means to sever communication with Cosmic direction. Such a person is like a gopher, eating the roots of plants and violating life.

Incarnation is a process of improving ourselves. Our Father asks, "My son, what did you learn in school today?" We answer, "I learned my ABCs." He says, "Tomorrow, learn to read. Tomorrow, learn more so that you graduate." Once we graduate from this planetary school, we will attend solar and galactic schools. Some day we will attend Cosmic schools, but they cannot be attended with the current bodies we have. We must leave something beautiful to earth in the form of higher and higher bodies, refining the elements of earth.

> **Question:** *How does one use self-will consciously without destroying his body? For example, I say, "I will do it," and give myself an ulcer.*

ANSWER: People in the western hemisphere have a very wrong impression which has penetrated to their bones, and they cannot rid themselves of it. They think that man has free will. He does not. There is only one will, and that is the Will of God. Christ said many centuries ago, "Thy Will, not Mine, be done." The only way to improve life is to understand that Will and to manifest It. Rid yourself of "will" because it is the urges and drives of your body, your glamors, illusions, vanities, pride, and separatism. These are not Will, but the "will" of the elements. There is only one Will. If you want to be Christ-like, you must say, "Not my will, but Thine be done."

This is renunciation of the ego. "My Lord, I no longer exist. Only You exist in me. My ego is gone. You can do anything with me You want because I am not me anymore; You are all." When a person begins to reach this consciousness, he will see how reality is very different from what we have learned.

I met a marvelous singer who used to come to our classes. I composed a piece of music for her to sing, and she performed it so marvelously. I asked her to work with me on the music, but she told me she was too busy singing for the opera. She gave me a ticket to go hear her, so I went to the performance. Her voice was good, but she was singing mechanically, and she was trembling on stage.

She came down after the performance to see how I felt about her singing. "Was I fantastic?" she asked. "You were trash," I told her. She came to see me later and asked, "What can I do?" "Let God sing through you," I advised her. "How is God going to sing through me?" she asked. "Let the song sing; let that power take over and sing. If God is on stage and not you, you will not have stage fright. When you are on stage and ten thousand people are looking at you, you have stage fright. Stage fright is a moment of egoism, separatism, where you become your tiny self. When you are not your tiny self, you present or express the Divine Presence; there can be no fear in you. Let God be on stage."

When I gave a seminar in Holland, two psychiatrists who had attended approached me and asked me if it would be possible for me to give a five-minute opening talk at a psychiatric convention that was going to be held the next day. I agreed and prepared a few opening remarks. Before the convention began, they put me in a dark room so that I could rest before going on. I felt very calm at first and began to go over my speech. "What am I going to say to these philosophers and professionals?" I asked myself. Then suddenly fear came to me, and I had to fight it off. I imagined that God was talking through me. When I took the podium, I opened my mouth and said, "Good morning. Psychiatrists are not helping humanity. You are destroying the brain. Do you know what you are doing?" I continued talking for fifty-seven minutes, and, even so, they asked me to continue. Afterwards a doctor came up to me and said, "We needed this shower." They praised me, but I said to them, "Who are you praising? I did nothing." "You are a true philosopher," they said to me. "Me?" I said, "There is only One Philosopher; there is only One Teacher; there is only One Life — that is God, not me."

If we can develop such a consciousness, we can evolve. If not, we remain as we are. In dealing with each other, we must develop the sense that God is touching God. When we love each other, we are touching God, which is what we are. Therefore, we must begin to take care of our body.

Let me explain how you gain liberation in the Higher Worlds. In the process of dying, you begin to talk less about what is going on around you, but you never lose consciousness — unless you are a very low human being or are surrounded by lots of karmic pollution.

A fainting phase comes in which you do not feel anything for a few days. As you are totally annihilated, this disappears. If you feel these things, do not be afraid. But if your continuity of consciousness is operating, you will never experience this phase; you will always be awake.

Two or three days later, you enter the astral plane. The astral plane consists of two sections — the lower and higher sections. The lower astral plane is hell. Hell is a state of friction between the astral energy and your aura. If you participated in wrong speech, wrong thinking, wrong feeling, and wrong action you violated the laws of love, justice, beauty, goodness, and freedom. Because of this, you accumulated a lot of pollution in your astral aura, which is flammable material. The instant this material comes into friction with astral energy, a tremendous explosion of fire occurs, which is the origin of the idea of hell.

Hell is not reality, in a sense. But hell exists because you create it. Your astral body burns until all the pollution in it is totally melted, at which point your astral body either dies or releases itself from the pollution and enters the higher astral level. In the higher astral plane you see greater beauty, greater freedom and liberation to use Cosmic direction as your own will. At these first stages you do not control what you want to do. As you proceed, you gain more control over your time, direction, and activities.

The higher astral plane is occupied mostly by artists, humanitarians, and those who sacrificed their lives for others. It is here where you meet your teachers and guides. Your Solar Angel immediately appears to you. In the lower levels It watches you as you go through the "valley of tears," the "valley of gnashing teeth," but It does not contact you at that level.

In writing about these levels, the Great Sage says that Urusvati heard the lamentations and grinding of teeth coming from the lower astral plane. The inhabitants at this level really suffer not for punishment but because they created it. Their pollution contacts the fire of the astral plane and creates a hell for them.

On the higher astral plane, you receive tasks and responsibilities from your Inner Guide. If you respond to this call, you can do something good for humanity. Great Teachers say that we can help Them every minute, because They are desperate for help. Sometimes you can perform greater works in the astral plane than you can on the physical plane.

Let us say that you were a tremendous singer in the physical incarnation, or a master ballet dancer. But when you became seventy-five years old, you lost the ability to sing well or dance. You tried to sing, but your voice was gone. With the body you have, you cannot dance. But when you enter the astral plane, you receive your youth. Most astral people have bodies that are like bodies of eighteen to twenty-two year olds; they are so pretty. So you can begin to dance and sing there. Because you are no longer restricted by clothes, age, pollution, and so on, you can really sing and dance. Your body does not tire; you can perform movements and reach notes you could never attain on the physical level. You can jump fifty feet in the air.

Those who have the opportunity to visit a music center or ballet center in the higher astral plane will see unique beauties. Great artists come to this level when they sleep and bring back tremendous creations to the lower levels when they return. Most composers, dancers, singers, and artists who are really advanced are unconsciously enjoying these levels. They consciously forget everything, but the impressions remain in their heart. These impressions express themselves as inspiration. A choreographer does not know why, but he says, "I am inspired to create this dance." If he were aware, he would see that he attended such a dance on higher levels, and he is trying to reproduce it as much as possible. Usually it cannot be reproduced one hundred percent; sometimes as much as eighty percent is lost in the actual performance. But the source of inspiration remains in his heart.

Some artists think that using drugs helps their creativity, but this is not true. If a great artist incarnates and begins to use drugs,[3] he paralyzes his eyes, ears, and etheric centers in subtle ways. When he travels to the astral plane, his astral eyes will be blinded, and his astral centers will not function. He will have a terrible time in the astral plane. That is why the use of alcohol and drugs is not recommended.

---

3. For further information, see *The Psyche and Psychism*, and *The Fiery Carriage and Drugs*. Also important information is contained in the video "Why Drugs are Dangerous."

Malice, slander, and gossip are also very bad poisons. It is important to keep the body, emotions, and mind in tune, elevated, and clear so that we can enjoy the coming years of eternal traveling.

When a person leaves the higher astral plane, he penetrates into the mental plane, which consists of two levels — the lower and higher levels. The mental plane is mostly prepared for those who are in the lower mental plane. The higher mental plane is a white flame in which no impurity exists. The lower mental plane is inhabited mostly by philosophers and scientists, those who suffered much, and those who had a lot of experiences. The higher mental plane is for second degree, Third Degree, and Fourth Degree Initiates. It is called the Fiery World.

If you are advanced, you do not follow this procedure. You will remain only one day in the astral plane, half a day in the mental plane, and then you will pass onto the Intuitional Plane.

There is a wall behind the mental plane called *Devachan*. Devachan means a hotel or resting place for devas and angels. From the human point of view, an angel is one who is not stuck in the astral or mental planes. They go to Devachan where they have the highest pleasure to meet Great Ones and see the most beautiful creations. This is a plane of inexplicable, unimaginable beauty. Many disciples who have been there cannot explain what they have seen because words are not enough.

The Great Sage says that some people, such as Helena Roerich, never enter Devachan because they think it is a waste of time to stay there for hundreds of years. When she passed away, she returned to incarnation after just a few days to work in a different field.

Question: *If a scientist enters the higher astral plane, does he have the same ability to create and dance, even though he was not a dancer or musician in his last lifetime, or does he start out as a beginner?*

ANSWER: He cannot dance on the higher astral level unless he has developed dancing on the physical plane. Whatever he cultivates on the physical level is valid on the higher levels. You must take initiation on the physical plane; you can be a genius or a talent on higher levels, but you cannot begin that process there. The cause and effect of it is created on the physical plane. That is why Jesus took the Transfiguration Initiation on the physical plane, not the astral plane. He took a physical body and resurrected Himself here. This is what all of us must do.

Proof of your advancement must come from the physical plane. If you start here, you can continue there. If the scientist likes art and starts to work along those lines, he has the foundation to work on the astral plane.

If a person does not believe in eternal life, if he totally ignores it and says there is no afterlife, he will not have an afterlife. When he dies, he will remain in a totally unconscious state until two thousand years later he again incarnates. If you think that you are going to have an afterlife, you will have one. If you do not, you are in a terrible condition.

It is mostly people who do not believe in an afterlife that create problems in our world. Eventually they go through so much trouble that they crack.

Question: *Is the two-thousand-year period you mentioned the same as earth time?*

ANSWER: Time is measured from our viewpoint, but two thousand years on the other levels is like one day there — no time at all. But on our scale, two thousand years have passed. For example, a lot of Atlantean souls are incarnating. They had atomic wars, laser beam wars, programming wars. Perhaps they are the ones who will lead us into an atomic war. When they were on the other side, they thought that they were sleeping and were born again in just a few days, when it may have been two thousand or eighteen million years.

There are two classes of "sleepers." The first class is not well-developed, a little above animals. They eat, drink, lay down, and forget everything. They are mostly asleep. The Bible refers to them when it says, "And they enter into sleep." The second class has no faith or any urge to be alive after death. Their religions teach that there is no afterlife; their philosophy says that when they die, they are finished. Because they build such a thoughtform, it does not allow them to be the opposite, so they do not experience the afterlife.

If we refine and demonstrate more service, more learning, and obey our Teachers, working more deeply in harmony with the Hierarchical Plan, some part of this activity remains in our heart. When we incarnate again, we want to pray, dance, and meditate at a very young age; we have an urge toward light and beauty. We go to the higher levels and see Cosmic beauties and then return. One percent of what we see remains, which is equal to what we do here.

The sign Pisces is symbolized by two fish, one looking in one direction, the other looking the other way. These two fish actually make up one fish. The first fish is going counter-clockwise, and then thinks it should go clockwise. It changes its direction again and travels counter-clockwise. The two fish are actually one fish going in two directions.

It is in the sign of Pisces that people change their direction. Clockwise direction takes them toward materialism, toward pleasure, greed, property, toward building bodies and enjoying life. Counter-clockwise, they detach from physical, emotional, and mental worlds and from separatism and travel toward wholism, toward Spirit, creativity, greater beauty, and glory.

In the clockwise direction, one fish is the Soul; the other is the personality. The two are tied together. Eventually the Soul says, "I am sick of the personality. If you are going in that direction, I am going the other way." They pull and push against each other. The smaller fish, which is the personality, reacts to this and wants to cut his relationship with the larger fish, the Soul. But when he reacts and is pulled back, the larger fish swallows him. When the Soul swallows the personality, he becomes a Soul-infused personality.

The two fish become one, and because the person is no longer divided against himself, he can determine his own direction. If he is separated into two, he cannot determine his direction. He is split mentally, emotionally, and physically, and he has no direction. The heart says one thing, the mind says another, and they contradict each other. This is the condition of humanity since the beginning of the Piscean Age.

As a human being travels through the Zodiac,[4] he learns a different lesson in each sign. Each sign is a school in which he perfects himself. For example, in Aries we learn willpower; in Taurus we cultivate wisdom; in Gemini we cultivate love. Once a person finishes his schooling in a particular sign, he does not return there.

For example, if a person is born in the sign of Scorpio, he has nine very heavy tests to pass. If he passes them, he jumps over Scorpio any time he comes near it. If a person is born in the sign of Libra, he is learning balance and equilibrium. When he becomes balanced between Spirit and matter, between force and action, inspiration and manifestation, he no longer needs to come to Libra. When he passes through and learns the lessons in each sign, his

---

4. See also *Symphony of the Zodiac* for detailed information on each of the signs.

circulation becomes faster because he skips those signs which he has already learned. When a person moves in the counter-clockwise direction, he accumulates everything he has achieved in each sign and actualizes it. He goes from Aries to Pisces, not Taurus. From there, he goes to Aquarius, once he proves that the Pisces lesson has been learned. He skips to the next sign, because he has already accumulated millions of years of experience. When a person chooses to travel counter-clockwise, he will demonstrate all that he has accumulated in the way of wisdom, tests, and the energies of each sign.

If by a determined time a person has not finished his clockwise round, his "goose is cooked." Most of us are traveling clockwise. When Jesus said, "Salvation is today, not tomorrow," the word "today" meant one clockwise rotation, not one life-time. He was speaking a symbolic language.

Whether we travel clockwise or counter-clockwise is determined by our own decision. The person takes a stand and says, "From now on, I am going to behave." We begin by traveling counter-clockwise daily, then weekly, then monthly, then annually, then through one life, then over a period of one hundred incarnations.

Q & A

Question: *Is it true that the month you die in is the month in which you return?*

ANSWER: Probably, but not necessarily.

> **Question:** *If an Aries dies and comes back in Aries, does that mean he did not learn his lesson?*

ANSWER: That is very probable, but in every case there are very distinct and individual choices and influences. For example, marriage changes this; different boyfriends and girlfriends change this.

For example, if I marry a Sagittarian and I am a Leo, I am no longer a Leo and she is no longer a Sagittarian; we blend. My chart as a Leo and my wife's chart as a Sagittarian are totally wrong; the charts no longer work because the chemistry is totally changed through mixing the different elements. This is why we must use caution and not mix our elements too much. By mixing fire with water, you have steam.

> **Question:** *Are there some signs that control us more strongly than others?*

ANSWER: Yes, but sometimes the weakest sign controls us more than the strongest. For example, you are a mother and you have a little child who is very naughty. Who is in control?

> **Question:** *If water and fire make steam, then couldn't that power be harnessed?*

ANSWER: That depends on how wise you are. If you are traveling counter-clockwise, it may be possible. If you are traveling clockwise, you may not have control over it.

All signs must be balanced and agree in harmony. Everything is possible, but somebody must make it possible. Who is that somebody? If a person's rising sign is not developed and his sun sign is not developed, there are two clashing energies which make his personality life miserable.

Astrology is a science which has not yet become advanced. Astrology looks at when the physical body was born; it does not tell you when you are really born, which means you have become a Third Degree Initiate. It is like addressing a letter to someone who does not exist yet. When an astrologer looks at your physical chart, he knows only a small part of who you are. Maybe in the seventh or eleventh year you are born astrally; then maybe you are born mentally at age twenty-one or twenty-seven. Each birth has a different sun and rising sign.

After speaking to a group of two hundred astrologers in South Africa about these ideas, a large number of them said they were going to resign from their astrology. One lady said, "I just paid seven hundred dollars for astrology books. I am going to give them all away." I told her not to do this because astrology is a wonderful exercise for the mind.

In *A Treatise on Cosmic Fire*, the Tibetan Master says that present-day astrology is nothing. It is advancing very beautifully. Someday astrology and astronomy will merge into the same science. Astrology is the mother of astronomy; now the son does not like the mother.

Future astrologers will be very clever, and they will develop a computation table to determine what sign dominates a family. They will be able to determine what percentages of the dominant sign affect the different family members.

In the future, a genius will create a laser beam machine which will be able to detect the moment of our astral birth and mental birth. It will also be able to watch our thoughts. The Great Sage says that the majority of humanity will hate that scientist.

It is important to know that the sign in which you are born is the exact place where you should be, and you should really try to master that sign. Once you do it, you progress a thousand years.

The decision to go counter-clockwise is made in Pisces. If you are not born in Pisces, then you can make that decision during the month of Pisces.

For example, let us say that a girl has fifteen boyfriends. Suddenly she decides, "No more." That is a counter-clockwise action. A boy steals here and there, cheating people, and then suddenly decides not to do this anymore. He shifts his direction. A person is lazy and does not do any meditation or study. Then one morning he awakens and says, "You know, I don't like my life. I am going to change my life. I am going to create." This is a counter-clockwise direction.

At the time of death, your computer prints out how many counter-clockwise efforts you made. The Great Ones note your progress. You are watched; every Great

One is watching you. "How is this girl doing? How is that man doing? Are they progressing, or going backward?" Our thoughts, actions, and emotions are all registered in the computer of Life.

A Great One tells us that Helena Blavatsky is now living in a very large cave in the Himalayas, with highly-advanced scientists who are three thousand years ahead of our modern sciences. In the cave walls there are little images which show who has reached various stages of initiation. When a person enters the first initiation, his image is entered. It is Blavatsky's duty to watch these images to see who is flickering, who is fading, who is coming alive. She then files a report with the Hierarchy. Any time a person's light increases, she sends light to him, and he feels enthused and inspired. When a person's radiance really increases, she takes his picture to the Hierarchy and says, "This person must take the Third Initiation." His picture is then moved into another hall where records are kept on the Third Degree Initiates. Other halls hold the images of Fourth and Fifth Degree Initiates, which are monitored by advanced Initiates.

We think that we are not being watched, but everything that happens in a person's life is recorded there. We are living in the eternal presence.

Question: *Is it just in marriage that there is a blending of the astrological energies, or is there an interchange in* any *sexual relationship?*

ANSWER: If a person is promiscuous, he takes on the energies of his sexual partners. I am not saying that promiscuity is a transgression and that promiscuous people are going to hell. But chemically-combined results create different effects. Young people must be very careful about what they are doing. They must try to find the best partner and continue with him or her. Sexual promiscuity can change future incarnations. If a person is not a liberated human being and he has a lot of different sexual partners, he will have trouble with these people in future lives.

In the future, great Masters who are astrologers, scientists, philosophers, and teachers will come to teach us. For example, when King Akbar was going to be born, five astrologers who found out when the conception took place, sought out his mother, Miryam. It is said that she radiated energy from her forehead for fifteen feet. When she asked why they were staring at her, they asked, "Did you put mirrors on your face?" When King Akbar was born, he was white with radiance.

Sex is very important; we do not know how really beautiful it is. In sexual activity, one combines karmic conditions. You can be a very beautiful man, but you go with a girl who is karmically loaded. While driving home, a car hits you because you share her karma, even though you did not do anything bad.

We have all "mixed our waters," so to speak. Now what can we do? We can take vows of celibacy and dedicate all our energies, transmuting them to higher development and slowly clean ourselves, or we can find the best partner and say, "This is it." If a person is physically celibate, but mentally imagining, there is no progress. If he is really celibate, physically, emotionally, and mentally, then he progresses. When St. Paul was asked whether it was good to marry or not, he said that if a person could do it, he should stay alone, but if he was boiling inside, he should marry. The person has to be the one to choose. No one else knows his own heart.

The opposite is also true. A boyfriend or girlfriend may help us advance ten thousand miles. Who can determine these things? It is better to take slow and careful action, so that you have time to think and observe and not hurry.

There is a great science of love — physical, emotional, mental, and spiritual love — which is not taught here. Most men and women do not know how to make love or what love is. They are producing children without knowing what they are doing. Sometimes they are forced; sometimes they are caught in a trap; sometimes there is no chance to escape. But this situation must end. In the future, we must have a university that will prepare men and women for sexual activity, marriage, and child-rearing.[5]

Let your light shine out so that everyone will see your light. Christ says that this glorifies the Father, not the personality or ego. In this way we develop humility, beauty, and resignation of the ego.

---

5. See also *Sex, Familly, and the Woman in Society* and *Woman, Torch of the Future*.

We are lucky to have great teachers from whom we can learn, seminars to attend, and books to read which are given or written by people who are hundreds of years ahead of us. Still, there is a lack in quality teachers. The greatest failure of humanity is human greed. We cannot improve the economy, we cannot change the economy, we cannot prevent exploitation, we cannot improve the economy in the future unless we clean greedy people. Because of greed, we do not have good teachers.

With help we will be able to build future temples for our children where they can learn right living. We have so much to offer, but money is killing us. We do not donate because of family obligations, or we are taxed to death. Our ideas about money are killing us.

• CHAPTER 27 •

Building the Human Being

According to the Ageless Wisdom, the human soul — collecting all the records of the physical and astral permanent atoms — and the mental unit — disappears eventually into the formless levels of the mental plane.

On his descent to reincarnate these records, as one frequency, are expressed as a voice which the human soul sounds to build his threefold vehicles. His voice is threefold, containing the notes of the physical, astral, and mental recordings. It is this voice that, according to its quality, tonality, depth, and so on, builds the bodies. Each note in his voice, reactivating in its turn the three permanent atoms and the blueprint of the future vehicles, begins to form and slowly "materialize."

In the esoteric Teaching we read that the human soul first sounds the voice, which synthesizes in it all the recordings of the permanent atoms. It then passes that voice to the Solar Angel. The Solar Angel then adds on it other elements and passes them to the transmitting devas who are connected with the three permanent atoms. The voice restimulates and further mobilizes the building devas to build the etheric, emotional, and mental bodies with etheric, physical, astral, and mental deva substance.

After the transmitting devas the voice goes to so-called listening devas who change the voice into mantrams in order to manipulate the four above-mentioned deva substances to build the vehicles.

The building process goes as follows:

1 2 3 4 5 6 7 Mental

  1 2 3 4 5 6 7 Astral (emotional)

    1 2 3 4 5 6 7 Etheric

      1 2 3 4 5 6 7 Physical

"...When...the co-ordination of the mental body is in its second stage, the first stage of astral concretion begins. ...Again, when the second stage is reached, a vibration is produced which awakens response in etheric matter on the physical plane, and the builders of the etheric double commence their activity. ...When the second stage of the work of these etheric devas is begun, *conception takes place upon the physical plane.*"[1]

---

1. Alice A. Bailey, *A Treatise on Cosmic Fire*, p. 938.

This means that the building process of the mental body must reach its fourth stage, and the etheric construction must reach its second stage in order that the conception takes place in the womb. What an intricate process it is of building the human form! How surprising that after the toil of these four kinds of devas people still use abortion. It is just like destroying a house in the presence of a great number of builders after the building is in its third or fourth phase!

The most important thing to see here is that the physical body is built after the model of the subtle bodies and, because of that, the physical body is absolutely related to the subtle bodies.

These building devas, after the baby is born, try to repair the bodies wherever a repair is needed physically, etherically, emotionally, and mentally. They work at all these four levels and try to do their best to repair and coordinate and integrate all the bodies.

When the time comes for the soul to withdraw, his voice gradually withdraws, and the transmitting, listening, and building devas no longer receive energy and commands from the soul. The disintegration of the body then begins. The soul withdraws from the physical body, then from the etheric, astral, and mental bodies, and the four bodies (counting etheric and physical as two) slowly disintegrate.

We are told that our mental unit and two other permanent atoms (physical and astral) are formed by devas which are the highest builders. These devas have a close connection with our Solar Angel.

Here is the pattern of birth:

- Voice of the human soul to the Solar Angel
- Transmitting devas
- Listening devas
- Building devas[2]

After the human soul incarnates, the human devas, who work in the physical, etheric, astral, and lower mental planes, continue their work under the control of the Solar Angel, Who possesses all past records of the human soul.

Also, the *Solar Pitris*[3] continue Their work in building the Chalice, its petals, and various networks of communication between the centers according to the striving, aspiration, devotion, dedication, and sacrificial service of the human being.

First we have transmitting devas, who are found on the fourth level of the mental plane, and also in the highest astral and first etheric planes. These devas are connected with the mental unit, the astral, the mental, and the physical permanent atoms. The human soul is thus related to four kinds of devas.

The building process starts from the mental plane and extends into the astral, etheric, and physical planes. After the birth, the devas work on the physical vehicle to

---

2. Note: If one does not have a Solar Angel, the voice goes directly to transmitting devas. (author)
3. *Solar Pitris* is the Sanskrit name for Solar Angels. See *The Subconscious Mind and the Chalice* for details of building the Chalice.

make it reach maturity according to the "lines of growth of subtle bodies." Then these devas work to repair the bodies so that the bodies last according to the purpose of the human soul.

The Ageless Wisdom says that the mental unit and astral and physical permanent atoms are built of the substance of the building devas. Such devas have a closer connection with the Solar Angel and are found "within the causal periphery" around the Chalice.

The next group of devas are those who build the vehicles and the third group of devas are those "who are built into the form."

• CHAPTER 28 •

The Soul and Its Vehicles

Whenever people write about the subject of reincarnation they speak about the reincarnation of the human soul or about the incarnation of the *scandas* — the material and psychic aggregations. In some books, *scandas* correspond to the human soul. It is the *scandas* that form the future personality.

Such an illogical doctrine prevails until today. People believe that the elements of the bodies of the present incarnation are responsible for their past merits or demerits — the bodies, not the human soul.

According to some Buddhists, the human soul does not even exist. But strangely enough the Tibetan Buddhists search for the reincarnation of a previous Dalai Lama, or for the great one who previously lived. Actually, what they are searching for is the incarnated lama

345

who is an aggregation of *scandas* because no one of the lamas has a permanent part in them, they are "empty."

The fact is that only a conscious individuality can be responsible in his actions, and this lama's soul reincarnates, life after life, according to his merits and demerits.

Not only the human soul as an entity incarnates but also his vehicles. For example, his astral body reincarnates with all its past tendencies because all its merits and demerits are recorded in the astral permanent atom. His mental body reincarnates with all its characteristics and tendencies cultivated throughout ages in his mental permanent atom. Thus we can see that the human soul reincarnates through the incarnating etheric, astral, and mental permanent atoms.

The Ageless Wisdom says that the entities reincarnating through the substance of the physical, astral, and mental bodies are being trained by the human soul. Eventually, the human soul will be able to emancipate them and lead them to the human Hierarchy, as the Solar Angel is leading the human soul to the fifth kingdom.

Merits and demerits are recorded in the permanent atoms, and each body accordingly pays its taxes. The human soul is also responsible for his thoughts, emotions, and actions due to the use of his vehicles, either ignorantly or consciously, in spiritually illegal actions.

The more a human soul is formed, the more responsibility he will have for the actions of his three vehicles until he totally transforms these entities and makes them channels of his light, love, and will power. It is true that for a long time the bodies were reincarnations to be ready to serve as vehicles for the human soul. During such a period the light of the Monad was providing to the aggregated elements instinct, attraction, repulsion, and tendency to action. The Monadic Ray, through thousands of incarnations and through the help of the Solar Angel, begins forming its individuality. Formation of individuality is nothing else but the formation of the human soul, the human being — besides his vehicles.

The Great Teacher said that individualization took place in the middle of the Lemurian Race when Solar Angels came to this planet to further the evolution of man. He also said that man is the Monad.

Previous to individualization, the Monad or the Monadic Ray had no individuality, and the show was run by physical and astral entities — though the Monad, "like a flame hanging from a thread," was emancipating the human animal. From the beginning the flame was there in material, vegetable, and animal kingdoms. In each successive kingdom the Monad gained more power until the middle of the Lemurian period, when Its power was reinforced by the Solar Angel.

The human soul, in due cycles, leaves his bodies and acts in the subtle bodies. The new formation of lower bodies is called the reincarnation of the human being.

The destiny of the human being is to

1. Be an independent individuality
2. Cultivate the lives of his vehicles and promote them on the path of evolution
3. Gain independence and know himself as a separate being from his vehicles and even from the Solar Angel
4. Cooperate with Cosmic Laws and Cosmic Purpose
5. Be a center in the planet or in the body of the Solar Logos
6. Know his oneness with greater and greater lives
7. Be universal but conscious of his identity

We are told that a human soul, a Planetary Logos, a Solar Logos, even a Galactic Logos reincarnate under similar laws and with similar goals in Their Life. All the lives forming Their body are responsible for Their individual labor.

The Law of Reincarnation clarifies our understanding of the process of life and inspires us to see righteousness in all that goes on in all universes.

• CHAPTER 29 •

Vehicles and Their Notes

All our bodies or vehicles have their own notes. In the evolutionary path these notes are purified, cleared, and eventually reach a state of pure harmony with each other and with higher spheres.

During the evolutionary process many disturbances occur among these notes. If a person is taken as a musical instrument, at this stage he is full of discord. He even sounds like noise. But during the progress of evolution, these notes go through a process of purification.

We must remember that each body sustains its life by its own *sound* or vibration. It is through the sound that the body attracts elements by which to nourish itself, and it is through the sound that the body eliminates, or burns away, all that is not needed.

As a person's consciousness focuses itself in a certain body, that body becomes the agent of increased attraction to various elements. As various elements aggregate in a certain body, an element may

— Become a factor of imbalance in the system
— Become a factor of harmony
— Disturb the harmonious development of the other bodies
— Thicken and lose its free function
— Take the lead for all other bodies
— Take the human soul as a captive and control its life

The Teaching says that the personality of man is an equal armed cross, called the "lunar cross," upon which the human soul is crucified.

The task of the human soul is to resurrect himself from that cross through sounding the note of pure light, love, and power and making the four bodies synthesize their notes with his note.[1]

The human soul must be enlightened in such a degree that it balances and purifies the notes of all those four bodies, preventing the accumulation of unneeded elements, and eventually tunes the personality as a musical instrument upon which the resurrected human soul can play his unique songs of light, love, and power.

---

1. The four bodies are physical, etheric, astral, and mental; they are sometimes called "The Square." (author)

As students of the Wisdom, we must try to understand that our actions are notes, our emotions are notes, our words are notes, our thoughts are notes. If these notes are sounded by wrong motive or in negative intentions, they draw corresponding involutionary lives or substances to themselves and make the progress of the human soul very painful and difficult.

Our anger, hate, fear, jealousy, revenge, slander, malice, treason, greed, vanity, egotism are nothing else but negatively polarized, destructive sounds, and they draw destructive elements to the personality. These are the causes of mental, emotional, etheric, and physical diseases.

The duty of the human soul is to purify his vehicles and their notes and free himself from their domination. It is after such a freedom that he can use them and these notes to build an environment which provides all possibilities for him to serve and to be highly creative.

Beyond the personality or beyond the lunar cross we have the higher vehicles which are again fourfold and are called

— Divine
— Monadic
— Atmic
— Intuitional

These vehicles also have their notes, but at such a frequency that the lower lunar vehicles cannot "hear" them unless they are purified, transformed, and spiritualized.

These higher notes manifest as virtues, as energies, and try to impress the human soul that he in fact is connected with the Higher Worlds. These higher notes work through will, purpose, motive, and intention. These are four energies that prepare the human soul and help him to redeem himself from the lower square.

The will energy puts the human soul in contact with the Cosmic Magnet. The purpose energy puts him in contact with the Purpose of our Solar Life. Motive is an accumulated purpose which manifests through that which we call intention.

The Great Teacher says, "Love is essentially a word for the underlying motive of creation. Motive, however, presupposes purpose leading to action, and hence in the group-life task of the incarnating Monad there comes a time when motive (heart and soul) becomes spiritually obsolete because purpose has reached a point of fulfillment and the activity set in motion is such that purpose cannot be arrested or stopped."[2]

Thus we have a fourfold process. We have will, we have purpose, we have motive, we have intentions. Purpose is the dominant note in our solar system; it is the foundation of the Will of the Cosmic Magnet in the Solar Field.

---

2. Alice A. Bailey, *The Rays and the Initiations*, p. 28.

Motive is the translation of the purpose; often it is called the plan. Intention is the actual carrier into actualization of this plan or motive.

The human soul often is forced by the will, purpose, motive, and intentions of the personality, or personality vehicles, and his *note* is not clear.

His purpose is wrong, his plan is wrong, his intention is not in harmony with the pure note of the Higher Spheres. His task is to withdraw himself from the chaotic noise of the lower planes and enter into the pure symphony of the higher spheres.

The human soul in his core has all the seven notes and their octaves — in audible and inaudible ranges.

The human soul creates the body through sound, through the permanent atoms which contain all records of the human deeds, emotions, and thoughts. If in the past life these deeds, emotions, and thoughts were harmful or destructive, they place a dark spot on the permanent atoms and chakras. As the sound is filtered through the permanent atoms and chakras, it loses certain of its notes, and the vehicles are created not as a result of complete notes but by partial notes. The lacking notes in the bodies become the areas of trouble and disease. The state of the permanent atoms and chakras reflect upon our consciousness. The defects appear in the sphere of our consciousness as dark spots.

Actually, if we analyze the speeches of people, we will see how they lack certain notes in their voices. The corresponding body organs that are lacking notes are the trouble spots in the body. These notes can be given artificially to cure the illness and raise the person's consciousness. But, because the sound is both destructive and creative, utmost care must be taken before the use of the sound.

The sound must be used in its destructive as well as its creative octaves: the destructive aspect to destroy viruses, microbes, germs, and so on and, at the same time, the creative aspect to strengthen the healthy cells and atoms in the vehicles.

• CHAPTER 30 •

Reincarnation and Individuality

There are three points about reincarnation:
1. The personality incarnates but the individuality does not.
2. The individuality does not disappear in the whole.
3. The individuality is not lost.

Let us take each of these into consideration.

1. It is true that the personality incarnates as the vehicle of the soul. The soul does not become physical, etheric, and astral bodies but builds them as his communication lines with the corresponding worlds.

2. The individuality does not disappear in the whole. It stays as it is. What would be the result of thousands of

incarnations when at the end all that one is becomes lost in the ocean of existence?

3. The individuality stays forever except when the laws of Nature dissolve him in the chaos. But we do not always have conscious individualities. We develop our individuality life after life.

Until we form our individuality, we identify ourselves — our individuality — with the bodies of our personalities. For a long time, in each incarnation, we are different beings, like a person who thinks he is the actor every time he plays a different role. Until he realizes that he is not the actor but the same person in each act, he cannot develop conscious identity or individuality.

The path of life has many stations. In each station we emerge with a new personality, with a new name, with our goals and duties. But this is an appearance. In reality we are the same person trying to develop our soul — or individuality.

The Monad is not an individuality. It is a Ray. It is universal. The Solar Angel's womb will be impregnated with this Ray and the individuality will form. The Chalice is the womb of the Solar Angel in which the future individuality is formed.

This future individuality is under the supervision of the Solar Angel, Who, life after life, nourishes and guides the human soul until he becomes a conscious individuality.

A conscious individuality is an individualized Ray, an individualized Monad. The human soul does not really incarnate but uses his lower three vehicles to collect experience and reach maturity.

In the Fourth Initiation the soul releases his Solar Angel and exists as a conscious individuality of his own. His Solar Angel can be replaced by an advanced Initiate who begins to lead him further on the path of perfection.

It is further possible that when the human soul reaches a certain degree of evolution — as an individuality or as an emancipated self — he creates illusionary personalities and controls them for certain services in certain places.

Human beings often cannot see that such advanced "individuals" are illusions. They think they are real, and they think they have superhuman power.

Most of such individuals do not die but disappear after their work is done. These are illusionary human beings who render many services otherwise impossible for those who have actual physical bodies.

It is also possible that such advanced, conscious individualities create illusionary persons in the Subtle Worlds who carry to the people of the Other Worlds certain messages from him. It is just like a person talking from a television station, broadcasting his image through many other television sets. Each image of each television set does the same thing, as the real person does in the broadcasting station.

There are many public reports of appearing and disappearing persons all over the world. These stories are not hallucinations but real facts of illusionary individualities.

It is observed that such appearances are frequent in primitive people because they need stimulus to go forward, or they appear in extremely confused places to guide people in the right direction. At the time of crises or cataclysms they appear, if the karma of the people permits. These are not Avatars or incarnations of their Archetypes. But they correspond to those who are born from the minds of Great Spirits.

Sometimes it happens also that a soul, instead of incarnating in a personality, creates a personality in the three worlds, but remains detached from it using it by remote control.

The illusionary personalities not only deliver the message of the real individuality, but also they serve as reporters to the Source. They are built as super computers — physically, emotionally, mentally — and because of a lack of ego, they transmit to the Source exactly what they hear, see, feel, and so on. Thus the Source expands His information and accordingly programs His future illusionary personalities.

Imagine that while watching television, your set reports to the station your mood, your talk, your ideas, and so on. This is what illusionary personalities do, keeping the Source completely informed without distortion of any information.

Sometimes such illusionary personalities move books, articles, and money not for their own use but guided by their Source to meet the needs of various people. They work in both the physical and subtle planes. What happens to the Monad when the human soul is born? The individualized soul is the individualized Monad. This individualized Monad will be called the Self when It reaches the Monadic Plane and stays conscious there. This is how the individuality of the Monad takes place.

The Solar Angels came to earth in the middle of the third Lemurian Race. People were confused about this. The Teaching intentionally did not reveal the mystery of the human soul until the year 1966. People thought that the Solar Angels were us, the human beings, despite many hints in the Teaching. People in the beginning of our chaos were endowed by a Monad. They had Monads even if they did not have a mind. Without Monads they could not exist.

Solar Angels came and indwelled in man as Guides, and, for a long time, it was the Solar Angels which acted as man. The Monad was concealed, and the human soul was in preparation for birth. This information was concealed for a long time.

The reincarnation of human beings and their relationship with lower kingdoms is one of the most interesting subjects. Karma decides the nature of reincarnation, and each reincarnation fulfills part of the karma created in the past.

Often people ask if the lower kingdoms have karma. This is a very intricate question. They are under the karma of the Planetary Logos, and on their level they share that karma.

But taken separately, it is possible to consider the following relationships. We have the mineral kingdom, the vegetable, and animal kingdoms, and the relationship going on between the forms of their kingdoms. Each form in these kingdoms is affected by each other, and by the interaction of man with them. The relation of a mineral and an animal makes the mineral change its composition and nature. Also a form in the vegetable kingdom changes its nature when related to an animal. Similarly an animal changes its nature when related with a member of the human kingdom.

The effects are various in regard to various levels of relationships. For example, if a tree is visited by a Sage who meditates or reads under the tree, the nature of the tree will change. The influence of thoughts and emotions or the physical influence of the Sage will change even the chemical constitution of the tree and further the growth of its essential nature. Similarly, a Sage will influence the evolution of His horse.

Such cause and effect relationships are not called karma until the life form has an individualized form of consciousness. From that moment on all his actions, emotions, and thoughts are in the Cosmic karmic computer.

The Law of Karma exists to bring human beings in harmony with the Law of the Cosmic Magnet.

The Cosmic Magnet symbolically is the source of all principles and laws that lead the manifested Universe to fulfill the Purpose of the One who stands behind the Cosmic Magnet.

Every time we act against the Law of the Cosmic Magnet, we fall into suffering, pain, and into various kinds of problems. Eventually we learn not to repeat those actions which prevent our expansion of consciousness and cause us suffering.

• CHAPTER 31 •

Incarnation of the Monad

The Great Teacher says,

...*the personal self (the lower threefold man) is such that the consciousness of the man occultly "awakens" in the Hall of Learning. For advanced man at this time these incarnations took place upon the moon chain and in some cases upon certain planets connected with the inner round. This is the circumstance which necessitated his "coming-in" during the Atlantean root-race. Men of this type refused to incarnate earlier, as the bodies were too coarse; this was the cyclic reflection (on the lowest plane) of the refusal of the Monads to*

> incarnate at the dawn of manvantaric opportunity.[1]

In the moon chain the devas and pitris prepared the tabernacle into which came the Monads. And these Monads achieved individualization without the help of the Solar Angels, who came in the Fourth Globe, the Fourth Round, in the Third Race. Those people who individualized on the moon — or on another planet — came again in the Atlantean Root Race. They could not come before because the parents could not offer advanced enough bodies for them — the "bodies were too coarse."

> ...The Monad, then, can be traced through the course of its pilgrimage and in its changes of transitory vehicles, only from the incipient stage of the manifested universe.[2]

Man was awakened in the Hall of Learning on the moon. For an advanced man his incarnation took place in the moon chain or upon another planet. These incarnated men "were *Monads*." They had not been visited by Solar Angels to be men. *Men of this type refused to incarnate earlier as the bodies were too coarse.*

> ...The Monad of an animal is as immortal as that of man.[3]

In the Lemurian times the case was different. There were those who were man-animal. They had their

---
1. Alice A. Bailey, *A Treatise on Cosmic Fire*, p. 825.
2. H.P. Blavatsky, *The Secret Doctrine*, Vol. I, p. 623.
3. H.P. Blavatsky, *The Secret Doctrine*, Vol. II, p. 552.

Monads. They needed only to have a mediator to individualize them, putting in them the "I consciousness."

The Master is referring to those Monads who incarnated on the Moon Chain or on other planets. They were not Solar Angels — Initiates of all degrees — but Monads. Referring to Solar Angels, the Tibetan Master says,

> ...*The goal for a man is initiation, or to become a conscious Dhyan Chohan, and in some distant cycle to do for the humanity of that age what the solar Pitris have done for him, and make their self-conscious expression a possibility.*[4]

In *The Secret Doctrine* we read that Solar Pitris embodied the fifth principle (see Vol. I, p. 241). Also we read that They gave consciousness to man (See Vol. I, p. 204).

> ...*Solar Pitris furnish the vehicle for the incarnating Monad, forming the egoic body.*[5]

> ...*Then comes a set time in the life of the planetary Logos wherein His centres become active in a particular manner; this is coincident with the incarnation of the Monads, and their descent into the three worlds [mental, astral, physical-etheric]. A systemic triangle is formed ... and through this setting loose of threefold energy, the work of the solar and*

---

4. Alice A. Bailey, *A Treatise on Cosmic Fire*, p. 836.
5. *Ibid.*, p. 837.

> *lunar Pitris is co-ordinated, and the three permanent atoms are appropriated by the jiva concerned, and appear at the base of the egoic lotus. Individualisation has taken place and the work of at-one-ment is completed; the fourth kingdom in nature is a "fait accompli;" the Monad has clothed itself in material sheaths, and the self conscious unit appears on the physical plane.*[6]

Notice that it is the Monad who in given time incarnates, assumes bodies, and eventually becomes visible by his vestures.

Solar Pitris — Solar Angels — and lunar pitris build the bodies, higher and lower. The Solar Pitris mostly are interested in building the Chalice with Their own substance. Then the three bodies are eventually built.

It is the *jiva* who coordinates three permanent atoms. Jiva is a Sanskrit word. It refers to the Monad who is acting in the bodies. We call it the human soul in the Chalice. It is the humanized Monad.

The *self-conscious unit* is the human soul, an individualized Monad.

The Solar Angel's duties are

1. To build the Chalice from Its substance
2. To plant the Spark of the Monad in the womb of the Chalice

---

6. Alice A. Bailey, *A Treatise on Cosmic Fire*, pp. 768-769.

3. To help with the growth and unfoldment of the petals
4. To watch the Spark in the Chalice so that it grows
5. To keep the sacred link between the Spark and the Monad and help the Spark to interfuse with the Monad
6. To withdraw from the Chalice during the last part of the Third Initiation and the first part of the Fourth Initiation and let the human soul learn to transcend the limitation of the Chalice and be a full grown man — an Arhat
7. To destroy the Chalice with the help of a divine being and with the fire in the Chalice; and to release itself from these obligations, thereby setting the man free

The three bodies of the personality are called lunar bodies. Lunar pitris are magnetically connected with our three bodies, and we unconsciously fall under their influence. Only those whose consciousness is focused in the higher mind, Intuition, or in still higher bodies can escape their influence. The lunar influence then cannot reach them and affect them. Hence the full-moon discipline.

We must remember that as human beings we are working from matter to spirit. There are also those who are trying to come down to matter and be individualized. These people are devas or higher than the devas. They come by building their vehicles from top to bottom. They build their mental vehicle, then astral, then wait for their final coat — their etheric body which will draw eventually the physical body. They have no Solar Angel, but they themselves are from high planes. They come down to learn to be human and gather experience in the three worlds.

As H.P.B said in *The Secret Doctrine*, "... in order to become a divine, fully conscious god — aye, even the highest — the Spiritual Primordial Intelligences must pass through the human stage."[7]

Thus, we have two forms of appearance on earth.

At the individualization of the earth people, Solar Angels came to help connect the Monad to its Spark in the mental plane and to help the Spark grow and unfold, drawing energy from the Monad until the Monad and its "reflections," the Spark, become one. At that time the Solar Angel is finished with Its work with man and departs for Its advanced duties.

> *Where man is concerned these solar Angels, the Agnishvattas, produce the union of the spiritual Triad, or divine Self, and the Quaternary, or lower self.*[8]

What the Master is saying is that Solar Angels, or Agnishvattas, produce the union of the Spiritual Triad with the personality, the quaternary — physical, etheric, astral, and lower mental. That is Their job.

Their job is to bring down a Spark into the monadic current and plant it in the Chalice, thus producing man on

---

7. *The Secret Doctrine*, Vol. I, p. 132.
8. Alice A. Bailey, *A Treatise on Cosmic Fire*, p. 698.

the physical plane. Unless They do that, the Monad will be an abstraction, and a conscious, individualized man will not exist.

We read further, ...*[Those] who gave the manasic principle to man, we must remember that they are the beings who, in earlier manvantaras have achieved, and who — in this round — waited for a specific moment at which to enter, and so continue their work. A parallel case can be seen at the entry — in Atlantean days — of Egos from the moon-chain.*[9]

These three groups are

a. *Those who refused to incarnate.*

b. *Those who implanted the spark of manas [in the animal man].*

c. *Those who took bodies and moulded the type.*

The second group, the intermediate, can be subdivided into two lesser groups:

a. *Those who implant the spark of manas,*

b. *Those who fan and feed the latent flame n the best types of animal man....*[10]

...This fifth Hierarchy of Agnishvattas in their many grades embody the "I principle" and

9. *Ibid.*, pp. 699-700.
10. *Ibid.*, pp. 700-701.

> *are the producers of self-consciousness. ...They enable him to build his own body of causes, to unfold his own egoic lotus, and gradually to free himself from the limitations of the form which he has constructed. ...Through Their work man can become conscious without the manasic vehicle, for manas is but the form through which a higher principle is making itself known.*[11]

Thus it is hinted that They are entities who occupied man to help his evolution. For a while They represented man until he matured and took his destiny in his hands.

The Monad is a Ray from space penetrating Spirit and matter and shining in the lowest plane of matter. It is the weaver of vehicles, after individualization, to climb the ladder of spirit to find Its essence.

All splendid vehicles are built by the Monad. The lower vehicles are masterpieces. The higher mind is a divine computer. The intuitional body is a shining star equipped with powers that are unimaginable. The atmic, monadic, and divine bodies are contact points with planetary, solar, and Cosmic communication, translations, and creativity. But the work of the Monad is not only on the Cosmic Physical Plane. It is also in the Cosmic Astral, Cosmic Mental, Cosmic Intuitional, and so on until It enters into the *Absolute Space*, the source of all, with individuality and universality.

---

11. *Ibid.*, p. 703.

The Monad's progress toward the Absolute is the Path. On this Path, the Monad is responsible for the transmutation of matter in order to prepare higher and more splendid matter in which to descend and ascend. Every Monad is a bestower of light, love, and power to the Universe.

The battle of the Monad in all these planes and levels with imaginable and unimaginable enemies is fierce. On each step It must destroy the limitation of matter, conquer the personifications of matter, and enter into the sphere of freedom to renew Its fight with more terrible forces of matter and with the formulation of these forces by the power of the human mind.

The refined substance the Monad creates on Its journey toward the Cosmic Magnet is the emanation and the remains of Its subtle vehicles, charged with Its wisdom and power, to be a blessing for those who will follow.

• CHAPTER 32 •

Past Lives

Various methods are used to make people remember their past lives.

Where are the events of past lives recorded? According to the Ageless Wisdom the best moments and attainments of past lives are recorded in the Chalice.[1] Also, our permanent atoms[2] are computerized by past lives, containing in symbolic ciphers the past life records. These recordings do not interpret themselves as events but are causes of future lives, as frequencies which control the building of our personality bodies.

The whole recording of our past lives is found in the Akasha.[3] Part of these records are in the subconscious mind

---

1. See *The Subconscious Mind and the Chalice.*
2. See *The Science of Becoming Oneself*, Ch. 12, "The Chalice and the Seeds."
3. See *Other Worlds*, Ch. 31, "Akasha."

in a very scrambled form. Akashic Records can be drawn down into the astral plane, but the astral plane is such a mess that any drop of reality that falls into this plane turns into kaleidoscopic phenomena, ever changing and fantasmagoric.

Past lives can be recorded by our consciousness when our consciousness can contact the astral plane. This happens very rarely, when our Solar Angel permits it for a special reason to help the individual in a serious problem or for his future striving. But such a revelation generally is very segmentary, and it may contain one or two short events of a past life.

It is also possible that our Master can stretch our consciousness to penetrate the Chalice and see a special event belonging in a past life or to recollect a few records in the mental unit or even from our subconscious mind.

In very rare occasions, a Master makes a person subjectively and temporarily clairvoyant to see a segment of his past life in the Akashic Records.

Some methods are used by psychics, mediums, and hypnotists to make a person see his "past life." But such revelations can have drastic consequences in the lives of the person involved.

Nature covers past lives for many reasons:

1. It prevents occupying a person with the past but instead enables him to forge toward the future, without being directly influenced by past events, relationships, and failures or defeats or victories.

2. It prevents the opening of sources of information that often cannot be stopped, thus making a person live in the past and forget about his present duties, responsibilities, and problems. Past events can even explode in the mind of the person with tremendous tension, which sometimes releases him or sometimes leads him to asylums.

3. An Akashic Record contains hundreds of lives which may suddenly reach an individual and devastate his life with tremendous confusion, burning his sanity and balance.

4. Subconscious trash can surface, leading a person into total imbalance.

5. Such revelations can bring back the experiences of the past in such a reality that the person loses his present opportunity to live a new life.

Most of the forced revelations of past lives, fortunately, are unreal. They are the result of the imagination or the result of a projection of a medium, psychic, or hypnotist.

But this unreality may be accepted by a person as a reality which gradually orchestrates a life built upon unreality. In such a life, present seeds of many talents and opportunities are lost, and the person tries to obtain goals which are not planned for this life. This way the program put in this present incarnation is disturbed and mixed with an artificial program. The result is that the person is slowly led to insanity or various physical, emotional, and mental disorders.

If you play two video tapes on the screen of your television at the same time, you can imagine what happens. The same thing happens when a pseudo past life film is mixed with the events of the present life in the same brain.

In order to stop the evolution of some advancing disciples, the dark forces attract and release certain past events from the subconscious minds of other people to make them believe that they are experiencing a past life. They can even show a video of events from the astral plane of a person who has nothing to do with him, but if he believes that the video tape is his past life he identifies with it and slowly lives under its control or enters into a desperate confusion. Visit asylums and you will see hundreds of such people who speak about their past lives or events that occurred in the past.

Some people make good money or gain high reputation by making people artificially see their past lives. But eventually they pay a heavy price for it.

We are told that a Master of Wisdom accidently saw the Akashic Records of a person. He immediately turned His face and averted His eyes so as not to see them. In writing about it, He further stated that even a Sixth Degree Initiate has no right to be involved with the past lives of other people, unless He has special permission for some important responsibility. But, at the present, many mediums are occupied with knowing and reading the past lives of others.

When your consciousness reaches a certain degree of expansion, Nature will allow you, under the guidance of your Solar Angel, to see certain segments of your past life.

In the Subtle World, it is even forbidden to be occupied with your past life so that you forge ahead to the future.

You can read how Buddha and Christ handled the problem of past lives. Christ and Buddha had enough psychic energy and ability to reveal the past lives of Their disciples or followers, but They related to Their followers in a way that affirmed the Law of Reincarnation, without making them stimulated or crazy for their individual past lives.

I assume that many of Their disciples had revelations of their past lives, but you do not find any record about them in their writings. But there are those at the present who present themselves as Jesus, as Saint John, even as Buddha, Cleopatra, Napoleon, Gesar Kahn, and even Einstein, without even having nuts in their brain.

I met a woman who, after going through past life exercises, suddenly proclaimed she was Moses, and she began to force people to believe her. Unfortunately, she devastated her family and ended in an institution.

It is a possibility that one can have some revelation about the past lives of his friends, children, or parents in a degree that solves a dark problem in his mind. Such revelations are possible, and the sign that they are given is that such a person never talks about it and keeps silence.

The Ageless Wisdom never encourages people to practice certain methods to dig up the events of past lives of people.

It is known also that some entities who possess people can reveal certain events of the life of the individuals they possess in order to make them a more obedient slave or to lead them into activities that prevent them from reaching sanity.

Some of our dreams and imaginations issue from past lives. The natural laws often release the unconscious pressure on the psyche of man by releasing pressure through dreams and imagination.

Some writers exhaust this pressure by writing stories and novels from their past lives, and they think that their creativity is the result of their artistic imagination. Of course, with the imagined events of past lives are also mixed fabricated events. These fabricated events can be related to the events of past lives of other people with whom the writer was related.

Some people, due to their excited imagination, create certain fabricated dreams, actors, and heroes. Ten, fifteen years later they dream or see in a vision their own former imagination, thinking that they are seeing their past lives.

Sometimes our fabricated imagination takes ten to forty years to legalize itself and reveal itself as events of our past lives. Even it is possible that we play out the imaginations of others as our past life events when psychic energy is weakened in our system.

The Teaching says that even some very rare chemical combinations make a man see a past event, but immediately when the chemistry changes, the person loses his ability to see.

To see consciously the past lives and use them for our further progress we must be a Fourth Degree Initiate. People start using their power of seeing past lives after they take the Third Initiation. At the Third Initiation a person has a direct access to the Chalice. His glamors and illusions have vanished and his subconsciousness is totally dry. In such a situation he has complete power of balance for any past life revelation.

Advanced spirits can benefit from their past lives if they are naturally revealed to them. They can review them and see the causes of their achievements and defeats. But for average people the revelation of past lives acts as a brake and bewilderment. Confusion sets into their life, pulling them back to the measures of past centuries.

Artificial revelation of past lives is a violation of the nature of the people. It is also possible for mediums, psychics, or hypnotists who are trying to reveal the past lives of people to be obsessed by the events of these past lives and connect themselves with their illusions, dreams, imaginations, or partial revelations. They create a heavy karma when they make people believe that which is not true. They mislead people by giving them the confidence that what they see is true.

Those who involve themselves in their past lives, whether true or false, can be obsessed by the events of these past lives. They often develop jealousy, revenge, hatred, or close ties with persons they think were associated with them in their past lives. Sometimes, they literally try to find such persons in order to take revenge or continue certain friendship with them.

I remember a woman whose life was ruined when she "found out" that her present husband murdered her in the past. From that date on the whole atmosphere of the family changed. She was continuously in fear and was cold toward her husband. He could not understand the cause of her actions. Eventually they were divorced. The children had a very hard time and the man, who was a very good and providing husband, died in misery.

Later the wife began to hate her three children because they were the children of a man who murdered her in the past.

An illusion of a past event can cause a drastic change in a relationship, especially if it is untrue and associated with past experiences of fear, anger, and crimes.

Most people try to identify their past enemies with the present people around them, making them their victims.

When the consciousness is ready, past lives slowly reveal themselves naturally in order to give a chance to a person to solve problems that were neglected in the past or to see the causes of present complications in his life.

When people have problems with each other, they can solve them through their reason and logic, tolerance, forgiveness, and the wisdom that they now have in their hands.

Searching past wounds in the light of modern days does not heal them but makes people continue to feel the pain and live in the pain of the past.

Many people discover their past imaginations as if they were their past incarnations. People imagine themselves in various positions and personalities. Some imaginations can go and enter into their subconscious mind or memory banks. Later they dream of their own imagination, mixing it with other associations, and then they have a "past life."

We must not think that such "past lives" are all imagination. They can be also true, or a certain percent true.

If such "past lives" are not real, then the person builds his present and future relationship upon an unreality, upon the imagination, which he will be forced to eliminate if he wants to proceed on the way to Reality. You can see how guilty those who build an imaginary "past life" within certain people can be.

The Great Sage says, "...We touch past incarnations only in cases of necessity, in order not to evoke the emanations of the past from Akasha."[4]

"Certain people remember the details of a definite epoch; when they dream of being a well-known person,

---

4. Agni Yoga Society, *Agni Yoga,* para. 230.

their remembrance of the dream molds the imagining of an incarnation. The resulting error is in the person, but not in the epoch. A child imagines himself a field marshal, and such a representation already sinks into his Chalice.[5]

"Only people with especially broadened consciousnesses can delve into the past without harm to their advancement. For a small consciousness, a glance backwards may be ruinous."[6]

It must be clear that no one is against knowing *one's own* past life. This is not the argument, but the argument is this:

1. No one must force another person, by using various means, to discover his past lives or to hallucinate about them.
2. No one must tell others about their past lives — as if he knew the facts of others' past lives.
3. No one must encourage people to investigate their past lives.

The reasons for this are as follows:

1. Any premature opening of the veil concerning past lives will have a very negative effect on the subject, and it may even lead him to astral and mental imbalance.

---

5. Agni Yoga Society, *Aum*, para. 491.
6. *Ibid.*, para. 535.

2. Those who think they know the past lives of others may be completely wrong about their assumption and mislead others into accepting their lies.

3. The only knowers of the past lives of others are Seers or Masters who are not interested in our past lives except if we are voluntary entering into the path of discipleship and initiation. In most cases, even They do not reveal our past lives to us but use our past lives to make decisions about us.

4. It is possible that certain people with various techniques can stimulate etheric vision or astral vision in us to see certain events. But these visions do not carry valid proof that one is seeing his past life. The probability is that he is picking up a station of events, identifying himself with the events, and misleading himself.

5. It is also possible that to sidetrack promising people from their right path, the dark forces show them fabricated or even real past lives which will totally upset their present life or create complicated problems in their relationships.

6. Teachers encourage us to strive toward the future. Every look at a past life definitely hinders our path toward the future.

Even our present life must be inspired by the future, not by the past. Our visions of the future, our aspirations, our contacts must control our present life — not the past.

When man is ripe enough, for certain reasons, Nature reveals certain events from the past. These are those moments of his past that can assist him to separate himself from the past or totally sever his relationship from past illusions, glamors, and crystallizations. If the person is not ready, any relation with the past pulls him into the problems of the past.

Nature guards the privacy of the past, and the Karmic Lords deal severely with those who knowingly or unknowingly mislead people or push them toward past lives.

We also have many dreams about other people and assume that our dreams are about their real past lives. Most probably our dreams are symbolic, not factual events, of the lives of others. Such a symbolic dream is set up by your Solar Angel (in your unconscious or conscious mind) in order to solve a problem with your friends.

You, as an individual, have no right to know the past lives of people before a certain major Initiation. Your Soul does not violate that law but orchestrates dreams in which the Soul helps you to have certain insights about other people.

In certain very rare occasions your Soul reveals certain events about the life of a friend for a very specific reason: when your Soul realizes that the secret will remain with you — only.

In some cases when the privacy of relations are violated, the Law of Karma severely reacts.

Of course, Initiates of high degrees live in the eternal presence, and They know all about each other. Such an elevated state of consciousness lives in the future. Despite the ability to see all the past, an Initiate's knowledge of the past neither builds a thoughtform about another, nor makes impressions on him to draw his attention to the past.

Great Ones are not occupied by the past because in all Their adventures toward the future They see reflections of the past.

You can see in the life of your friend those lines of influence which are from the past — negative or positive — and you encourage him to develop those energy lines which help him to proceed toward the future.

To see the past in the future is a totally different approach than to see the past in past lives.

The Great Sage says,

One must thoroughly realize the future. Labor does not end in the works already predestined, but continues endlessly.

Reaching toward Infinity is the most beautiful striving.[7]

---

7. Agni Yoga Society, *Agni Yoga,* para. 493.

• CHAPTER 33 •

Resurrection

In learning a given Teaching, knowledge misleads us unless we experiment with that knowledge. We must try to experiment with what we learn. Knowledge is like eating food. If a person fills his mental stomach with food and does not digest it, it will cause him trouble. The same is true of wisdom; we must understand the technical side of wisdom, which is knowledge, and try to experiment with it as much as possible.

For example, if you experiment with only one percent of your knowledge, your knowledge has greater value. That one percent of experimentation has more value than all of your knowledge combined because it is knowledge obtained through experience.

The whole world is suffering because of theories that are not applied. The same is true of the Teaching of resurrection. We must apply the idea of resurrection in our lives as much as we can. Every day we must strive to penetrate a little more deeply into the meaning of resurrection, and we can do this only through experimentation. We must work upon ourselves. If a person does not work upon himself, he can collect a lot of information and never proceed on the path of evolution. He will be a nice puppet or, as the parable says, he will adorn himself with peacock feathers and look very pretty — until a gust of wind comes and blows all the feathers away.

Experimentation leads to realization or actualization. You will be able to say to yourself before you die that you really know what resurrection is if you enter death without fear. There are a lot of techniques which help us realize or actualize resurrection. It is not going to be a theory, but we are going to understand it in actuality, step-by-step.

There is an idea that in resurrection a person is immediately taken away into heaven. But is this really resurrection? It may be part of it, but resurrection begins when the Spirit in a mineral atom passes into the vegetable kingdom. When that atom passes to the vegetable kingdom and becomes a fragrance-giving flower, it progresses. This process continues throughout Nature, until the atom becomes a human being.

In the human being the Spirit, the Self, is initially stuck to the physical body. A person is stuck to his body like an oyster is stuck to its shell; he cannot rid himself of it. Eventually he must detach from that shell. Unless a person has the experience that he is not the shell, all his wisdom and knowledge are worthless; all his prettiness, books, libraries, astrology, psychology, physics, and chemistry become nonsense because they do not pass through the doors of death.

Self-actualized people pass through the doors of death. That part of a person which has become immortal will penetrate through those doors. It is this part on which we must work. Our amusements, pleasures, and joys in this world are very beautiful indeed, but they are not of prime importance. The path of resurrection is of prime importance.

The path of resurrection extends from the atom to the Solar Logos. We are walking that path, whether we like it or not. Eventually, every person is going to resurrect himself. If he is late on his path or fooling around on his path, he will increase his own misery and pain in the same proportion. If he wants to be on time, in tune with the cycles and rhythms of Nature, he will work to resurrect himself.

Imagination and visualization have been given to us by Nature to prepare us for actualization. We visualize, we imagine; then we create. Without visualization and imagination, we cannot create. This means that we must first expand our consciousness; consciousness then affects matter, molding matter to fit the design of our imagination. In other words, whatever a person thinks, he is.

To experiment with this process, the following visualization exercise is given, which is very healing:

Exercise

1. Close your eyes and relax your face and body. Release all tension.
2. Say the following mantram:
   > *More radiant than the sun,*
   > *Purer than the snow,*
   > *Subtler than the ether,*
   > *Is the Self,*
   > *the Spirit within my heart.*
   > *I am that Self;*
   > *that Self am I.*

As you repeat this mantram, visualize that you are more radiant than the sun. Visualize that your Inner Self is so radiant. You may start seeing a little spark in your head after this process. Visualize that you are in the sun. When you put yourself in the sun, see that your radiance is greater than that of the sun. One minute of the psychic energy which comes to you during this visualization can purify your whole aura and body.

See yourself purer than the snow. No matter what you have done, what you have thought or felt, all will evaporate in the sun. In essence, you are purer than the snow. Do not admit any feelings of guilt.

See how subtle you are, just like an electrical wave. You are more subtle than the ether, faster than light. All of this is the Self within your heart. Do not visualize the physical heart. See a Lotus six inches behind your back. Within that Lotus, see a shining Spark, a diamond; this is the Self. Identify with that Spark, with that Self. You are that Spark. Forget your other bodies.

3. Place the Lotus containing the Spark on top of the highest mountain, and visualize yourself shining on that mountaintop. Millions of miles away, your light can be seen like a beacon.

4. Slowly open your eyes to complete the exercise.

Visualization and creative imagination are beyond the mind. The mind cannot conceive the value of visualization because visualization is the ability to translate Cosmic realities that are beyond the mind. Visualization is, in a sense, a sense.

Some people have a sensation of pain when they use this exercise. This means that impurities are being thrown out and the person is becoming purified.

The personality will still try to pull you back to the former state of consciousness; it is a fight between Spirit and matter. You are on the verge of detaching yourself from past personality attachments, glamors, illusions, past karma, deeds, and thoughts while in the meantime you are feeling the Self. The physical, emotional, and mental bodies are the grave of the Spirit.

A single eye, or a gland in the body, can be more pure or sensitive than the others. The other eye or glands are less sensitive due to pollution, certain experiences, attacks, or accidents over the centuries. For example, if you had an accident ten million years ago and lost your hearing, there is a blockage there. You need slowly to wash this away. The best way to do this is to concentrate in the True Self. From that point you can clean whatever needs to be cleaned.

During this exercise if you feel as if something is touching your hair like a wave, it means that your head center is slowly opening and receiving energy. **Do not work on specific centers; instead, expand your consciousness and become the True Self. The flowers of the chakras will take care of themselves as we do this. If we force our chakras, we create a tremendous reaction which attacks our bodies, glands, and aura.**

A person will experience to the degree that he is. We cannot give him a pill and take him to the astral or mental plane; such pills are disastrous. Through doing visualization exercises, one can slowly make a breakthrough. One little breakthrough on the path of resurrection is worth three hundred incarnations.

Do not think so much about the effects on the bodies. Think of the Self. Who cares what we did for millions of years? We are going to become spiritual millionaires and pay our past debts. To be a spiritual millionaire means to be the radioactive Self. Only then can we purify ourselves and pay our debts. We are not going to be stuck with them and hinder the path of resurrection.

The Self reflects Itself in the head, with the mind or brain, and then identifies with the mind or brain. The Self thinks It is the brain, the mind, so It starts to think. But It is not the brain or the mind. We must make this distinction. The brain and the mind are like a television set, a radio, or a machine that we use.

The secret to resurrection is that we must realize that we are not the form. A person puts on so much make-up and looks at himself in the mirror, saying, "Aren't I beautiful? Look at my beauty; look how beautiful I am." Suddenly he identifies with his body. When he does this, he cremates himself. After sixty years of looking in the mirror and saying, "I am that," he becomes stuck and identified with the image, the form. He becomes his nose; then it takes him six thousand years to detach from that nose.

Our entire civilization, our advertising propaganda, schools, universities, and colleges are trying day and night to make us turn our backs on the path of resurrection and become our bodies. This is the curse under which we are working. We must eventually come to the realization that all we are seeing is unreal. This is what happened to the prodigal son.

Christ worked for the path of resurrection. The greatest plan of Christ was to establish and build the path of resurrection, nothing else. He told us the story of the prodigal son, who said, "Good-bye," to his father, to become a "thief" — the densest matter. One day he awakened and said, "What am I doing here? My father is so beautiful. Let me return to him." At this point, the path of resurrection begins. Of course, along this path we sometimes are distracted, or we reflect on the crazy things we did. When we reach the top of the mountain, we will see how many people we destroyed. The path is very difficult.

People are joyful in killing their enemies, but in esoteric science there is no enemy; there is only the Self. We need life, not killing. It is very healthy to experience coming back to the unreal world, realizing that it is unreal. One little touch of this puts a seed in our consciousness which grows. But one must experience that he is living in an unreal world before he wants to return to the real world.

This is very difficult because the body has its own dramas and tragedies. The emotional body has its phantasmagoria; the mind has its own labyrinth. The phantasmagoria is that we create so many imaginative things that we are caught in their network; no matter which way we go, we are caught by this big octopus. The mind has a labyrinth which we enter from one door and after traveling through a myriad of corridors find that we are totally lost and do not know where the door is.

It is not easy to find our way through all of this mess. The moment we begin to try, our friends, our boss, our lover, our own emotions, thoughts, and actions come into play. Any time a person begins the path of resurrection, he awakens antagonism from matter. But we must be courageous and conquer the world.

We experience karma when we are identified with our bodies. That is why it is important not to be lazy and begin working on our meditation and studies. When the Spirit is identified with the body, it is shocked, it is dead. Billions of people are nothing more than corpses. We think that we are alive, but we must return home through resurrection. Whenever a difficulty arises on our path, we must say, "This belongs to matter; I am going to conquer." One inch of progress is worth three hundred lives.

There are seven Rays in the Spark which radiate the colors of the rainbow. In *The Psyche and Psychism*, it says that man is a little Spark which radiates seven colors, seven powers, and so on. When we have an experience at this level, we are registering our own transformation. Awareness of our transformation is our experience. It is the Self that registers transformation. A great Sage tells us that just as it is difficult to watch and record the growth of a blade of grass, it is as difficult to see our own expansion. It is a slow and beautiful process. You cut the grass one day, and the next day it is so tall. When did it grow? We grow in the same way, subtly, but very beautifully. It is most important to take action toward that great goal.

If the religious teachings of the world begin to emphasize the resurrection of the Spirit in mankind, it will result in the growth of those religions. Emphasis should be placed upon the livingness of the Christ-nature in every human being. Using will to bring forth the living transfiguration of the lower nature will be proof of the risen Christ.

Resurrection is the radiant way, the lighted way which lives from one great expansion of divinity in man to another. It is a way which expresses the light of intelligence, the radiance and substance of true love, and inflexible will which permits no defeat or withdrawal —intelligence, love, and will. Defeat comes from matter; will does not recognize any defeat because will is from Spirit. We must not be defeated by our material side.

The Spirit of Resurrection is an extra-planetary Being, a member of the Council Chamber of Shamballa. He is a chosen Emissary Who carries healing in His wings, Who carries life-giving energy which contradicts death. This vision gives incentive to life; it gives us a vision of home which can restore all nations.

In 1945, it was the duty of the Spirit of Resurrection to create an urge in humanity toward resurrection. From that date until now, we can see an awakened interest in spiritual matters. Millions of little groups have formed, searching for answers. The whole planet is stirring in order to resurrect toward that great vision.

The moment that Spirit started to work for resurrection, the black lodge[1] sent millions of its agents to halt any progress. The first attempt it made was drug use. This trapped many people. Then it introduced acid music, rock 'n' roll, forms of jazz, and so on. But the Spirit of Resurrection was not defeated. He is still pumping an urge for betterment into humanity.

---

1. See *Battling Dark Forces, A Guide to Psychic Self-Defense*.

In speaking about resurrection, the Great Teacher says:

> ...*The Spirit of Resurrection will intensify, and is already making its presence felt. More and more people are beginning to be forward-looking and to hope with greater conviction and courage for a better world set-up; their hitherto wishful thinking and their emotional desire are slowly giving place to a more practical attitude; their clear thinking and their fixed determination are far more active and their plans better laid because both their thinking and their planning are today based on facts; they are also beginning to recognise those factors and conditions which must not be restored, and this is a point of major importance.*[2]

Resurrection from two things, materialism and selfishness, is the goal of the Hierarchy. We must have resurrection to rid ourselves of materialism, but there is another pitfall, which is selfishness. As long as a person is selfish, he is an obstacle on the path of resurrection. We must defeat these two enemies. The Hierarchy works with all Its disciples to create that consciousness within humanity which will lead it out of materialism and selfishness. Those who want to be resurrected are going to be co-workers with the Plan of the Hierarchy.

---

2. Alice A. Bailey, *The Externalisation of the Hierarchy*, p. 459.

Each initiation is a greater step and advancement toward resurrection. The first initiation is a great advancement on the path of resurrection; this is the moment a person feels he is the Spark and not the body.

As a consequence of this awareness and consciousness, a person begins to purify himself and, when he does so, he takes the second initiation. First he establishes the foundation that he is the Spark. Immediately thereafter, he has a center, a core, a goal or destination. After determining the destination, he tries to purify his vehicles and make them ready to walk the path of resurrection. In the Teaching, it is said that the second initiation is basically the purification of the emotional body, but it is more accurately a purification of all three vehicles — physical, emotional, and mental.

The Third Initiation is when the mind is impressed to such a degree that it is capable of translating the Spark. The person cultivates his mind to such a refined state of matter and vibration, that it realizes the Spark. The Spark then begins to shine through his mind. Because the bodies are purified, the Spark also shines through the emotional body, but It is anchored in mental understanding when a person consciously, mentally, and intelligently realizes that the Spark is present. It is the Spark which is now able to reflect on the mental plane, affirming the translation that the mind makes confirming the existence of the Spark. It is not the mind that is thinking; the mind is becoming aware. The Self is reflected in the waters of the mind. When a person completely mentally translates the stage of development achieved through the mind, through the Self that is transfiguration. He can now see his true face in the mirror of the mind.

When a person sees his face in the mirror of his mind, he has achieved the Third Initiation. Through the mind he is now able to translate that kind of achievement and experience. When the mind grasps and does not create any hindrance to reflect that Spark, when it translates, explains, and convinces, it is the True Self that it is convincing.

The mirror convinces the person that he is seeing his face. If the mirror is broken, it cannot convince a person of his reflection. The mental body, the mental consciousness must reflect Sparkhood, Selfhood, the beauty that the person is. When the mirror has reached a high degree of refinement in which the real beauty of the person can be reflected, that person is a Third Degree Initiate because he now mentally realizes that he is the Self. In the physical body, he dreamed about this and was shocked. In the emotional body, he felt it. In the mental body, he knows it.

In the Fourth Initiation, the Spark dedicates Itself for the service of One Humanity. All cleavages are counterproductive; they are all glamors and illusions. There is only one value: to dedicate to the service of humanity. This is not a dream or a plan at this stage; it is an actualization. It is the practical application of the Self in world affairs. It is practical application of the consciousness of the Self in daily relationships. Whatever a person thinks, feels, or does is inspired by the Self for the service of the One Life.

In the Fifth Initiation, the Initiate hears the voice of Sirius, and he returns the call Home. His path of resurrection is totally intensified because he sees his destination. His responsibilities increase a thousand times.

In the Sixth Initiation, he sees the glory of the Self in the Atmic Plane. He sees what a beautiful genius he is, what a glorious being he is, that he has the capability of traveling ten thousand miles in one second.

In the Seventh Initiation, the person leaves the Monadic Plane behind, and with it the entire Cosmic Physical Plane to become a traveler of the Cosmic Astral Plane.

This process of initiation is the path of resurrection. It is not going to the tomb and seeing that Christ has risen; that is the easy part. Ask Christ how He worked for billions of years before this, how He dreamed of resurrection at the beginning and then eventually attained it.

We celebrate Easter and other religious events, and then the moment we leave the church, we return to our old destructive ways. Of course, it is good to celebrate and recognize these events because it directs our minds toward these ideas. But it is also necessary to take intense action not to know so much about resurrection but to be actually resurrected human beings.

We can accomplish this in various ways. From the first sensation of temptation, we must resist it. When a person feels that the body, emotions, and mind are trapping him, he must resist this because he cannot resurrect himself if he is trapped. He must strive toward the highest sublimation at work, in his personal relationships, with his body, emotions, mind, ideas, and determination. When anything is activated in his life against resurrection, from the first moment of this awareness a person must be on guard. This is how the door of initiation and resurrection opens. We are the key to the door; we must turn ourself and open the door.

The first step begins when you open your eyes in the morning. Begin the day with something positive and beautiful. Make plans to finish something unfinished, or plan to help someone. Then when you arrive at work, be on guard against the thousands of "flies" that will come to distract you.

When an argument or tension begins, do not allow yourself to be caught in that trap. Remember that you are resurrected Spirit. By applying these ideas, step by step, you will gradually resurrect yourself. By not being drawn into an argument, the smallest argument even, this becomes a door leading you toward resurrection. The secret to resurrection is hidden within the argument, if you can conquer it.

The second step in daily life is to resist any pull to identify with your bodies. If you are sick, do not say, "I am sick." Say, "My body is feeling a little crazy." Do not identify with it.

By applying these ideas to our daily life in a practical way, we break the identification with the bodies and take a step on the path of resurrection. The octopus of matter has millions of arms, and we are in its grasp. But we can break its hold. Resurrection is like a beautiful rain. Look how the flowers are resurrected after the rain. Wisdom is the rain of resurrection. We must bloom like the flowers.

The most tense point of identification occurs the moment a person says, "I can't." This is the moment when one must help himself.

One day a disciple asked his Master, "Why don't You ever appear to me?" to which the Master replied, "Why should I appear to you? You have not even learned your ABCs yet; what can I talk to you about?" Imagine if you walked into your kitchen and saw your Master sitting there. What would you say to Him; what would He be able to say to you? Have you conquered yourself? Did you pass the test?

Our current-day theologians and philosophers often translate renunciation in a painful way, saying that it is sad and miserable, or they do not mention it at all. They are ashamed to talk about it because they feel that people would think they were ridiculous. Only Descartes mentioned it in half a sentence. Renunciation is the process of increasing joy because the person becomes more Spirit and less matter. The Great Sage says, "Traveler, My companion, as we climb to the mountaintop, rid yourself of the burdens you carry on your shoulders." If we do not do this, how can we climb to the summit?

We do just the opposite; we continually load ourselves. The moment a person realizes that he must climb, does he put the load down, or does he begin to cry, "My chair, my girlfriend, my boyfriend, my money"? If he wants to keep his burdens, let him sit down with them and stay; he has lots of time to pass there. But when is he going to climb? He may try to climb with a chair on his head, his sofa on his back, and two or three buckets of money hanging from his tail. If his Master asks him why he is carrying all this excess luggage, he will reply, "I need them."

If we do not learn to renounce, all that we have will be taken from us. It is not a matter of prophecy but a matter of accounting. Our property does not belong to us; our money does not belong to us. The Hierarchy will teach us the lesson that we are stuck to matter and say, "Come on, child; walk."

The moment you become aware that something is hindering your path toward resurrection, put a stop to it. This will save you millions of dollars and energy because every burden saps your energy. There is only one burden of the heart which does not sap energy; that is the burden of responsibility, which really makes you greater and greater.

Religious and spiritual traditions throughout all ages have mentioned resurrection. In seeing that the religions of other countries contained ideas about resurrection certain early Christian fathers accused them of speaking to Satan because there was, in their opinion, no resurrection except Christian resurrection. Who said so? God has many children. There were thousands of resurrected beings before Christ was born. Christ was the first from the human family to be resurrected; that is why He is sometimes referred to as the "only resurrected one" in Shamballa.

For example, tradition says that "Krishna rose from the dead," that He did not die, and He existed thousands of years before Christ. A great light enveloped the earth and illuminated the whole expanse of the heavens; it was through this light that Krishna ascended to His native skies. We also have records that an incarnation of Vishnu ascended into heaven, resuming His Divine Essence. Why should we ignore these traditions? On the contrary, these resurrection stories give credence to the resurrection of Christ.

When Armenia became Christian in 324 A.D., a zealous man became the pope in Armenia. For five months, he burned all the previously-existing temples and all their manuscripts, holy scriptures, and treasures because he thought the only scripture was the Bible. God gave many Teachings before the Bible; why burn them? Through this action, we lost a great source of tradition and history.

God's seeds are everywhere. It is crazy to say to one mountain, "Give the only flower." Go to the Himalayas and see what mountains are. The foundation of tolerance and acceptance grows in God's garden.

Tradition says that Lord Buddha was placed in a coffin prior to His cremation, but when the coffin was opened, He was not there. Zoroaster ascended to heaven, after which He was called the "Living Star." He was a powerful, fiery man who brought us the worship of celestial fire, as symbolized by natural fire.

Apolonius was a Greek sage, and tradition says he rose from the dead. They were carrying his body and he spoke to them from his coffin, asking them what they were doing. They all escaped and he walked away.

The resurrection of Adonis was celebrated at Alexandria with the utmost display. His image was carried with great solemnity to a tomb where he was given his last honors. Before singing his return to life, there were mournful rites performed in honor of his suffering and death. The large wound he had received was shown, just as the wound made by the thrust of a sword in the side of Christ was shown. The feast of the resurrection of Adonis was celebrated on March 25th.[3]

Lao Kiun, the virgin-born, ascended bodily into the paradise above when his mission of benevolence was completed on earth. Since that time he has been worshipped as a god.[4]

Zoroaster, the founder of the religion of the ancient Persians, who was considered "a divine messenger sent to redeem men from their evil ways," ascended to heaven at the end of his earthly career. To this day, his followers mention him with the greatest reverence, calling him the "Immortal Zoroaster."[5]

---

3. Dupuls: *Origin of Religious Beliefs*, p. 161.
4. See *Progressive Religious Ideas*, Vol. I, p.72.
5. See *Bible Myths*, by T. W. Doane.

There are many such Great Ones, such as Aesculaphius, Adonis, Horus, Atys, Bacchus, Hercules, Memnow, Baldur, Quetzalcoatle, and many others who were virgin born and resurrected to heaven.

These resurrection stories were accounts written thousands of years before Christ. In Alexandria, the Syrians and Arabs of the time worshipped Adonis by carrying his image with great solemnity in a procession to a tomb. The same custom is carried out in Greece and Rome today in many little villages. They observe this also in some parts of Russia.

• CHAPTER 34 •

Healing Through Approach

In life, people always meet with various resistances: resistance from the weather, from psychic elements such as thoughts, emotions, vibrations, and so on. There is a way to meet such resistances, and it is called *approach*. We approach the Almighty Presence with our heart and spirit so that He helps us perform our tasks, duties, responsibilities, and creative work and helps us overcome our obstacles.

When we initiate a creative work or any labor that is very creative and beautiful, when we make a great decision, or when we encounter danger or rejection from people in our environment, we can use the method of approach, rejecting the opposition and conflicts around ourselves. Whenever we begin a project, we see that there are many obstacles in our mind, in our heart, emotions, and aura. But we can pave the way for creative thinking, blissful and joyful feelings, and successful activities through the method of approach.

Our main obstacle is harmfulness; we hurt others. Whenever we hurt someone — their feelings, their body, mind, spirit, evolution — we create a barrier in our soul, just like closing the windows to sunshine.

The second obstacle is not forgiving others when they hurt us. When we are wounded, any intentions, directions, or inspirations coming from the Soul are distorted. A hurt feeling is a wound in the aura, in the soul. When any impression comes, either from the outside or from the inside, from the Higher Self, that wound creates static which prevents clear reception, impression, inspiration, and response. This is why great Masters tell us to clear up such matters before we begin any new endeavor. To clear these matters up is called "approach."

Approach is also repentance and renunciation. What is it we must approach? We must approach the creative forces in Nature. Once a person learns this secret, he will see how successful his life will become, how happy he will be.

Exercise

There is a very ancient ceremony which teaches us to approach. This ceremony only takes two or three minutes to perform and is very beneficial if performed prior to making any major decision or beginning a new service project.

1. Kneel, holding the spine erect, and raise your hands. Notice how this makes you feel as if you are tuned in, as if something is going through your spine and head. Kneeling in this fashions opens the avenue to approach. Raising your hands symbolizes renunciation.

2. Close your eyes and feel the presence of God, a Master, Christ, your Solar Angel — any holy one that you want.

3. Begin by apologizing for any wrongs you have committed. By ridding yourself of this accumulated negativity in your subconscious and aura, you approach Divinity — Light, Love, and Power; you approach the beauty that is within you and without you.

4. Renounce by repeating:

> *My Lord, with all my heart,*
> *I forgive every person who has hurt me*
> *with his thoughts, words, or deeds.*
> *May the blessings of my heart reach him.*
> *I forgive him.*

5. Send your blessings to those who have hurt you. Then repeat:

> *My Lord, I feel deeply sorry*
> *for those I have hurt*

with my thoughts, words, and deeds.
May Your blessings heal them,
enlighten, and lead them.

My Lord, so many times
I have hurt my mind,
my heart, my body.
I realize my errors and failures.
Give me the strength
not to repeat my errors.
Give me the light
not to hurt others.
Give me the wisdom
to stay in harmony with You.

My Lord, let me not put faith
in possessions, knowledge, or power,
but only in You.
Let Your creative energies
inspire and impress me.

OM   OM   OM

6. Now sit on your knees and place your left hand on your solar plexus and the right hand over it. Then rest a few minutes.

When you create harmony within yourself, with God, with others, then your path opens. If you do not clear the records before beginning a new enterprise, you will make mistakes; you will be hurt, mislead, or exploited.

Let us say that you are going to write a book or some music, or create a painting or sculpture. Perform this ceremony before beginning the project, and be really sincere in forgiving others.

When you clear away the obstacles and hindrances that you created between yourself and the creative forces of Nature, you tune yourself, just as you would tune a musical instrument. Because contemporary man does not do this, he is going deeper into turmoil and imprisoning himself with his own problems, binding himself with threads of his own actions, words, deeds and thoughts. When we clean these things in our mind, in our heart, we see the world differently. The creative forces of Nature work with us. Approach is simple; we approach the Divine Presence.

The success of this ceremony depends upon the sincerity of the person performing it. When he forgives, he must really mean it and not hold any resentment. This brings subconscious wounds to the surface and heals them.

Q & A

Question: *If you concentrate on the spirit of forgiveness, do you clear that channel, or do you have to think about specific instances when you have been hurt? Is it necessary to specifically forgive each instance?*

ANSWER: You can do that, but you can also be more general and really mean it. For example, if there are three people that I have hurt, I can send blessings to each of them and apologize to them during this ceremony. If you can be specific, it is more effective. That is why visualization must accompany such prayers and exercises. It is very good to do it mentally, emotionally, and with your physical actions. But if you cannot remember specific instances and are really sincere, your forgiveness and blessings will automatically reach the persons and they will feel as if something has been resolved or lightened.

If you are sensitive, you will also feel that something has been released. Let us say that a person is thinking badly about you and sending you lots of dark thoughts. When he says, "Forget it," the pressure that was psychologically coming to you is now relieved. If one is sensitive and observant, he will see many things that happen.

Question: *Are there other ways to demonstrate forgiveness without performing this ceremony?*

ANSWER: The way you do it is up to you. Great philosophers say that whatever you think in your heart, that is what you are. When you forgive someone with your heart and mind, your reactions and relationships will automatically change. You do not need to use force. Force becomes artificial, showing-off, and perhaps even harmful.

For example, if you hurt someone very badly, and then you buy some goodies to take to his home and ask for his forgiveness, if I were him, I would throw them in your face. I would say, "You hurt me, and now you are bringing me gifts?" It is wiser to wait until he accepts your repentence by very subtly and subjectively helping him. You can even send money to him, but without forcing. There are millions of ways to do this, but inner orientation, tuning the instrument through approach, will make the car go the right way.

Exercise

The next exercise, which I learned from my Teachers in the monastery, is a very ancient ceremony for sun-healing. The sun must be shining, or you can visualize the sun shining.

1. Sit cross-legged and make your spine very erect. Place your hands on your knees, palms up and open to the sun.

There are large chakras in your palms; the left hand has a healing chakra. The right hand has an energizing chakra.

2. With your thoughts, absorb the rays of the sun into your hands. Imagine that the rays of the sun are hitting and energizing your hands. Visualize that the sun is filling your palms with Light, Love, and Power.

Or you can imagine that God is standing in the sun, sending this energy to you.

Feel the energy coming through your hands, filling your Chalice with solar energy that heals, purifies, creates. The energy of the sun is the source of life on this planet; without it, we are all finished. Feel your hands filling with Light; see that the bowl of Light is increasing. Next, feel your hands filling with Love and then tremendous Power.

3. Now visualize a triangle, the apex of which is a point above your head and the base of which is a line formed by your two hands. Let Light, Love, and Power circulate within this triangle.

4. Take your right hand and place it on your left shoulder, while repeating:

Let the energy of the sun pass through my left shoulder to my right side, purifying, healing, regenerating, and transforming it.

This takes the energy from your left shoulder to your right side, and this energizes your left side.

5. Then take the left hand and place it on the right shoulder, repeating:

Let the energy of the sun pass through my right shoulder to my left side, purifying, healing, regenerating, and transforming it.

You are energizing your whole being, infusing both energies together.

6. Now put your left hand on your heart, and then the right hand over the left hand, repeating:

> *Let my hands rest upon my heart, and through my heart fuse the healing energy of the sun throughout my entire body, throughout my whole aura, purifying, healing, regenerating, and transforming them.*

7. Slowly place your hands on your knees and repeat:

> *Lord, bless us; keep our integrity in harmony with You. Let the health of the body, the purity of the heart, and the creativity of the mind express through our thoughts, words, and actions.*

Doing this exercise in the sun is very effective, especially if you are depressed, emotionally down, or you are suffering from inertia or irritation. These problems will evaporate immediately.

Index

A

Abortion 79, 284, 341
Action, right
  defined 215
Actions
  repeated 165
  right 120
Adonis 405
Advanced people
  and Subtle Worlds 279
Advanced person
  defined 291
Advancement
  and physical plane 327
Afterlife, belief in 327
Agnishvattas 368
Akasha 374
Akashic Records 173, 227, 213, 226
Akbar, King 336
Aloofness 147
Analysis
  how done 129
Animal Monad 364
Animals
  and suffering 296
  incarnation of 296
  killing of 297
Antahkarana 208
Antenna
  of Great Ones 160
Apolonius 405
Approach and healing 407

Arguments 401
Arhat(s) 367
  how made 305
Armenia 404
Armenian prayer 89
Artists
  and astral plane 325
Ashrams 145, 146
  and antenna into 161
Astral games
  being trapped in 225
Astral plane 323
  and bodies in 324
  and death 275
  and entities 281
  and initiations 227
  and soul 82
  being aware on 228
  communicating in 274
  consciousness on 309
Astrological energies
  how mixed 335
Astrology 333
Asylums
  and bad karma 34
Atlantean shocks 306
Atlantean souls 328
Atoms of bodies
  and our role 311
Attacks
  how to avoid 128
  and karma 166
Attitude & karma 52
Aura 11, 231, 261

417

and emotional crystallizations
    23
  as mirror of life 86
Aura, astral
  and pollution 323
Aura, mental 311
Avatars 358
  and karma 124
Awake, being
  levels of 101
Awakening
  and astral plane 228
  ways of 87
Awareness
  conditions of 158
  field of 157

B

Bailey, Alice 250
Ballet dancer
  and care of body 313
Battle and karma 145
Beauty
  and natural methods 32
Beingness 157
Birth
  as planting seeds 262
  and death
    law of 229
    of solar system 230
  astral & mental 334
  pattern of 342
  place of
    and karma 212
Births & bodies
  and signs of 333
Blavatsky, Helena
  and caves 335

Blessings 288
Blood transfusions 172
Bodies
  as computers 200
Bodies, advanced
  use of 248
Bodies, all
  caring for 248
Bodies as house
  building & destroying 316
Bodies, dramas of 394
Bodies, higher
  notes of 351
Bodies of others
  use of 257
Bodies, three
  accumulations in 261
  and perfection & freedom 318
  and virtues in 54
  conditioning planet 319
  creation of 153
  purity & attachment to 316
  relation in incarnation 341
Body, emotional
  how used 197
Body, etheric 78
Body, mental
  as mechanism 199
Body, physical
  control over 210
  purpose of 197
Body, trouble in
  and lack of notes 354
Boomerang 11
Buddha 404
  bodies of 247

C

Calamities 315
Cataclysms 164
Cause
  how exists 71
  how to be 140
  and effects 14, 100, 165
Celibacy 337
Centers and exercise 392
Centers, etheric 78
  and past life 155
Chakras, healing 413
Chalice 367, 373
Changelessness 133
Channeling 27
Cheek, turning 237
Chemical combination
  and past lives 379
Chemicals
  defined 168
Child, unborn
  sequence of 285
Choice, power of
  and karma 165
Christ
  and vehicle of Buddha 314
  livingness of 395
  sacrifice of 26
  time of working & teaching 318
  and resurrection 393
  initiation of 282
  risen 395
Circuits
  how to destroy 193
Clairvoyance, temporary 374
Clairvoyants 24
Clockwise round 331
Communication links
  and advanced bodies 312
Compassion
  and responsibility 98
Compensation
  defined 17
Complaining 21
Conception
  and incarnation 340
  preparation for 286
  and life 284
Conscious living
  defined 81
Consciousness
  and Higher Worlds 155
  continuity of 254, 269
  defined
    and levels of matter 315
  expansion of
    and karma 139
    and sacrifice 26
  level of
    and liberation 307
Cosmic Magnet 139, 361
Counterclockwise efforts 334
Creativity, defined 223
Criminal & pollution
  defined 319
Criticism
  and karma 129
Cross, lunar 350
Crucifixion 26, 132
Crystallizations
  how to break 172
Cycles of birth 234

D

Dalai Lama
  and incarnation 345
Dark forces 48, 127, 166
  and karma 62
  and past lives 376
  and resurrection 396
  and soul 287
  and unborn child 285
Daydreaming 96
Death
  and zodiacal sign 331
  preparation for 292
  preparing for 249
  ecstasy of 264
  of child
    reasons for 290
  phases of 323
Debts
  why to pay 22, 235
  and karma 308
  kinds of
    why to settle 250
  of departed 270
  payment of 113
Departed person
  and speaking evil 295
Depression
  exercise for 415
Destiny of human 348
Devachan 276
  defined 326
Devas
  and incarnation process 340
  and process of incarnation 367
Dhyan Chohan 365
Disciple, accepted
  and sacrifice 178

Disciples
  and imposition 167
Discrimination
  and karma 148
Divinity
  and karma 138
Dreams 228
  symbolic 384
Drug use
  and artists 325
Dying
  long process of 263
Dying person
  last thoughts of 253
  steps to help 266

E

Echo in Pyramid 15
Ego and vanity
  and karma 147
  defined
    and problems with 304
  source of 308
Elijah 247
  and mantle 312
Emotional body
  wounds in 88
Emotional condition
  and karma 23
Emotional plane
  learning from 88
Emotional body
  creation of 154
Emptiness, defined 304
Enemies
  and karma 38
  dealing with 147
  and esoteric meaning 394
  how to treat 38

Energy
  electromagnetic 302
  and death 271
  spiritual 303
Enlightenment 185
Entities
  and past lives 378
  and centers 78
  astral 280
Eternal Presence 54
Etheric body
  problems with 279
  and health 86
Etheric plane 79
  and learning 95
  exiting from 99
  expansion of 94
Evolution
  and karma 61
  and Other Worlds 81
  path of 217
Exercise:
  of renouncement 301
  of renunciation/learning to
    approach 408
  visualization of sun/healing
    with sun 413
Experience
  defined 56

F

Failure
  non-identification 267
Faith, defined 128
Fanatic
  defined 178
Fearlessness 259, 266
Fiery World 326

Fifth factor 74
Fire in space 11
Forgiveness 41, 237, 250, 267
  and karma 57, 134
  and dying 277
Freedom
  and karma 35
Friendship
  and karma 148
Full-moon disciplines 367
Future and karma 74
Future life 234

G

Genius
  and Other Worlds 82
Ghost 280
Glamor, defined 226
Glory, body of 312
God
  as a vacuum 304
  righteousness of 204
  as love 319
  fear of
    and karma 106
Great Bear 72
Greed 338
Grief
  and departed ones 295
Group
  affiliation and karma 146
  association and karmic debt
    170
  karma 51, 110, 145
  members and sharing karma
    171

H

Hall of Learning 364
Harmony 15
Hatred 199, 260
Healing
  and approach of 408
Heaven 215
Hell, idea of 323
Help by others
  and karma 127
Hero and karma 140
Hierarchy
  and resurrection 397
  as Solar Angel 178
Higher Worlds
  & reasons to return from 84
  and liberation in 322
Hitler 180
Holy Communion 258
Homosexuality 284
Hope, defined 201
Human misery 51
Humanity
  as throat center 230
Humility 299
Hurt by others
  and karma 127
Hypnotic suggestion 192

I

Identification 402
Identity, conscious 356
Illnesses
  causes for 261
Illumination
  defined 169
Illusionary personality 357
Imagination 96, 389, 391
  and emotional body 24
Immortality, belief in
  and subtle planes 252
Immortality, secrets of 248
Immortals, defined 258
In vitro fertilization
  and soul 285
Incarnation
  and planets 222
  defined 219
  of soul & scandas 345
  three laws affecting 233
  as process 320
  preparing for future 293
  periods and a person's responsibility 309
  causes for traps 306
Incarnations
  and gender 283
  as schooling 202
  number of 72
  times between 94
Indifference, divine 30, 175
Individuality
  and incarnation 355
  conscious 357
Individualization 347
Initiate
  subtle body of 314
  and Law 164
  female 283
Third
  and real birth 333
Initiates
  and incarnation 291
  records of 335

Initiation
 Fifth 400
 Fourth 227, 357, 399
 and gender 283
 second 226
 Seventh 400
 Sixth 400
 Third 398, 399
 and path of resurrection 398
 and physical plane 281
Initiations, higher
 and past lives 379
Inner Guide
 direction of 162
Insanity
 as contagious 21
Intention 352
Intoxication 308
Intuitional awareness 191
Intuitional light 191
Intuitional Plane
 and consciousness 157

J

Jealousy 115
Jesus
 last lecture 297
Jiva 366
Joy
 and relation to will 117
 and karma 35
 and sacrifice 26
 defined 28
Jupiter and Venus 214
Justice
 vs. righteousness 43

K

Karma
 and attitude toward 52
 and dark forces 288
 and flow of consciousness 138
 and grouping of people 143
 and indifference 146
 and levels of 119
 and Other Worlds 90
 and Purpose of Lord 169
 and reincarnation 169
 and right decisions 173
 and Subtle Worlds 100
 and three worlds 146
 and ugliness 32
 as a computer 79
 as a law 10
 as action & inaction 47
 as compensation 16
 as contagious 21
 as energy disturbance 79
 as fluid 125
 as key to liberation 39
 as Moving Scales 20
 as protection 10
 being freed from 303
 changing of 164
 exhaustion of 37
 facing of 43
 how adjusted 42
 how altered 168
 how created 19, 100, 102
 how dissipated 124
 how formed 128
 how it works 9
 how multiplied 28
 how paid 126

how repaid 237
how revealed 22
how reversed 145
how to change 147
how to face 140
how to overcome 41
knowing & cooperation with 164
lessening of 98
of lower kingdoms 360
overcoming 91
relation with reincarnation 213
result of inaction 75
triple action of 120
accumulated
   dissolution of 111
and future 74
and history 68
and office 67
and self 124
and success 162
and Teaching 61
and vices 32
as chemical 168
collective 52, 122
control of 124
defined 13, 16, 119
destruction of 160
experience of 395
group 51
how paid 55
impressed 170
increase of
   and subtle bodies 35
   in subtle levels 30
Law of
   and path of advancement 158

how to teach 104
and stages of evolution 45
three essentials 44
and justice 27
lessons of
   and labor 135
merited 128
motion of
   and will 170
national 73
of Lord 151
overcoming 291
paid 83
secrets of 72
shared 109
victory over
   and achievement 140
Karmic Lords 53, 59
   and dealing with past lives 384
Karmic recordings 67
Karmic waves 158
Kerlian photography 78, 231
Kingdom of God 244
Knowledge
   and experience 387
Krishna 404

L

Lao Kiun 405
Law of Absolute Justice 120
Law of Action & Reaction 119
Law of Cause & Effect 10
Law of Causelessness 185
Law of Compassion 10, 11, 185
Law of Compensation 16
Law of Conscience 39
Law of dates 168
Law of giving & receiving 302

Law of Inevitability 189
Law of Justice 27
Law of Karma
    9, 11, 45, 68, 91, 360, 384
    and tolerance 190
    and transformation 37
Law of Love 129
Law of Payment 21
Law of Pralaya & Manvantara
    230
Law of Reincarnation 348
Law of Righteousness 43
Law of Sacrifice 26
Law of Self-Made Traps 20
Law of the Cosmic Magnet 361
Law of the Echo 15
Law of the Mirror 17
Law of the Universe 80
Laws, man-made
    and karma 43
Lemurian 364
Lemurian shocks 306
Liberation & Higher Worlds
    how gained 322
Libra
    lessons in 330
Life
    as mirror 17
Life cycles
    evolutions of 234
Light, increase in
    and changes 305
Loneliness 147
Lord, karma of 152
Love,
    defined 132, 337
    law of 319
Lunar bodies
    and influence 367

M

Magnetism
    thought and emotions 307
Magnetized thoughts 309
Manipulation 23
    dealing with 174
Mantram
    "Lead us ..." 100
Manvantara 303
Mark
    & soul's destination 56
Marriage
    why sacred 286
Masters
    and refinement 245
Materialism 397
Maturing process
    and reincarnation 233
Meditation
    and cultivating Intuition 174
    reasons for 395
Mediumism
    dangers of 215
Memories 157
Mental body
    as mirror 399
    reality of 89
Mental condition
    and karma 25
Mental plane
    and death 275
    levels of contents 326
Mental unit
    and devas 341
Millionaire, spiritual 392
Mind
    creation of 153
    higher 191

Miscarriage 285
Mission, defined 93
Mistakes, kinds of 84
Mohammed 250
Monad 315
 and birth of soul 359
 and individualization 364
Monad as Ray 347, 356
 and building bodies 370
Money, ideas on 338
Morality 261
 new
  and karma 123
Moses 297
Motive 352

N

Nirvana 303
 and relation to karma 74
Non-attachment 175
Nonresistance 38
Nosiness
 and karma 131
Notes, complete or partial
 and forming bodies 353
Notes of vehicles 349

O

Obsession
 and past lives 379
Obsession & possession 166
Obstacles
 how paid 166
Office, position of
 why important 66
Opposites, pairs of 72
Ordination
 words to candidates 63

Organ transplants 172
Orphans
 care for 295
Other Worlds 77
 and karma 169
 and landing there 97
 and learning in 82
 and physical works 79
 and refusal to follow 104
 as an effect 100
 momentary awakening in 90

P

Pain & suffering 53
Pain and exercise 391
Pancreas 261
Parental death 276
Past life 155
 pseudo 376
 when revealed 384
Past lives 158, 196, 213, 219,
  220, 224, 227, 373
 access to 379
 and Christ & Buddha 377
 dangers in knowing 382
 when seen 381
 why covered 374
Patience
 defined 49
Patterns, brain
 changing of 96
People, five kinds of
 and levels of consciousness 80
Perfection
 striving toward 248
 defined 246
 of bodies, and knowledge
  associated 203

Permanent atoms
   53, 232, 339, 373
   and sound 353
Persecuting others
   and how to help 54
Personality
   as a cross 350
Petals, unfoldment of
   and incarnations 73
Physical body
   creation of 154
Physical condition
   and karma 22
Pisces
   and decision 334
   and direction in life 329
Planes, astral & mental
   being awake in 98
Planes, three
   and work in 146
Plans of departed
   and completion of 294
Pleiades 72
Pollution
   and energies of Universe 300
Population explosion 315
Position
   as a reward 63
Pralaya 303
Pranic triangle 154
Principle and bodies 311
Principles, three
   working together 230
Privacy, real 54
Prodigal son 393
Progress, levels of 222
Projection & karma 101
Promiscuity 336
Psychic energy 160

and result of weakening 378
Psychics
   and astral plane 226
   and illusion 224
Psychological exploitation 131
Purification of bodies 351
Purpose
   and perfection 201
   and Solar Life 352
   and karma 151
   of life
      being awake 87

Q

Q & A 93
Queen
   example of 88
Quotes:
   from Bhagavad Gita 220

R

Radiation 307
Recording of life 219
Refinement 260, 313
   as part of life 243
Refinery, human 310, 312
Reflection in mirror
   and real change 18
Regeneration 301
Reincarnation 302
   and karma 306
   and perfection 249
   and refining bodies 243
   and soul/personality relations 355
   and tolerance 287
   three kinds of 208
   Law of 303

dealing with 207
nature of
and karma 359
Religions, various
idea of incarnation 219
Renunciation 299, 402
self 25
Repentance 41
Responsibility
defined 93
Resurrection 26
and other traditions 403
as rain 402
defined 388
path of
antagonisms on 394
steps of 401
Retreats 292
Right and wrong
waves of 158
Right human relations 110
Righteous
defined 85
as a measure 29
Roerich, Helena 313, 326
Roerich, Nicholas 249

S

Sacrifice 166
and expansion 26
and love 132
Sage
effect on nature 360
Salvation 99
Sanskrit
and effects 16
Scandas 345

Schools of life 218
Science, defined 82
Scientist
and astral plane 327
Scorpio
lessons of 330
Self
and mind 393
defined 222
Divine, blinded and ego 304
little, and levels of consciousness 303
True 399
Self-actualization
and death 389
Self-defense
and karma 38
Self-image
and Other Worlds 103
Selfishness 397
Service
and karma 144
and will 118
defined 25, 131
Sex and karma 336
Sexual partners
and karma 35
Sexual thoughts
and karma 35
Shocks
and renunciation 306
Shower, inner 300
Singer
and care of body 313
Sleepers
classes of 328
Sleepwalking 99
Sodom & Gomorrah 85

Solar Angel 54, 58, 90
  after our death 271
  and astral plane 324
  and birth of soul 356
  and guidance 167
  and incarnation 340
  and karma 177
  and lack in devas 368
  and training bodies 346
  being without 178
  guidance of 282
  job of 368
  and group & family 273
  duties of 366
  teaching on 359
Solar Logos 389
  karma of 72
Solar Pitris 342, 365
Soul and personality
  detached from 358
Soul development
  and karma 25
Soul, human
  and conception 286
  and consciousness levels 156
  and incarnation 346
  and notes in 353
  and relation with bodies 346
  and service 214
  and sound of 350
  as self-conscious unit 366
  incarnation & voice of 339
  path of 218
  when immortal 169
Soul-infusion 330
Sound and bodies
  and attraction 349
Space, forces in 119

Spark 398
Seven Rays of 395
Spirit of Resurrection 396
Spiritual diary 263
Spiritual life
  defined 31
Stage fright 321
Story:
  about lawmaker 65
  of Akbar/trusting God 163
  of Arjuna 220
  of auto accident/karma saves 34
  of being fearless 259
  of Buddha & Arhats/renunciation 305
  of choking boy/karma & protection 288
  of cholera/karma 128
  of continuity of consciousness 254
  of Damodar 203 of dying man/teaching immortality 263
  of earthquake/karma 126
  of graduating student/importance of teacher 66
  of Hindus/leaving bodies 203
  of ignoring warnings 48
  of Judas 297
  of King & enemy/debt owed 270
  of man & wife/karma in action 206
  of man and sex/spending resources 22
  of martyrs/ecstasy in death 264
  of massacre/repaying debts 238

of molester/vices 286
of monastery & lecturers/
   readiness 317
of old man & trees/future life
   235
of Omar Khayyam/God's
   creations 205
of passing of Teacher/karmic
   time 163
of pharmacy/being saved 32
of remarks in Holland/God's
   Will 321
of Sanjaya/refinement 313
of serving Teaching/paying
   karma 64
of singer/God's Will 321
of Socrates & his wife/repaying
   karma 239
of Sodom & Gomorrah 29
of T.S. & auto accident/karma
   125
of T.S. & enamored girl/
   protection 289
of T.S. father & charity/karma
   pays 34
of TS dream/wars & incarnation 262
of watch and boys/recordings in
   bodies 262
Striving & karma
   defined 42
Subconscious mind 373
Subconscious recordings
   and death 278
Subjective life
   and problems 278
Subtle Worlds
   learning in 91
   and fear 267

Surgery
   and Ashram 162

T

Taijasi
   defined 169
Teacher
   and karma 29, 144
   good, lack of 338
Teaching
   as a gift 65
   reason to assimilate 195
   and karma 61
   as law 63
Temptation 400
Thinking
   and incarnation 233
   three kinds of
      and cause & effect 307
Thought atoms 311
Thoughts
   how to change 308
   pure
      how affected 161
Tolerance
   defined 48
Traitors 62
Transfiguration 399
   defined 245
Transformation
   and karma 137
   awareness of 395
Transmutation
   moment of 38
Traps
   how built 20
Treason & slander 114
Triangles of karma 72

True Self 133
  -see also, Self

V

Vices
  and alcohol & drugs 326
  and karma 28
Virtues and vices 50
Visualization 96, 389
  as a sense 391
Voice
  of human soul 339

W

Wars 237
  and karma 38
Watched, being 335
Waves, electrical
  and karma 159
Will energy
  and Cosmic Magnet 352
Will, free
  and greater will 320
Willpower, defined 117
Wisdom, defined 131
Workshop of life 246
World citizenship 110

Y

Young age
  and urge toward light 329

Z

Zodiacal signs
  and changes in person 332
  and lessons learned 330
Zoroaster 404

About the Author

Torkom Saraydarian (1917 – 1997) was born in Asia Minor. Since childhood he was trained in the Teachings of the Ageless Wisdom.

He visited monasteries, ancient temples, and mystery schools in order to find the answers to his questions about the mystery of man and the Universe.

He lived with Sufis, dervishes, Christian mystics, and masters of temple music and dance. His musical training included the violin, piano, oud, cello, and guitar. It took long years of discipline and sacrifice to absorb the Ageless Wisdom from its true sources. Meditation became a part of his daily life, and service a natural expression of his soul.

Torkom Saraydarian dedicated his entire life to the service of his fellow man. His writings and lectures and music show his total devotion to the higher principles, values, and laws that are present in all world religions and philosophies. These works represent a synthesis of the best and most beautiful in the sacred culture of the world. His works enrich the foundational thinking on which man can construct his Future.

Torkom Saraydarian wrote a large number of books, many of which have been published. All of his books will continue to be published and distributed. A few have been translated into Armenian, German, Italian, Spanish, Portuguese, Greek, Dutch, and Danish.

He left a rich legacy of writings and musical compositions for all of humanity to enjoy and benefit from for many years to come.

Visit our web site at *www.tsg-publishing.com* for interviews and additional information on Torkom Saraydarian.

Other Books by Torkom Saraydarian

- The Ageless Wisdom
- The Aura
- Battling Dark Forces
- The Bhagavad Gita
- Breakthrough to Higher Psychism
- Buddha Sutra — A Dialogue with the Glorious One
- Challenge for Discipleship
- Christ, The Avatar of Sacrificial Love
- A Commentary on Psychic Energy
- Cosmic Shocks
- Cosmos in Man
- The Creative Fire
- Dynamics of Success
- Education as Transformation, Vol. I
- Education as Transformation, Vol. II
- The Eyes of Hierarchy—How the Masters Watch and Help Us
- Flame of Beauty, Culture, Love, Joy
- The Flame of the Heart
- From My Heart — Volume I (Poetry)
- Hiawatha and the Great Peace
- The Hidden Glory of the Inner Man
- I Was
- Joy and Healing
- Karma and Reincarnation
- Leadership Vol. I
- Leadership Vol. II
- Leadership Vol. III
- Leadership Vol. IV
- Leadership Vol. V
- Legend of Shamballa
- The Mystery of Self-Image
- The Mysteries of Willpower
- New Dimensions in Healing
- Olympus World Report… The Year 3000
- One Hundred Names of God
- Other Worlds
- The Psyche and Psychism
- The Psychology of Cooperation and Group Consciousness
- The Purpose of Life
- The Science of Becoming Oneself
- The Science of Meditation
- The Sense of Responsibility in Society
- Sex, Family, and the Woman in Society
- The Solar Angel
- Spiritual Regeneration
- Spring of Prosperity
- The Subconscious Mind and the Chalice
- Symphony of the Zodiac
- Talks on Agni
- Thought & the Glory of Thinking
- Triangles of Fire
- Unusual Court
- Woman, Torch of the Future
- The Year 2000 & After

Booklets

- The Art of Visualization — Simply Presented

- The Chalice in Agni Yoga Literature
- Cornerstones of Health
- A Daily Discipline of Worship
- Discipleship in Action
- Duties of Grandparents
- Earrings for Business People
- Earthquakes and Disasters — What the Ageless Wisdom Tells Us
- Fiery Carriage and Drugs
- Five Great Mantrams of the New Age
- Hierarchy and the Plan
- How to Find Your Level of Meditation
- Inner Blooming
- Irritation — The Destructive Fire
- Mental Exercises
- Nachiketas
- New Beginnings
- Practical Spirituality
- Questioning Traveler and Karma
- Saint Sergius
- Synthesis

Booklets
(Excerpts and Compilations)
- Angels and Devas
- Building Family Unity
- Courage
- Daily Spiritual Striving
- First Steps Toward Freedom
- Prayers, Mantrams, and Invocations
- The Psychology of Cooperation
- Responsibility
- Responsibility and Business
- Responsibilities of Fathers
- Responsibilities of Mothers Success
- Torchbearers
- What to Look for in the Heart of Your Partner

Videos
- The Seven Rays Interpreted
- Why Drugs Are Dangerous
- Lecture Videos by Author (list available)

Music
- A Touch of Heart (CD only)
- Dance of the Zodiac
- Far Horizons
- Fire Blossom
- Go In Beauty (songs by Torkom Saraydarian sung by choir)
- Infinity
- Lao Tse
- Light Years Ahead
- Lily in Tibet
- Misty Mountain
- Piano Composition
- Rainbow
- Spirit of My Heart
- Sun Rhythms
- Tears of My Joy
- Toward Freedom
- 1994 Annual Convention Special Edition — Synthesizer Music

About the Publisher

T.S.G. Publishing Foundation, Inc. is a non-profit, tax exempt organization. Founded on November 30, 1987 in Los Angles, California, it relocated to Cave Creek, Arizona on January 1, 1994.

Our purpose is to be a pathway for self-transformation. We are fully devoted to publishing, teaching, and distributing the creative works of Torkom Saraydarian.

Our bookstore in Cave Creek and our online bookstore at our web site *www.tsg-publishing.com* offer the complete collection of the creative works of Torkom Saraydarian for sale and distribution. Our newsletter OUTREACH contains thought-provoking articles excerpted from these books. We also conduct weekly classes, special training seminars, and home study meditation courses.

Torkom Saraydarian Book Publishing Fund

Torkom Saraydarian dedicated his entire life to serving others in their spiritual growth. At the time of his passing, more than 100 manuscripts had been written and prepared for publication. This work represents a seamless tapestry of Wisdom and we are dedicated to publishing the entire collection.

Torkom Saraydarian had the unique wisdom and dedication to write all of these magnificent books in one lifetime. Now it is our turn to do the work. Together we can make his dream a reality and bring his legacy to fruition.

We depend on contributions for the publishing of the books. A special fund, *The Torkom Saraydarian Book Publishing Fund* has been established for the completion of this legacy. Contact us for details about the *Book Fund* and an update regarding remaining manuscripts. You can contribute funds for an entire book, or give any amount you wish on a continuous basis or a one-time contribution.

Your contribution will entitle you to devote an entire book to a loved one, or share the dedication with others in the *Book Fund*.

Thank you for your loving and continuous support.

Participate in the Vision for the Future
Contribute to
The Torkom Saraydarian
Book Publishing Fund

My Pledge:

❏ One-time: $ _____   ❏ Annually: $ _____   ❏ Monthly: $ _____

Name: _____
Address: _____
City / State: _____ Country: _____
Tel #: (_____) _____ – _____
E-mail Address: _____

Method of Payment: ❏ Check/U.S. Money-order   ❏ Visa   ❏ MasterCard
Account # _____ – _____ – _____   Exp. date: ____ / ____
(If using credit card, please include account number & expiration date)

Please send to:
T.S.G. Publishing Foundation, Inc. • Attn: Book Fund
P.O. Box 7068 • Cave Creek, AZ 85327 • U.S.A.
Tel: (480) 502-1909 • Fax: (480) 502-1909
Web site: *www.tsg-publishing.com*
E-mail: *webmaster@tsg-publishing.com*

T.S.G. Publishing Foundation, Inc. is a tax-exempt, non-profit organization.

❏ I would like to pay for the publishing of a book in its entirely.
  (Please tell us what you want on the dedication page.)
❏ Please include my name on the list of donors.
❏ No name please, just add this donation to the Book Fund.

Ordering Information

Write to the publisher for additional information regarding:

— Free catalog of author's books and music tapes

— Complete list of lecture tapes and videos ($2 postage for each list)

— Placement on mailing list for continuous updates

— A free copy of our newsletter *Outreach*

— **Join our Book Club at no charge. (Receive a 20% discount with each new release by Torkom Saraydarian. Each new book is mailed to you automatically as soon as it is released.) Send us a written approval to include you in the Book Club.**

Additional copies of *Karma and Reincarnation*
U.S. $25.00

Postage within U.S.A. – $6.00 plus applicable state sales tax
International postage: contact us for surface or air rates.

T.S.G. Publishing Foundation, Inc.
P.O. Box 7068
Cave Creek, AZ 85327–7068
United States of America
TEL: (480) 502–1909
FAX: (480) 502–0713
E-Mail: webmaster@tsg-publishing.com
Web-site: www.tsg-publishing.com